About the editor

LeRoy Marceau is labor counsel for the Standard Oil Company (New Jersey). He is a member of the Ohio Bar, of the Bar of the Supreme Court of the United States, and of the New York Bar. Prior to his affiliation with the Standard Oil Company, he was special counsel to the attorney general of Ohio, regional attorney for the National Labor Relations Board in Indianapolis and New Orleans, member of the Louisiana Labor Mediation Board, and member of the Personnel Board of Baton Rouge. **Dealing with a Union** is Mr. Marceau's second book in the field of labor relations.

Dealing with a Union

DEALING
WITH A UNION

Edited by LeRoy Marceau

American Management Association, Inc.

Introduction

THIS BOOK IS ADDRESSED TO EMPLOYING COMPANIES OPERATING IN THE PRIVATE sector with only the average amount of government regulation. It assumes that the workers are represented by a union, affiliated or independent, and that the employer is not trying to dislodge the union. It assumes that the employer wants peace with the union, flexibility in management decisions, and moderation in labor costs—objectives not always compatible. It then asks: How are one's objectives thwarted or achieved? What governs what will happen in the labor relations world?

College professors, thinking about labor relations, perhaps without taking part in them, attribute developments to general causes—as though natural forces ruled with an iron hand. Negotiators, taking part in labor relations without thinking too much about them, attribute developments to their own decisions—as though the strings they pull were, as de Tocqueville puts it, "the same as those that move the world." There is something to be said for both the professor and the negotiator. This book acknowledges both the "power of ideas" and the "responsibility of man." It recognizes a great many immutable principles in labor relations, but suggests that in the hands of skillful men those principles—like the immutable laws of natural science— can be used to produce magnificent change.

In trying to assist the employer toward his objectives, this book refrains from pontifical advice. It seldom says, "Do this," or "Don't do that." Instead, it points out the plausible alternatives that are open to the employer and marshals the arguments that can be made for each alternative.

5

In the hierarchy of any employer there are likely to be one or more professional labor relations people who already know almost everything this book teaches. We address ourselves primarily to the less specialized member of management—such as the president, vice president, or director—who wants to understand the labor relations world without mastering every detail. In order not to confuse them, we have held to the main highway, resisting those tempting byways that by their oddity lure the sophisticate. Nevertheless, we believe this book will interest the professional, too. Even though one may have mastered the details, even though he is familiar with each separate piece in the puzzle, he must occasionally step back—or step up—to obtain a panoramic view. One who would formulate a strategy must know how the separate pieces fit together.

In dealing with a union the employer cannot face his problems one by one as they arise. He cannot, as employers so often boast of doing, decide each successive problem "on its own facts." In deciding today's problem he must know what he intends to do tomorrow, and so he must know a little about what tomorrow's problem will be. If tomorrow's management decisions are not within his knowledge and control, he cannot make a decisive management decision today; he can only hedge against innumerable possibilities so as to preserve, for an unknown successor, far more flexibility than he himself would need. This book tries to put tomorrow's problem within his knowledge. His superiors must put tomorrow's decision within his control.

Sophisticated readers will notice a few omissions in this book. Thus arbitration, although an important facet of the union-management relationship, is omitted. There is a reason. Rather than try to discuss everything, and thus perhaps to overcondense everything, we have carefully omitted a few segments—like organizational drives, arbitration, mediation, and litigation —segments so clearly defined, so easily separable from the mainstream, that they have been singled out and discussed exhaustively in other books. We prefer to treat in some detail those more elusive facets of the union-management relationship that the textbook writers have slighted.

This book suggests that there have been some serious faults with labor relations in the 1960's. Specifically, there has been too little respect for ancient wisdom and modern science; too much respect for salesmanship and public relations gimmicks; overemphasis on force—especially by government; overemphasis on self-interest—especially by labor and management; and over all too much jargon, too little order or stability.

Finally, this book admits that it is written for the decade, not for the age. Had it been written a decade ago, or a decade hence, it would have been written differently. In labor relations, change is the enduring reality, resistance to change the enduring problem, and management of change—alas—the rare human ability. A labor relations executive, living as he does in these latter years of the dark ages, must be content with a fragmentary wisdom and must often look back over his shoulder—with qualms and trepidations —as he stumbles toward new answers.

LeRoy Marceau

Contents

Labor Relations
in a Critical Era

Vincent R. D'Alessandro

INDUSTRIAL RELATIONS—LIKE ALL HUMAN RELATIONSHIPS—CONSTITUTES A MOST challenging area of business management. The employer-employee relationship, in times past a fairly simple person-to-person matter, has been fantastically complicated by the very confusion of modern-day life itself—in numbers, in conflicting forces, in sheer overall growth.

This chapter outlines some of those complications and examines the contending forces: the unions, the government, and the changing workforce. Thus it portrays the background against which industrial management will operate in the near and not-so-near future. The picture is not an encouraging one. But, with the diligence and hard work of which intelligent management is capable, success can be achieved.

GENERAL PERSPECTIVE

Labor-management relations do not exist in a vacuum. The total environment—war, peace, depression, prosperity—has always strongly influ-

VINCENT R. D'ALESSANDRO is director of industrial relations of Sinclair Oil Corporation.

enced what takes place at the bargaining table and in day-to-day employee relations.

In this "activist" era, environmental influences tend to make management's problems more acute and complex than ever. There will be no easy solutions; in fact, the collective bargaining process will be dramatically tested as it never was before.

While unions have now *gained* a hitherto unmatched "power grip" on the nation's economy, union leaders have in great measure *lost* their grip on the union membership. The mood of "action now" enters the picture too, as does the relatively youthful composition of union membership. In general, these young people bear no depression scars. Their working lives have known only years of unmatched prosperity with high employment rates. The job insecurity their predecessors of the thirties (and earlier) lived with has evaporated. The youthful overconfidence which has resulted ranges from simple insubordination and rejection of leadership to outright illegal action. Now, if the cause seems just, any means to achieve it—however illegitimate—may be adopted. Today's union members have little patience with traditional collective bargaining methods.

As a result, many union leaders approach negotiations under a strange new pressure—with a tacit confession that some agreements they reach will not win rank-and-file acceptance unless their membership has first had a chance to "demonstrate" by strike. Until such catharsis occurs, they feel, "meaningful" negotiations are impossible. Indeed, there have even been instances where companies have acquiesced in this approach and have put up with a premature strike in order to let workers feel the negotiations are meaningful.

Unfortunately for such firms, any offer they made before the strike becomes a bargaining floor when negotiations are resumed. Simply stated, the traditional bargaining procedure is now often reversed: Get an offer, reject it, then strike and up the ante. In other instances, the union leadership simply misjudges the temper of the members and reaches an agreement in good faith, only to see it rejected. The ratification process can no longer be considered routine once an agreement is reached with designated union officials.

Another aspect of the youthful union membership is its almost total lack of identification with the employer's interests. This, too, is a result of the relatively prosperous times the young people have experienced in their working lives. Add to this employee independence the general increase in population mobility, and you have a situation where there is little impulse to put down permanent roots in a particular company. This lack of identity, along with the high rate of mobility, has a strong practical implication for the bargaining process. It has resulted and will result in greater pressures for the establishment of industrywide programs covering vacations, pensions, health and welfare benefits, and other similar fringe benefits—with the employees carrying their benefits with them as they move from job to job.

While there is ample evidence of union weakness in controlling membership action, union power vis-à-vis the employer has been significantly bolstered by judicial and Labor Board decisions in recent years. These restrictions imposed on employers tend strongly toward union-employer codetermination, making it difficult—often impossible—for management to achieve desperately needed efficiency in plant operation.

Labor Board precedents dating from the few years of relative balance between unions and management in the fifties have now been ignored or expressly overturned. For instance, the Labor Board now sanctions certain secondary boycotts, questionable picketing practices, limited picket-line violence, and oppressive union penalties imposed upon members who cross picket lines or exceed production quotas. Also, the Labor Board all too often applies one free-speech standard to employers and another to unions, harking back to pre-Taft-Hartley-Act days. A whole raft of Labor Board decisions sets down strict obligations which companies must observe during plant shutdowns and relocations. Of course, appeal to the courts is possible; but it is expensive, time consuming, and seldom practical for the small employer. Generally, wrongs are not righted through litigation until long after the fact, no matter how big the company. Certainly, the Labor Board's recent decisional trends offer strong support for the establishment of labor courts to replace the board.

In view of the Labor Board's chronic tendency to overturn precedent, it has become almost impossible to predict what view it may ultimately take toward specific employer action or how far it may stretch the definition of the statutory obligation to bargain on "wages, hours . . . or other conditions of employment." Thus the management of labor relations demands greater sophistication and more expert attention than ever before. Constant evaluation of new developments and of the most effective approaches to adopt in dealing with them is essential. The American Management Association's many labor relations and personnel courses afford management the means to keep attuned to these problems and their possible solutions.

GOVERNMENT'S ROLE

"Free collective bargaining," the classic ideal for resolving labor-management differences, has been endangered by escalating government intervention in recent years. The role of the government used to be that of mediator—no more than a catalyst. Nowadays, however, the executive branch tends more and more toward active participation rather than mediation. As a result, settlements are often coerced instead of freely negotiated.

In the past, the government rarely took an active part in working out settlements short of a threat of national emergency. Recently, however, "emergency" seems to mean "public inconvenience" stemming from a heightened political sensitivity to the public's expression of irritation. Therefore, it can be expected that government intervention will become even more frequent and more forcible.

Currently, federal intervention in labor disputes customarily begins with the announcement that the executive branch will appoint an ad hoc committee of "impartial," blue-ribbon labor relations statesmen. This announcement itself is usually enough to stop negotiations cold. What follows then is a time lag during which the panel members are appointed and publicized and hold preliminary talks among themselves. Rarely, if ever, do the negotiating parties settle privately once the word is out that a committee will be appointed.

The ad hoc committee's usual procedure is to issue an executive summons to the parties, who know that they must either respond or risk the wrath of the executive wing—which can take stringent action against either side by invoking a host of statutes in a repressive manner. Hordes of government investigators stand ready to move in on a recalcitrant management, and the union risks imposition of a Taft-Hartley Act 80-day injunction.

Once discussions begin, the pressures that the executive branch can apply regarding settlement are countless and virtually irresistible. Such coercion can be screened from public view by adroit employment of the good offices of the ad hoc committee. Add to that the government's power to mold and mobilize public opinion, and the parties' respective freedom to accept or reject becomes illusory.

Seldom, however, have these pressures been directed equally against labor and management. The relative political power of the disputants is an element that no politician can comfortably ignore. Indeed, the mere convening of an ad hoc committee is an implicit gesture of government partiality, since employment of this technique forestalls use of the Taft-Hartley Act injunction—an anathema to unions. A good example is found in the government's reluctance to invoke the Taft-Hartley Act injunction in the 37-week 1967–1968 copper strike, even though we were then *de facto* waging war in Vietnam and copper was a vital military component.

Executive refusal to use the Taft-Hartley Act injunction cannot be ascribed to a belief that the 80-day cooling-off period does not work. History records otherwise: Of the 28 instances where the injunction has been invoked since 1947, 22 were settled by the parties before the 80 days ran out; the remaining six were settled soon afterward.

Settlements worked out under the aegis of ad hoc committees have been of mixed quality. Some have been advantageous to the public without unduly depriving the disputants of their freedom or property; but many more have sacrificed the legitimate interests of one of the parties without appreciably achieving a public benefit.

On balance, one must conclude that the ad hoc committee technique is unsatisfactory—certainly it is not impartial. As a practical matter, this device impairs free collective bargaining in two ways: First, disputants, aware of this last resort, often fail to work hard enough to reach settlements on their own; second, strikes are often unnecessarily prolonged while the parties mark time waiting for the ad hoc machinery to get rolling.

Despite these readily recognizable deficiencies, the ad hoc committee is too convenient a political tool for the government to renounce. For the future, however, this settlement technique can only mean more and more restraint of economic freedom.

Today's Unions

The old-line, bread-and-butter attitudes of traditional unionism have fallen by the wayside. Instead, there is a strongly developing trend toward the more "cosmic" in union objectives and goals. After more than 30 years of successful organization and recognition, most unions are now solidly entrenched as collective bargaining representatives, despite the family squabbles between the Reuther supporters and those representing the Meany philosophy. Management can derive no comfort from intraunion or interunion conflict; union competitors representing disparate schools of thought vie with each other to get results which are always paid for by management.

Like the people they represent, many union leaders typify the younger generation. These youthful officers of labor are concerned with broader goals than the more elemental organizing and cents-per-hour preoccupations of their predecessors. The fact is that today's younger union leaders chafe at what they regard as the backwardness and conservatism of the old timers. The new aim is to exert union strength to achieve "community" goals—that is, to cope with social problems, civil rights, and housing, as well as to improve education and training and to forge stronger links with free-world trade unions.

Since the familiar "basics" have already been attained, modern labor officers argue that the unions' efforts should now be devoted to the attainment of broader benefits. Indeed, Steelworkers president I. W. Abel predicted in 1966 that, before long, areas of negotiation would include benefits traditionally restricted to white collar and executive people. Abel cited stock options, portal-to-portal pay—from home to plant—employer-purchased homes for transferred workers, guaranteed annual wages, and profit sharing.

This prediction is, of course, in tune with current union aims to organize the white collar worker. Although to date there has been comparatively little progress in such campaigns, the success of the union movement in the teaching profession and among government employees (the implications of which have not been lost on state and local workers) has whetted appetites among industry's professional and technical employees. Walter Reuther, for his part, has mapped out plans to "make agricultural workers first-class citizens" and to help other disadvantaged groups to build "community unions" where they live.

The clash between the antipodal philosophies of Reuther and Meany has led to a split by UAW from the AFL-CIO. It can be expected that UAW will be successful in wooing other AFL-CIO affiliates to join it. As the gap between these organizations widens, many managements may once again face the troublesome byproducts of the intense rivalries that heated up labor relations during the 20 years between the founding of the CIO and its merger with the American Federation of Labor.

"STRATIFIED" BARGAINING

Prompted, they say, by the broad emergence of conglomerate companies, unions have been working out pragmatic expedients of cooperation to achieve companywide or industrywide bargaining through "coalition negotiations," even when members of the coalition are intense rivals. In some instances, for example, union components of these coalitions formerly competed to represent each other's people in Labor Board elections. Typical coalition structures are amalgams of two or more international unions to negotiate at one sitting with a single company. Thus local negotiations are replaced by national bargaining when multiplant companies are under contract with several different bargaining agents.

Beyond the obvious difficulties of having to negotiate with a strengthened multiunion bargaining team is the more subtle problem for management of neglecting local issues, inherent in such top-level bargaining. As each union local transfers some of its power to the broader-based group, the gap between the rank and file and their representatives is widened. Local issues are not permitted to take up the time and energy of the coalition people bargaining at the lofty level of companywide negotiations.

Even if the will to do so were present, top-level coalition negotiators cannot truly get at local problems as plant-by-plant negotiators can. The inherent danger, of course, arises from the intense emotional content of the local dissatisfactions (real or fancied) with which employees have to live from day to day—far more indeed than from most so-called major issues. Since local strikes are thus an ever-present threat when coalition bargaining is attempted, union officials cannot safely neglect these local issues. This situation will logically result in several different levels of bargaining, all interdependent: the coalition level, the international union level, and the local level.

Some possible consequences of coalition bargaining are readily discernible: greater union strength in numbers, greater "savvy" in negotiations, and greater buildup of central strike power. Such strike power will, in the nature of things, lead to major work stoppages—both in scope and in duration—and will often cause national emergencies calling for government intervention. Greater central strike power does, however, result in *pressure* intervention, with most of the pressure applied to management. In short, Taft-Hartley Act 80-day emergency provisions should not be expected to be invoked.

While union mergers are fundamentally distasteful to the entrenched leadership, they may occur where the coalition bargaining device does not succeed. We must therefore be prepared to face the paradox of internal union division on the one hand and interunion cooperation on the other.

But management's major problem with respect to coalition bargaining and its divisiveness is the day-to-day one of closely observing the mood in the plant, anticipating employee irritations, and promptly dealing with them to reduce or remove unrest. In short, *employee* relations rather than *union* relations deserve management's closest attention under these circumstances. The obvious need for effective supervision thus entailed necessitates closer ties between the executive and department-head levels and the front-line supervisors. The latter will require constant, systematic retraining in their methods of dealing with the workforce.

WORKFORCE FLEXIBILITY

It is important to distinguish between workforce flexibility and initial high skill level. The technological changes of the past ten years or so have tended to decrease the proportion of low-skilled, one-operation, mass-production jobs. Although the dismal predictions of mass unemployment owing to machine take-over never materialized, there has been a noticeable upward trend in the skill specifications of new workers who must be equipped to handle the sophisticated equipment now in use. Even these higher-skilled people, however, find that they must be adaptable to radical changes in technology. Many will have their job requirements upgraded several times in their working lives.

While technological change is not new, the pace at which it will proceed in coming years will force management to continually train and retrain its employees so as to attain maximum efficiency and avoid losing otherwise valuable personnel through skill obsolescence. Such training will not be easy. There are widely recognized deficiencies in the nation's basic educational processes at all levels—elementary, secondary, academic, and technical. In many cases, management will, in its own interest, have to fill fundamental educational gaps left unfilled in the normal educational curriculum.

Otherwise, unions will clamor for expensive contract provisions covering such needs or will look to government to step in and do the job, with the kind of interference such action implies. Other union obstructions to technological improvements will take the form of extraordinary, expensive provisions for beefed-up retirement benefits, severance allowances, guaranteed annual wages, and the like.

Astute managements will get the jump on these problems by installing economically sound training and educational programs of their own choosing, suited to their own specific needs. As for the overall economy, the real concern will be with companies that adopt a complacent attitude and do not try to do for themselves and their workforce what they can and should do better than any other agency. If those companies fail to take the initiative, the economic damage will not be confined to their own enterprises but will spread and generally impair the prosperity of many other companies.

Durable Contract Provisions

Once written into a contract, the life of a provision is all but everlasting. In those rare instances where a company has been able to negotiate a provision *out* of an agreement, it has had to pay a high trading price. And those durable provisions also have a way of expanding to cover situations that management, at least, had not thought were contemplated at the time of their writing.

Contract clauses which originally seemed to be only minor restrictive concessions have too frequently turned out to be Frankenstein monsters that hamper management prerogatives as their interpretations have been stretched and expanded over the years. Often, management consent to such clauses resulted from the conviction that they covered situations that would never happen; they seemed inexpensive bargains as against the cents-per-hour demands that could be traded off for such management concessions. Yet many a company entrapped by such clauses has paid a far higher price than a few cents per hour would have cost over the years.

As stated earlier, the total environment influences union-management relations. Companies must consider everything that is going on in the nation if they are to achieve effective relations with employees, their unions, and the community. Management horizons cannot be limited to the walls of the plant.

This need is especially urgent in the current intensifying atmosphere that pervades the nation. Minority group demands will strongly influence company actions for years to come. In many cases, jobs will have to be created for the minorities. The basic dilemma is how to do this and at the same time operate efficiently and profitably. While there are no doubt some companies and unions that are not ready to assume this responsibility, many more companies regard the problem as a matter of self-interest.

But even the companies that are ready to come to grips with the problem from the highest social motives often find their efforts hampered in many respects. There are so many agencies—government and private—involved in this area that it is understandable why managements can be confused, to say the least, as to what course they should adopt. Often, agencies with the same professed objectives operate at cross-purposes. Many managements are under simultaneous barrages to *do something,* even though the something that Group A insists on conflicts with what Group B wants done.

Pressures to make seniority adjustments, for instance, to accommodate minority members bear on unions as well as on managements, with little or no regard for the proprietary interests of long-service employees. Similarly, demands for waiver of essential testing requirements present difficult managerial problems. These are isolated yet vital examples of the kinds of problems facing management and unions. Reconciliation of these divergent interests will be among management's most difficult challenges in the years ahead. They will not easily be met. Clearly, the minority problem will affect most phases of the bargaining relationship and create added conflict in an already accentuated atmosphere of contentiousness.

✦   ✦   ✦

The chapters which follow suggest practical methods of dealing with the problems management faces in the administration of its industrial relations. Prepared by men who have successfully faced the issues in their day-to-day pursuits, the following chapters—as well as the foregoing comments—should serve as guides in dealing with unions and managing employee relations.

Organizing
the Enterprise

Frank P. Doyle

WITHIN THE PAST YEAR, A HANDFUL OF GRIM-FACED LABOR RELATIONS EXECU-
tives of a major American corporation sat down with a half-dozen
high-level representatives from several international unions for a critical
negotiation. The meeting, on the surface at least, was merely a local negotiation for a contract covering only one small plant of the company. Actually,
as all the participants knew, it was much more than that—it was to set the
pattern for contracts in most other plants of that diversified, multimillion-dol-
lar company. In the end, the two sides could not reach an agreement; the joint
demands the unions were making were too great a threat to the firm's
entire corporate plan. A disastrous strike ensued, followed by a settlement
which—it was clear to all—settled nothing and left the battle to be fought
again.

What went wrong? The plain fact was that the real conflict was not
between the company and the unions, but between the company and its own
industrial relations organization. The firm—whose aggressive, enlightened
management had some years before made a basic business decision in favor

FRANK P. DOYLE is vice president—public and employee relations of the Western Union
Telegraph Company.

of decentralization—was still represented in labor matters by a highly centralized industrial relations staff that exercised close control over all local contracts. As a direct result, the once-separate unions also developed a common approach and the bargaining muscle that went with it. Labor relations was dominated by a headquarters staff from within and union internationals from without. Theoretically autonomous local managers were thus denied effective control over the central element of their operation.

The situation reached an impasse. The company could not relinquish its (correctly assumed) commitment to decentralization; the unions would not relinquish their demands for common contract terms. Today, and for years to come, the entire corporation must suffer from the fact that its industrial relations structure effectively prevented the realization of its corporate goals.

DELUSIONS OF INDUSTRIAL RELATIONS

There is a natural temptation in industrial relations, as in all other disciplines, to cling to a self-centered scheme of values. The assumption that the world revolves around the bargaining table, however, is likely to result in a rude awakening. For labor relations professionals, detachment from reality manifests itself in a number of ways.

The brothers-under-the-skin syndrome. It can happen (and has, notably in the steel industry) that labor relations professionals on both sides become so involved with the artistry of their craft that they end up having greater rapport with their opponents across the bargaining table than with the interests they represent. They become alienated from their constituencies, and when this occurs the agreement they work out bears little relation to the needs of the business. Nor is the agreement responsive to employee needs (which, after all, is a legitimate function of a labor contract), making the union an inadequate channel for the employer-employee relationship.

When employee needs are not met, the rebellion may strike either union or company; but in the end it is the business that suffers. The skilled-trades turmoil in the auto industry—at first only a threat to the United Auto Workers—now hangs like a cloud over every contract negotiation in industry.

The labor relations of convenience. This is reflected in the subcontract approach: Get rid of your labor problems by passing them on to someone else. Essentially, this is an abdication of the industrial relations function—not only is the problem surrendered, but so is all control over its solution.

If, for example, maintenance tradesmen are hard to manage, you can decide to subcontract maintenance and construction projects. You and the union will fight the bloody battles of contracting out; then you will subcontract the work and breathe a sigh of relief. Remember, however, that the subcontractor lives and works under the restrictions of construction-trades contracts, pays construction-trades rates, and serves *his* industry first—not yours. And you may end up wishing you had your unmanageable maintenance men back again.

What should you have done? Recognize the existence of the problem and come to terms with it as best you can. If you can't swallow the fact that you don't win them all, you don't belong in industrial relations.

The insolence of office. Here we find one of the most common characteristics of the industrial relations department: the administrative stranglehold it has over the entire enterprise. Can the marketing vice president's secretary get a raise? The verdict is given by a functionary in a cubicle behind the file cabinets at headquarters. May a production foreman retire early? Again, the universal administrator gets his chance to exert influence.

While this may be an orderly process, it is not the best way to handle personnel management. While it may, indeed, be convenient, very often relieving the line manager of some tedious or unpleasant chores, it is not responsive to employee needs. Sooner or later, these unanswered needs explode into a red-hot grievance fed by years of frustration. Personnel management is best done by the supervisor closest to the situation. It may not be so neat and professional, but pragmatically it makes more sense.

In labor relations administration, the entrenched bureaucracy is characterized by blanket uniformity in work-practice enforcement and depersonalized answers to employee grievances. In short, the "personnel department" intrudes upon the supervisory relationship in a way that denies the supervisor an effective role in the very thing that makes him a boss—the authority to manage the people who work for him.

PHILOSOPHY OF MANAGEMENT

The sad fact is this: Once you recognize that the enterprise does not center on the industrial relations function, you realize that there is no single model for appropriate industrial relations. Instead of viewing industrial relations planning as an intellectual exercise, it should be seen as a response to the business situation. The organization of industrial relations must be analogous to the organization of the business and must serve the business—not itself.

Discussed in this chapter are three basic forms of business organization—the conglomerate (a multiplicity of small or large self-contained businesses, each its own profit center, independent of the other elements); the process-integrated system (in which the elements, while they may be in different industries, are to some degree interdependent); and the single system (the classic, one-industry corporation). Special problems of the single-plant company will also be touched upon. Each form of enterprise has its own appropriate contract relationship; and for each contract relationship a different employee relations organization is required.

A management or manager moving from one form of organization to another must recognize that, with a new form of enterprise, an entirely new labor relations approach may well be demanded. Provision for an appropriate response should be made at the very first stages of organization planning. In fact, a problem-solving group representing as many levels of responsibility for industrial relations as possible should be created to formulate a coherent approach.

In broad terms, the most effective philosophy is to keep decision making as far down on the local level as is possible without anarchy. Responsiveness and responsibility are the key words here; the closer a response is to the actual situation, the more appropriate it can be. Personnel management, in other words, should arise from the supervision of people. For this, a deliberate organizational effort is required. Managers responsible for industrial relations—all the way down to first-line supervisors—must be trained, kept informed, and made comfortable with staff assistance.

The obvious approach—in the name of "backing up our people"—is then to espouse the doctrine of managerial infallibility, defending every line decision regardless of its worth. This should be avoided. Indeed, the key to democracy as a philosophy of management is to create an atmosphere in which managers are not afraid to make mistakes because they know that their mistakes can be corrected without recrimination. Even though democracy and local decision making are the ideals, the reality may vary according to the business situation. Above all, the form these ideals should take depends upon the structure of the enterprise.

THE CONGLOMERATE ENTERPRISE

The contract relationship. In a conglomerate enterprise, the ideal contractual arrangement is a series of individual contracts that have separate expiration dates and are negotiated with different unions. With a conglomerate, the bargaining advantage is that, if there is a shutdown in one plant or industry, the remainder of the enterprise can still function normally. Loss of income is thus minimized and the amount of pressure the union is capable of bringing to bear is therefore limited. With separate expiration dates, a whipsaw situation is less likely to occur. With separate unions, negotiations are more likely to be with people sympathetic to the problems of the particular business.

It can easily happen that the labor conventions of one industry get in the way of the operating necessities of another. For example, craft-union standards could be imposed upon assembly-line production. Once this happens, it is difficult to redress.

So the cardinal rule in organizing labor relations for a conglomerate is: *Keep the contract local and separate.* It seems a pitifully simple axiom; yet the alternatives are tempting.

Consider, for example, how convenient it would be for a central employee relations staff to administer only one pension plan instead of a dozen. The savings would be formidable; everyone would benefit. In order to sell this reasonable proposal to your 12 suspicious unions, you offer them a concession—say, common expiration dates. About a year later, your unions, having thought it over, conclude that they would be much stronger dealing with you as one body. If, they reason, they have one pension plan and one expiration date, why not have one negotiation? When you protest that they represent separate industries with separate problems, they accuse you of hypocrisy, of trying to keep them weak. You have chosen, for your own convenience, to deal with them jointly in one area—now you may be forced, to your discomfort, to deal with them jointly in all areas.

The landmark case on coordinated or coalition bargaining at American Radiator & Standard Sanitary Corporation, for one, grew out of a common pension plan negotiated on coincident or closely aligned dates. The unions found it easy to stall settlement, bringing all the dates together. Then, having discovered how profitable it was to bring their combined weight of membership to bear in winning a better pension plan, they extended the practice first to a hospitalization plan, then to other areas. In three short years the decentralized labor approach, which seemed most appropriate to American Radiator's business organization, was seriously undermined. A series of bargaining maneuvers, Labor Board actions, and court decisions have not resolved this major conflict between bargaining pattern and business organization.

Organization of the employee relations department. The employee relations department exists to support the contractual superstructure and must be organized accordingly. In a conglomerate enterprise, this is a difficult and delicate task. A balance between local responsibility and central professionalism must somehow be struck.

The local employee relations manager has probably had limited bargaining experience—in a small company, with infrequent negotiations—compared to his union counterpart. Thus the temptation is strong for the headquarters employee relations staff to move in with all its expertise and experience whenever a difficult problem or critical negotiation takes place. As soon as this happens, the first step has been taken toward centralized labor relations in the enterprise. This inevitably leads to a standard, uniform approach to bargaining, which, in turn, leads to countervailing efforts to coordinate union bargaining.

Once the union coalition is formed and can bring the cumulative weight of its membership's strike threat to bear, the company succumbs. There is left only the empty solace of speeches denouncing union monopolies and never-heeded appeals for new labor legislation.

How can this trap be avoided? How do you derive the benefits of your professional central staff without losing the advantages of decentralized bargaining? By establishing the unequivocal supremacy of the local employee relations manager. He negotiates the contract. He has the final authority on all labor matters. He may or may not take the advice of the headquarters pro, whom he may or may not call upon for assistance.

The only authority the staff man can wield is the authority of expertise; if he's good enough and helpful enough, the local manager will call upon him when he needs back-up assistance. One does not report to the other, nor must one be in a position to hire or fire the other.

Staffing. First-rate men are needed on all levels to staff the employee relations function of a conglomerate enterprise. The local employee relations manager, responsible as he is for all administration and negotiation, must be able and well rounded. At headquarters there must be a small staff of seasoned professionals capable of wielding and deriving the authority of knowledge.

How is this intrinsic authority developed, considering the gulf between the outlook derived from single-contract, single-plant experience and the subtlety and sophistication required at staff level? The gulf is bridged by a conscious staff-development program in which plant-level industrial relations men are moved from facility to facility, from industry to industry, until they have broadened their base of knowledge sufficiently to operate confidently in a multiple-contract, multiple-union setting.

Given this kind of staffing and stressing a continuing sensitivity to the need for decentralized decision making, the conglomerate enterprise should have labor problems that are less difficult to handle than those in the original, preconglomerate components.

THE PROCESS-INTEGRATED ENTERPRISE

The contract relationship. Many aspects of local decision making which characterize the conglomerate are retained in an integrated enterprise. The basic difference, however, is that now the various elements are functionally related and interdependent; if one part breaks down, the entire system is affected. Thus, for example, a union could cripple the entire enterprise with one small strike in a strategic location.

For this reason, the aim is for a contract arrangement exactly the opposite of the one desired by the conglomerate. What should be sought, ideally, is a single national contract (amplified by local supplements) negotiated with one union. With such an arrangement, the union finds a strike as costly as the company does.

If the firm should find itself with numerous local contracts and several unions, its best strategy is to give them all a common expiration date. At least, in that case, its labor calendar will not be dotted with one strike after another.

Organization of the employee relations department. Once again, the goal is to keep decision making local. The plant industrial relations manager should have complete authority over his local supplement. With a national contract, however, many questions must be referred to corporate headquarters for handling under the national-level grievance machinery. In this situation, the role of the plant industrial relations manager is more investigative and less authoritative, but no less critical.

As the union will have an in-plant representative who is thoroughly familiar with the contract and who will report on all grievances in detail, the company cannot afford to be any less knowledgeable. Each facility must have an industrial relations man capable of investigating every case and submitting intelligent, detailed reports to the headquarters staff—which, in turn, will make national-level decisions based on these reports. The local industrial relations man therefore becomes critically important, albeit limited in authority; he is required to understand, interpret, and apply a contract he is relatively powerless to create.

The contract itself is the work of specialists whose direct concern with it ends the day it is signed, for it is the economists, actuaries, and industrial engineers whose expertise shapes the outline of the agreement. All the local man can do is keep up a steady flow of reports from the plant to relate the national contract to local-level operating problems.

Staffing. Presenting its own peculiar problems, staffing the industrial relations department of an integrated enterprise begins at the base level, where the need is for a great many local representatives who are not much more than leg-men. At the very top, there must be a handful of peerless negotiators backed by a large corps of functional specialists. In between these two levels is a void.

There is no logical middle step between the plant level and the headquarters staff because, with real decision making so centralized, a large staff (such as is required in a conglomerate) is unnecessary to support the local managers. The plant man is there to support the headquarters staff, not vice versa. Therefore, in this type of situation there is real difficulty in developing second-line talent capable of taking over the top.

The problem is compounded by the fact that, when the crisis of actually negotiating a contract comes, the responsibility devolves upon one or at most two men. No one else gets any real bargaining experience; no one has a chance for the kind of minor-league seasoning that produces a top negotiator. Unions, on the other hand, do not face this problem. Their men can use the entire industry as a training ground, getting experience and making mistakes with small, less critical negotiations.

For the integrated company negotiating a major contract, too much is at stake to permit the luxury of learning by error. Management must therefore make a conscious effort to groom a successor to the top man by creating an "anointed" second who, little by little, is permitted to take on more responsibility.

THE SINGLE-SYSTEM ENTERPRISE

The contract relationship. The single system, like the integrated system, suffers from acute sensitivity to local upsets. A breakdown anywhere along the line damages the entire operation. In addition, with a basically unitary operation, labor troubles are not likely to be localized; a grievance in Tonawanda is likely to be a grievance in Duluth as well. For this reason, a single national contract with one union is essential. Local supplements are usually unnecessary and undesirable.

The most serious labor threat to the single-system enterprise is union organization along craft lines. And, all too frequently, this is precisely what we find—the newspaper industry, the airlines, the railroads are all nightmare examples of disproportionate labor leverage. No further comment need be made on just how seriously these industries have been hurt; their labor problems are chronicled daily (when the newspapers are not on strike).

Management's responsibility—and opportunity—is to provide discipline and coordination even when competing unions have found that "solidarity forever" is a meaningless slogan from the past. Common or closely aligned expiration dates, the bane of the conglomerate, become a positive good for the single-system enterprise. Unquestionably, the problems do not lend themselves to easy solution; nevertheless, they must be faced. The industries thus afflicted are too vital in our political and economic system to be allowed to suffocate under the weight of collective bargaining failures.

A possible breakthrough has come from, of all places, civic government—traditionally so benighted in labor management. The Office of Collective Bargaining (OCB) of the City of New York, established under the Lindsay administration, is pioneering a rational and creative handling of a near-impossible situation.

The very creation of the legislation under which OCB was established reveals how broad a concern this type of labor conflict can arouse. A tripartite team made up of city management, labor, and public sector representatives hammered out the legislation and overcame resistance within their respective groups before the law was actually submitted for approval. As enacted, it establishes a comprehensive and continuing program in which the city, labor, and impartial mediators work together to avert strikes. It provides for a seven-man board to meet at least six times a year to consider grievance procedures, review fact-finding machinery, and recommend solutions in case of contract-talk stalemates.

Thus, in long-range planning and for a good part of the citywide administration of a variety of labor agreements, this representative group can bring its moderating influence to bear. Mediation panels are selected, bargaining units are defined, and arbitrators are chosen for resolution of contractual disputes.

In addition, both with OCB and with the city's basic labor relations approach, there is a genuine attempt to achieve a consensus on those items which cut across bargaining-unit lines. These include pensions, holidays, and sick benefits. What has been achieved is something very close to a single-contract ideal. The contractual structure becomes an exceedingly loose framework within which a variety of once-competing unions can negotiate more responsibly and with less danger of disruptive whipsawing.

New York's sanitation workers' strike of 1968 was the first real challenge to OCB. There will undoubtedly be others. Nevertheless, the Office of Collective Bargaining presents the most hopeful sign yet that this type of labor difficulty is not hopeless.

Organization of the employee relations department. Let us assume that you are fortunate enough to have a single national contract. You will now need a highly centralized industrial relations department, capable of quick response to local grievances and characterized by a close relationship with *non*-industrial-relations field personnel. This last point is the basic difference between employee relations of an integrated enterprise and that of the single system. With no local supplements to administer, an in-plant industrial relations specialist is really unnecessary. Feedback to headquarters, in the form of investigative reports, is minimal. Nor is the actual labor responsibility inherent in the job sufficient to justify his existence in this capacity alone.

The local man, charged with whatever labor relations exist, will probably have other functions while exercising day-to-day administrative authority in labor matters. When problems arise outside this purely administrative area, he should be able immediately to call upon a force of field-located labor relations experts for assistance. These traveling consultants should work closely with the line organization, but only as trouble-shooters. They should assume no day-to-day responsibility, which is left entirely to the in-plant man. The consultants' function is to supply emergency assistance along with the benefit of their expertise. In this manner, local decision making and quick, appropriate response are preserved.

Staffing. In the single-system employee relations organization, the out-of-house traveling labor experts are a sort of noncommissioned officer corps. They must be seasoned generalists as well as solid, well-rounded persons; but no more than that. After all, they have no bargaining responsibility; their function is merely to protect the existing contract.

At the very top, however, a group of expert negotiators is needed, backed by an extensive research staff. Here, as with the process-integrated enterprise, everything rides on a few weeks of face-to-face bargaining. There is no margin for error and no allowance for sloppy preparation. Contract decisions are based less on local factors than on economic and industry considerations.

The Single-Plant Company

A microcosm of the other organizational forms, the single-plant company can produce under one roof a diversity of products, related products, or one product. Depending upon the case, industrial relations are organized along the lines of those in the conglomerate, the integrated system, or the multi-plant single system. Still, there are important differences. Employees of a single-plant company are far closer in all respects than those in a far-flung business; and the labor relations reflect this fact.

There are few secrets in a one-plant company. Employees must therefore be dealt with consistently, making a uniform approach to labor relations a necessity. The industrial relations manager must, however, be careful that this consistency does not become a straitjacket for the individual foreman, preventing him from meaningful decision making. And, since consistency is a knife that cuts both ways, the industrial relations manager must at the same time be alert to union attempts to make a single favorable decision by one foreman the rule over the entire plant.

Three basic rules are useful in organizing industrial relations in the single-plant company:

1. Establish, through the contract, a grievance procedure under which decisions by individual foremen do not set precedents.
2. Train first-line supervisors in effective labor management through informal meetings and discussions in which the foremen themselves can establish patterns for supervision. (This, in fact, is sound procedure in *every* type of enterprise, since the bulk of real labor relations decisions are made not by labor relations professionals, but by foremen and other first-line supervisors.)

3. Give first-line supervisors the professional help they need by making industrial relations staff people accessible and visible at all
times. Let the industrial relations man walk up and down the
production aisle several times a day. Not only will it do him good,
as long as he doesn't intrude in the supervisory relationship, but
it will also raise the quality of day-to-day contract administration.

Above all, the foreman must not be made an errand boy for the front
office or a mouthpiece for the industrial relations manager. This will, in the
long run, limit his effectiveness in all areas. Labor relations on the production floor is an integral part of the production process. Why try to separate
it? If the nature of the production process is such that the foreman has
latitude in structuring work and making assignments, he should have equal
latitude in contract interpretation.

Similarly, on a different level, the role of the industrial relations manager
should also be seen as a vital part of the production process. He should
report directly to the plant manager, so that labor and production considerations carry equal weight. His role should be, not one of defense—reacting to
labor problems as they arise—but one that is both cogent and creative. For
this, he must participate in weekly production-planning meetings and be a
vital part of plant management.

The cohesiveness of a single-plant enterprise can be a problem or an
opportunity for creative industrial relations, depending on how the situation
is handled.

THE ENTERPRISE OF INDUSTRIAL RELATIONS

We have discussed in broad terms the type of industrial relations talent
needed in each form of enterprise. Where is this talent to come from and
how is it to be developed?

The day is not long past when personnel managers were drawn from the
ranks of deserving payroll clerks and production men who could no longer
cut the mustard. More recently, the field attracted a sanguine breed who
liked to deal with people and chose to be personnel men because they didn't
care for the rigors of sales work. Their techniques were seat-of-the-pants;
their zest was for the eyeball-to-eyeball confrontation. They were the corporate equivalent to the old leather-jacket flyboys.

Today, with labor relations a more and more critical concern in every industry, corporations can no longer afford the luxury of the dashing amateur. Men must be trained specifically for careers in the field. They should enter it, preferably, with a strong academic background. Failing this, it is best to select a bright young trainee and send him to school.

The classic training program for a top industrial relations man should follow these lines: He should start as a trainee in the headquarters industrial relations department, then be shifted to a line job supervising union employees. Having had his baptism under fire, he can then return to industrial relations in a post that will let him be involved first-hand in grievance machinery. As soon as possible, he should assist the company's top negotiator in a contract session, participating, along the way, in arbitration cases to sharpen his understanding of the importance of contract language.

Finally—and this should be as early as possible in his career—he should be permitted to negotiate a contract entirely by himself. There is no substitute for total responsibility.

As he nears the top, he should be given opportunities to sit in with the highest councils of corporate decision making. He will thus give men from other departments the benefit of his knowledge of labor relations and gain a more acute awareness of the needs of the entire business. With the interchange of ideas will come a more rational approach to his own work and a better understanding by others of the problems he faces.

Since so much in industrial relations depends upon past practice, it is difficult to operate within the framework of present, let alone future, business needs. Yet the industrial relations department should, by virtue of its influence on all segments of the business, be in the forefront of change.

The department can anticipate business needs through the enabling aspects of the contract. Many corporate programs are hamstrung by outmoded labor practices. It is the creative function of the negotiator to prepare for those programs in advance. For example, if the man responsible for labor relations knows that a major change in corporate structure may occur within five years, he can prepare for it by negotiating a nationwide seniority system in his next contract to allow the company flexibility in transferring personnel. This type of advance work is possible only if the contract, the department, and the entire function are understood within the context of the business as a whole.

Many costly labor problems could be avoided if the responsible industrial relations person had a voice in policy making. This holds as true for the production foreman as for the vice president of employee relations. Placing industrial relations in the mainstream of the enterprise is as important on the production floor as on policy-making levels.

Labor management should not be merely a defensive process of reacting to union attacks. It should be an honestly creative function by which personnel are managed to achieve productivity. This is the enterprise of industrial relations, and this is what the organization of that enterprise must achieve.

Bargaining Power

Walter H. Powell

COLLECTIVE BARGAINING ASSUMES MUTUALITY OF AGREEMENT SANCTIONED BY
the potential expression or exercise of power by either party. In extreme cases, this power may be used to close down the enterprise through a strike or lockout. Whether either party will go to such lengths depends on its ability to muster adequate strength in the attainment of ultimate objectives.

These ultimate objectives are normally economic, although ideological questions or even the simple desire to punish the other side may, at times, assume importance. But even where the issues are not economic, the final struggle will be fought and resolved in the economic arena. For example, early struggles prior to the passage of the Wagner Act were often based on the right of self-determination. The issues of wages and working conditions, while possessing economic overtones, were secondary to confirmation of the right to organize. Conversely, many industrial organizations have accepted strikes (and the acceptance of a strike as opposed to an overt lockout is a matter of semantics, not a question of who took the initiative) because they felt compelled to take a stand on such matters as the union shop, compulsory union membership, and other issues which were emotional, not economic in origin.

WALTER H. POWELL is vice president of industrial relations at IRC, a Division of TRW Inc.

Tactically, final refusal to accept an opponent's adamant or fervent position will force the use of ultimate strength by either party. Proper judgment of the adversary's position will determine whether fundamental issues will be discarded in favor of an agreement or whether a bargaining impasse will result.

Bargainers for either party will engage in many maneuvers, ploys, and expressions of strength in the choreography of the normal negotiation. As extreme positions become isolated, judgment factors must of necessity measure the seriousness of the position, the adversary's demand and the consequence of absolute refusal, the alternatives, and the simple process of bargaining it into decay. Some issues will continue with obstinacy; only a resolution of such an issue will meet the parties' objectives. Without such a resolution, bargaining becomes meaningless and the parties may resort to the free use of bargaining power.

There are many nuances, flavors, and hints which can render avoidable these ultimate positions. However, whether such positions result from the political concepts of the union, the political aspirations of its leadership, or the will of its members, the positions may become obdurate. Similarly, management's team may be restricted emotionally or economically where compromise from its preconceived position spells defeat. Thus the adherence to a final position incapable of resolution calls for a strike, an invitation to strike, or a lockout. Any of these choices means a work stoppage.

Work Stoppages

The consequences of a work stoppage run the gamut from mere discomfort to the finalities of never reopening, bankruptcy, or capitulation. Both parties must assess what the costs of such action will be. Since the parties, of necessity, operate from different bases, strategy and tactics must be examined in terms of their unique positions and not in joint terms. While bargaining power may be used because of peculiar economic advantages to one party, those same advantages may have no value or even be disadvantageous to the other party. For example, an off-seasonal disruption of work could have little effect upon the seasonal manufacturer; conversely, seasonal disruption would be greatly advantageous to the union.

Advantages to one side, however, are not always disadvantages to the other. In some instances, there will be a counterpull on the opposition; in other instances, there will be no important results. In other words, each party's position must be examined according to its own particular criteria.

Strengths and weaknesses cannot be arbitrarily computed on a balance sheet; each party, within the totality of its action, can bring greater or lesser degrees of influence on the other through a work stoppage. The union's prime weapon is the threat of a strike. A decision by the union to provoke a strike is an acceptance of the alternative of a secondary weapon. Once a work stoppage has occurred, a whole new set of criteria comes into being which pits the relative economic strength of the union against that of management.

Thus, understanding the union's position and its problems is an absolute necessity for management's final-decision makers. Indeed, comparison of the relative bargaining and relative power alternatives of one's opponent is essential in all forms of opposition, whether it be games, war, collective bargaining, or power politics. Whenever the decision depends on relative strength and power, the opposing moves, tactics, and strategy are all based on intelligence and countermoves.

The very makeup of the union's membership may be the most compelling factor. If, for example, a company operated in a rural community with predominantly female help—most of whom were second wage earners in a family—the prospects of economic hurt from a work stoppage would be minimal. Families would continue to eat and many employees might even relish the idea of an enforced vacation enabling them to complete their spring housekeeping, stay home with their children during the summer, or assist in the fall harvest. In such a case, therefore, the urgency of returning to work would not be a factor propelling the union leader into a quick settlement.

STRIKE SETTLEMENTS

After a strike, settlements depend on the makeup of the workforce—young or old, male or female—and the extent of the union treasury and its strike fund: Is the particular local a member of a large international union? Has the national or international a good treasury, or has it recently been depleted?

Just as the assets of the corporation must be examined, so must those of the union. Borrowing capacity of the employees—individually and collectively—within the community, sympathies of local unions, and actions to assist the union will, in part, set the limits of its staying power.

This staying power, in itself, may have deeper psychological influences, depending on the reaction of the union membership. If, for example, the issues of disagreement have a highly inflammable emotional content, the time of settlement will be delayed. Thus, when seniority is threatened as opposed to mere additional pennies in the settlement, the very core of unionism, along with its past victories, is at stake. Vitalizing an issue, for the union, will give it strength nurtured from within, far beyond its economic capabilities of maintaining and sustaining a long strike.

Management's behavior during a strike can prolong the situation by giving sustenance to the reason for the breach, just as management's approachableness and reactions to employees, even in contrived contacts, can shake the solidity of the union. Behavior patterns of management prior to and during the collective bargaining sessions will often determine the length of a stoppage.

Good or bad morale and the employees' regard for their employer are not such trite factors that they are of no importance to relative bargaining power. While morale is rarely the aggressive, outspoken force of reason and rationality, in the face of opposite attitudes it often becomes the voice of restraint and sometimes the face-saving device needed by more indignant members.

Union officials are faced with comparisons of political power, aptitude, and results; the perpetuation of their powers is hardly distinguishable from the continuity of management. Successful strikes are built upon the union leaders' desire to gain capitulation to their point of view. Thus their battle tactics must include an unswerving belief in what they are doing. And this belief must not only be sold to the union members, but must also be adhered to and supported by them. In today's affluent society, however, union members are often at odds with their leaders, willing to pursue strikes and economic power not so much for the pursuit of further economic gain, but as a release from the drabness and boredom of the status quo.

While loss of control over its membership can be devastating to a union's position, it does not always redound to management's advantage. Such loss of control can lead to the emergence of a leaderless mass out of control, out of reason, and beyond reparation for resolving ultimate agreement.

PREPARING A SHUTDOWN

Management's strategy in accepting a shutdown, whether by action or reaction, must always be directed toward an ultimate resumption of work.

Resorting to a plant shutdown requires as much planning as any other facet of the business operation; for not only will the consequences of such an act shape the future of the union-management relationship, but it will also have long- and short-run effects on the very nature of the business.

Preplanning for a shutdown may permit advance shipping to customers, advance billing, and strategic relocation of inventories to insure continued product flow and thus minimal disruption of customer goodwill. Of course, extensive preplanning and preshipping may not always be feasible, depending in large measure on the distribution channels and policies of the enterprise.

Too often, management does not consider its true bargaining strength and power. The emotionalism of a particular issue or the price of a specific demand so outweighs the desire to compromise that the decision to accept the ultimate is not balanced against the true costs. Such costs—including inability to make deliveries and temporary and possibly irrevocable loss of customers to competition—may be difficult to measure.

Management's decision to exercise its bargaining power requires new forecasting and planning to overcome the breach in normal company life. Although revenue is lost during a strike, many costs will continue, such as capital flow, certain salaries, inventories, insurance, rent, and other fixed costs. These, however, are predictable and should provide the basis for the action taken and the decisions made.

Collective bargaining cannot exist without constant review of the ultimate decision to strike. The whole economy reacts to certain major negotiations six months to a year in advance. For example, steel stockpiling for users occurs from six months to a year before the parties even enter hard-core negotiations. Critical parts and components are tracked down by purchasing men to insure continuity of production in their plants and to insure against work stoppage in their suppliers' plants.

Since the economy has accepted the possibility of work stoppages, certain mechanisms are now in existence to diminish their impact. On an individual basis, a management may well decide to continue full or partial operations in opposition to a strike.

Here, too, preplanning provisions must consider the solidarity or lack of solidarity of the workforce as well as the political climate of the community, police protection, and judicial proceedings. These factors may all work together to permit or prohibit plant operation. In a highly unionized community, it is very unlikely that the local police will give support or protection to strike breakers; whereas, in a rural community or right-to-work state, the climate might permit plant operation. Again, ultimate bargaining power becomes an individual exercise, depending on the circumstances, timing, and alternatives available to the particular establishment. In a multiplant situation, production might be transferred; on the other hand, multiple unions might prohibit it.

ULTIMATE POWER DECISIONS

Exercise of the ultimate power should always bear a relationship to its alternatives; and adherence to an alternative, once it is adopted, is imperative. Retreat after the initial action will often give rise to a lasting division of loyalties and irreparable hard feelings.

The use of ultimate power, as contrasted with the mere threat of it, requires constant attention to all the variables which first brought such a decision into being. Adherence to the decision must be not simply a blind obedience but a rational action without the fallacies, emotions, and retributions which ordinarily give rise to such a course of action.

Too often, when both parties believe that a strike will be short-lived, failure to settle quickly causes real distress. Hopelessness replaces hope, and lack of planning for this contingency results in serious doubt being raised as to the justification for the original action. Many ploys and counterploys disturb the original plan if a strike continues for an appreciably longer span of time than had been expected.

Union leadership, without any fruits of victory, cannot find a face-saving mechanism to rationalize work resumption. Management, feeling the impact of meeting salaried payrolls and ongoing costs in the face of no income, is distressed over the defeat that must be accepted. Punishment by means of loss of income may cause employees to develop adverse attitudes which remain for an extended period after work is resumed.

Somewhere short of the ultimate in bargaining power is the basis for sound collective bargaining. Often, the exercise of final power is a demonstration of weakness and lack of discipline rather than a positive, planned course of action.

Sometimes, management is faced with an unplanned action: Labor engages in partial shutdowns, slowdowns, or mass absenteeism to disrupt production in the late stages of negotiation. Conceivably, a partial strike could cause the same disruption as a full-scale strike. Again, management's power alternatives are a complete shutdown, disciplinary action, recourse across the bargaining table, or calling a halt to negotiations until the situation reverts to normal. Partial strikes have the same potential bargaining power as total strikes, and management either reacts to their impact or takes positive steps to deal with them. Management's response, while spontaneous in point of time, should be based on the same alternatives with which the realities of a total strike would be faced. More often than not, strength from management at this point will offset the union's partial exercise of power.

COORDINATIVE TECHNIQUES

Often, one can follow the leader without participating in determining one's own future. In the more sophisticated industries, however, techniques have been used to counter union whipsawing action. In some instances, companies have banded together through industrywide bargaining, with one negotiating team bargaining for all companies. In other instances, industry councils have been created offering a complete interchange of information and wage structures, as well as a general agreement on the type of action the lead company should take in wage negotiations. Protective mechanisms are established among the companies to protect the lead company. In such sophisticated industries as the airlines, strike insurance has been provided so that if any one line is struck, the other companies will help to maintain the profitability of the struck company during the course of the strike.

While the use of coordinative techniques is a means of expanding companies' bargaining power, these techniques bring certain responsibilities to bear upon the participating companies. Often, the combinations pose legal implications wherein companies may not unilaterally remove themselves from the coalitions; and, sometimes, the price of a bargain may be greater than that which could have been negotiated individually. Profitability, in fact, tends to be an industry average rather than a unique bargaining tool for an individual company.

In general, bargaining power from the corporate point of view must be weighed in the context of the total objectives of the company. Its use and abuse are dependent on the particular situation at the particular time in line with the attainment of management's ultimate goals.

Evolving
Management's Objectives

Walter H. Powell

AN ACCURATE PICTURE OF THE JOB OF MANAGING WOULD NATURALLY INCLUDE planning in a long-run sense. Attempting to clarify company objectives and their relationship to the planning process as a whole assumes that these objectives are primary purposes toward which the company is directing its activities.

Too often, however, collective bargaining objectives have been taken out of the mainstream of company planning. The collective bargaining philosophy—if, indeed, one exists—has been regarded as an expedient to restrict the thrust of a union's demands rather than an overt expression of management's hopes and aspirations.

The very words "collective bargaining" assume a mutuality of purpose within and from which the ultimate bargain arises, rather than merely a restraint or negative reaction to union proposals. Thus the successful management negotiator of tomorrow has a huge task ahead of him—one that is conceived in objectives and philosophy, not in a mere minimization of union demands.

Structuring management's preparations for its relationship with a union encompasses a program which can effectuate management's basic objectives.

Perhaps it is oversimplifying to state simple objectives and then build upon them to formulate the plan of philosophy, the program, and the strategy to be followed. But top management planning will enumerate the company's direction in stimulating growth, increasing profitability, insuring survival, and achieving greater operational stability.

Attaining these objectives requires a philosophy of positive collective bargaining. Such bargaining is more than mere haggling in the marketplace; nor is it the Eastern bazaar where parties are governed by the ancient precept, let the buyer beware. The ultimate agreement is between two parties who will continue to live with the fruits of their negotiations.

In the past, the success of a negotiator was measured by his dubious victory in obtaining settlements for pennies less than others. Negotiators prided themselves on the tremendous savings to management in pennies per hour and in the prevention of work stoppages. Too often, however, the price was far in excess of the cost because restrictive work and plant practices were easily traded, dissipating management's freedom to manage and concurrently increasing the cost of operations.

While the prime objective facing any negotiator is the reduction of labor costs, a secondary objective is the maintenance of equitable wage scales which are balanced internally and externally as part of the negotiations—and this in no way contradicts the basic objective of reducing labor costs. A very small group of companies stands out as such pattern makers in present-day wage negotiations.

FOREIGN COMPETITION

Research plus the positions of individual firms will guide negotiators in framing their wage package in absolute terms, in managerial concurrence, and in furtherance of their own objectives. Often, however, a new and cogent variable has been introduced at the bargaining table by an absent member—one whose wage scales and labor costs are in direct competition with the operation of the particular enterprise or the particular industry. The name of this absent member is foreign competition.

For many industries, foreign competition has evolved from a threat to an actuality. Acceptable foreign products made by skilled workmen with a high order of technical ability are making inroads into our markets. Wage differentials between domestic and foreign sources have become increasingly important in determining the tactics of the negotiator.

Thus, to formulate a price objective as part of the bargain, the competitiveness of the particular workforce must be compared to domestic and foreign rivals, as well as to local and national wage scales.

REDUCED LABOR COSTS

Reducing the wage package to a palatable sum is only a small part of the total of bargaining objectives. The quest for reduced labor costs will necessitate a minute examination of the existing contract.

While it is well to speak of reclaiming management's rights and management's prerogatives, the question at hand is the examination of clauses having a cost influence on operations. The problem is to present to the union the necessity of reducing labor costs and, at the same time, increasing wages. Many practices contained in the union contract represent real cost and financial obligations on the part of the company, with little financial gain to the union or its individual members.

Consider, for example, the cost of intraplant movement. In most companies, it represents a staggering figure and a definite increase in labor and absolute costs through training, retraining, loss of productivity, waste, and the significant friction that accompanies change. Sometimes, such movement is unavoidable—for example, when it is caused by a seasonal or cyclical demand for the product; but much of it is caused by the unnecessary bumping and bidding required by the contract. Restriction of voluntary movement, whether it be lateral or downward, will curtail unnecessary rises in costs. Yet this problem is so fundamental that it is often overlooked as a possible avenue to pursue in seeking reductions in labor costs.

Another deterrent to reduced costs is the fact that every contract contains clauses which have long outlived their usefulness. They exist in the contract as a bar to management's future action and were originally created to protect union members against some managerial indiscretion in the past. Such clauses for protection against past sins remain in the contract as a bar to nothing and do in fact increase costs.

Also contributing to increased labor costs are the many contracts which provide for premium payments or just straight-time payments—dollars either way—in rewarding people for time not worked. The gamut of payments for jury duty, sick leave, death in the family, and so forth, plus holidays and vacations, are vital factors in increasing labor costs. Of course, it is not feasible to simply drop benefits which have been created to improve the welfare and health of our industrial society. It is important, however, to relate these benefits to direct costs before extending them in the future.

Past provisions for washup time and delay time and obscure allowances may well have outlived their purpose. For example, in areas where hygienic conditions have replaced dirty operations, washup time may be as obsolete as the dodo bird; but the clause and the expense accruing from it linger on.

FUTURE GOALS

The parameters of future negotiations will have to go beyond the traditional economic strengths of the parties. Negotiators must thoroughly acquaint themselves with the economics of manufacturing and the problems of production and production costs. The time-honored instruments of negotiating union demands are not enough; bargaining is an art embracing well-established scientific tools. And objectives can be attained only through the use of these tools and techniques, so that the full application of computer technology, statistics, profit-volume curves, and breakeven analysis may be factored into the decision-making process.

Many companies are engaging in pre-collective-bargaining sessions where issues can be reduced to bargainable terms so as to eliminate the vitriolic animosities of outmoded negotiations. Permanent bargaining sessions and all-year sessions are supplanting the crisis bargaining of the past. Bringing participative management techniques to the collective bargaining process in this way is a logical extension of sound management practices. After all, the behavioral sciences have contributed to a better understanding of man in the work situation—why not a natural extension of this understanding to an area where mutuality is at a premium?

Mutuality of objectives between labor and management is more than a shibboleth. The strident voice of labor basing its demands on industry potential, business acumen, and profitability underscores the realization of sound business practices. Too long have the prejudices of the past and the inbred biases of antiunionism been incorporated into management philosophy. Management should analyze the labor movement and, more specifically, the unions which confront it with the same regard that it uses to analyze its competitors.

These very same competitors join together in trade associations to root out and solve industry problems. They exchange information on wage rates. The trade press publishes details on marketing techniques. And, more often than not—without collusion and antitrust actions—competitive companies either follow or lead each other in price determinations. Often, these same companies share the market and their customers' favor because the sage buyer does not wish to put himself at the mercy of a single source.

Unions are similar competitors striving for a greater proportion of the expense dollar and more abundant profits. They want management to penetrate more markets, thus increasing the supply of jobs. Jobs are always part of cost reduction campaigns, and these campaigns are becoming a way of life in most negotiations.

Commonality and mutuality ought to be the foundations for assessment of the objective. A momentary victory, while not without some satisfaction to the negotiator, may prove costly in terms of future activities and expenses. Short-run gains, which have often been the shallow victories of a particular negotiation, may later lead to massive retaliation—too often at a time when more meaningful objectives are the criteria of success.

The flat cents-per-hour increases across the board, which were the fashion not too many years ago, satisfied the absolute cost requirements of top management and, in particular, the cost accountants and financial men. Yet the havoc wreaked upon future negotiations by forcing wider differentials in pay for both skilled trades and recognized crafts as well as payment of other status differentials has been far more costly than the pennies saved.

Similarly, the relaxation of care over nonfinancial encroachment on running the business as a softening-up process has been most expensive in the long run. The give-and-take over the bargaining table has veered from the objectives to the victory of the moment.

Objectives may disappear under the impact of the bargaining situation, but each retreat should be carefully measured against its immediate as well as future cost. Too often, emotional issues introduced or adhered to by either party bring about stalemates that require drastic deviations from other objectives in order to work out the ultimate settlement.

Clear objectives, well conceived, well thought out, and well presented, can set the tone and direction of the negotiation. Pride and rigid adherence to managerial prerogatives are deterrents rather than adjuncts to sound bargaining practices. Thus adherence to principles must be analyzed in terms of alternatives and the ultimate achievement of the original objectives.

Merely nullifying the union's position or lessening the cost of a settlement is negative rather than positive collective bargaining. And it is only through positive bargaining that objectives can be attained.

Understanding
the Union

Maurice S. Trotta

LABOR-MANAGEMENT RELATIONS OPERATES ON TWO LEVELS: INSTITUTIONAL AND human. Thus disputes may arise because of conflicting personalities, differences in institutional functions and objectives, or differences in subjective value judgments and attitudes.

A representative of management cannot deal effectively with a union unless he comprehends not only its economic functions but also the thoughts and feelings of its members. Also important is an understanding of internal union politics.

Since the objectives and problems of a business executive are different from those of a union member or leader, some conflict is inevitable. However, the economic welfare of business, labor, and the country as a whole requires that ways and means be found to reduce the area and intensity of that conflict. New and better methods must be found to resolve labor-management disputes.

There is an insistent and growing demand by representatives of both labor and management that present methods of collective bargaining and

DR. MAURICE S. TROTTA is professor of industrial relations, management, and law at New York University and an arbitrator of labor disputes.

settling contract disputes be improved. Widespread dissatisfaction exists re-garding all-night crisis bargaining and strikes which often result in huge losses in wages and profits as well as in public inconvenience. But formulat-ing new methods of dealing with labor-management disputes—based upon the concepts of free management and free labor—is not easy. There are, however, two essential ingredients of improved labor-management rela-tions: a better knowledge by each of the other's economic functions and problems and an understanding of the human and political aspects of the relationship.

ECONOMIC FUNCTIONS OF UNIONS

As an economic institution a union has certain specific economic func-tions to perform. Union leaders believe that a union is necessary for labor to obtain a fair share of the gross national product, and they do not believe that an individual worker will receive wages commensurate with his contribution unless he bargains collectively. It is argued that, under normal conditions and in the absence of a union, workers compete with each other for available work and employers will pay, not what the services are worth, but the lowest wages possible. Union economists point out that mass purchasing power, which is the basis of a growing and prosperous economy and increased profits, depends on good wages. Economists reason that it is bad for business when a disproportionate amount of the gross national product is retained in the form of capital and invested in new productive facilities, because more products will be produced than can be consumed. They also feel that labor's participation in increased productivity is necessary for an expanding economy.

Labor points out that part of its economic function is to obtain higher real wages and such economic benefits as paid holidays and vacations, pen-sions, sick leave, hospitalization, and insurance. In the absence of a union, labor concludes, management will usually not grant these economic benefits even when the individual firm and the economy can afford it. Unions argue that even when an individual employer wishes to increase wages and other economic benefits, he may not be able to do so if others in his industry, with whom he must compete, refuse to follow suit. But a union, by dealing collectively with an industry, can make these benefits possible.

The economic insecurity felt by all employees in the plant when manage-ment lays off workers regardless of seniority is another problem that a union attempts to cope with. Unions believe that by laying men off according to seniority the worker with long years of service has some degree of economic security. Moreover, since foremen do not always promote on the basis of ability but frequently base promotions on friendship, the principle of seniority is needed to avoid discriminatory practices.

Unions contend that foremen and other representatives of management frequently discipline or discharge employees unfairly, which may seriously affect the employee's ability to obtain other employment. Thus, unions conclude, a grievance procedure terminating in arbitration is needed to prevent and correct unfair management decisions.

POLITICAL ASPECTS OF UNIONS

The president and other top local union officials are elected by the members of the union. A shop steward is also usually elected by the men in his department. Officers of the national unions are elected at conventions. Many of these elected officials receive good salaries, exercise wide powers, and perform important and interesting work. Participating in union politics is a means of increasing income, acquiring power, improving status, and satisfying the urge to be a participant—not merely a spectator. There are also political rivalries among the national unions within the AFL-CIO.

The realities of union politics must be understood by management. Politics may explain why certain demands are made, why particular union officials maintain certain positions during collective bargaining, why it is possible or impossible to agree on the terms and conditions of a new contract. A strike may be called for political as well as economic reasons.

In order to win votes, a politically oriented shop steward may pursue a grievance which has little if any merit in order to obtain the political support of the grievant or to show the other union members that he will fight for their rights. An insecure union president who is running for reelection may make demands or take certain attitudes toward management which he would not ordinarily do.

The negotiating committee of a union may refuse to accept a management offer, in spite of economic realities, if a rival union has won a larger wage increase. Sometimes, a settlement made by a local may be an important political factor at the national convention, and political rivalries on the national level may well affect the whole national economic situation.

Politicians, whether they are in a local union or in the state legislature, must, if they wish to be reelected, follow the same rules. To obtain votes, a politican must be aware of the problems of his constituents and try to solve them. To obtain the political support of others, he may have to make promises. His political image is important and he is constantly seeking ways to discredit his opponent.

To understand unions, then, management—on all levels—must be cognizant of union politics.

History of American Labor Unions

The Philadelphia Cordwainers, organized in 1794, was probably the first genuine trade union in the United States. It successfully struck against a cut in wages in 1799; but, when it struck again in 1806, the court convicted its leaders of criminal conspiracy. This destroyed the union. These early unions were local in nature and consisted of skilled craft workers.

The year 1827 marks the beginning of a real labor union movement, when various unions in Philadelphia joined to form the Mechanics Union of Trade Associations, which, in 1828, started the Mechanics Free Press—the first labor newspaper. Similar organizations were founded in New York, Baltimore, and Boston. In 1828, the Philadelphia Association founded the first labor party, the Workingmen's Party. Its platform advocated public education, free suffrage, abolition of imprisonment for debt, and a ten-hour day. It collapsed in 1832.

The National Trade Union, organized in 1834, was the first attempt to unite all unions on a national scale. The first permanent national craft unions, which are still in existence, were organized in the 1850's. The Typographical Union was formed in 1850, the Stonecutters in 1853, the Hat Finishers in 1854, the Molders and Machinists in 1857. Because of its political activities, the National Trade Union ceased to be effective after 1872.

It was succeeded by the Noble Order of the Knights of Labor, which was started as a single secret society of Philadelphia Tailors in 1869 and grew rapidly until its membership reached 700,000 in 1886. Its objective was to weld all workers, regardless of race, creed, nationality, sex, or skill, into a single economic and political organization. It succeeded in winning several strikes, including one against the Jay Gould railroad system in 1885. But in 1886 it was charged with participating in the Haymarket riot in Chicago and was discredited.

The national craft unions felt that the Knights of Labor's policy of admitting unskilled workers was a threat to their bargaining power and thus their very existence. Therefore, in 1881 they started a movement to form a federation of craft unions which became, in 1886, the American Federation of Labor. The A.F. of L. was a loose federation of skilled craft national unions with primarily economic objectives. As Samuel Gompers, its first president, expressed it, unions wanted "more, more, more, now." They sought higher pay, shorter hours, and better working conditions. Political activities were limited to economic interests. They lobbied for the eight-hour day, child labor legislation, apprentice regulation, and restriction of immigration.

In 1886 the A.F. of L. had only 150,000 members; in 1898 membership had risen to 278,000; by 1904, to 1,682,000; by 1917, to 2,457,000; and by 1920 it had a membership of 4,093,000. As a result of the lack of an aggressive organizing campaign (particularly among the semiskilled in the mass production industries), a drive by industry to weaken unions during the 1920's, and the economic depression, membership fell to 2,318,000 in 1933. It increased to 9 million in 1945 and close to 11 million in 1954.

Considerable disagreement existed among the national unions as to the wisdom of trying to organize the semiskilled and unskilled. Many believed that because of their poor bargaining position they would weaken the entire labor union movement. When the A.F. of L. convention refused to support the organization of the semiskilled along industrial lines, ten large international unions led by John L. Lewis and the United Mine Workers—in itself an industrial type of union—formed the Committee for Industrial Organization to organize the mass production industries. These ten unions were promptly expelled from the A.F. of L. for dual unionism. When attempts to reconcile the differences failed, the Congress of Industrial Organizations was formed in 1938 as a permanent rival federation.

The national unions affiliated with the C.I.O. pooled their funds for a vast organizational drive which was successful in organizing the steel, automobile, rubber, oil, textiles, and electrical appliance industries. By 1942 the C.I.O. had more than five million members, and in 1945 its membership had topped six and one-half million.

The split in the labor union movement lasted until 1955 when both organizations agreed to merge into an organization called the American Federation of Labor and the Congress of Industrial Organizations (AFL-CIO). In 1966 total membership in the AFL-CIO was 16,150,000.

Local Unions

The basic unit in the union structure is the local union. In 1966 there were 76,496 local unions in the United States. When an employee becomes a union member, he joins a particular local, pays initiation fees and dues to it, and attends its meetings. He participates in the political affairs of the union by running for office and voting for the officials of the local. He may serve as a business agent or shop steward or as a member of the grievance committee, the negotiating committee, or other committees. At union meetings he has the right to express his opinions on all union affairs and vote on any matter brought before the membership including whether to go on strike or to ratify a contract negotiated by the negotiating committee. If he files a grievance that is submitted to arbitration, he is entitled to representation by a union official or a union lawyer at the arbitration proceedings.

With some exceptions local unions are granted charters by national and international unions. (Some national unions are called international because they have locals in Canada and Mexico. Here, the word "nationals" is used to refer to both.)

Some local unions decide to disaffiliate and become independent; others are initially independent and not affiliated with any national or other labor organization. The national will appoint a trustee to control the funds and affairs of the local if local officials violate the provisions of the union's constitution or commit unethical or illegal acts. The degree of control exercised by the national over the local in such matters as contract negotiations, calling of strikes, and arbitration varies from one union to another. In general, the industrial type of national union exerts a greater degree of control over local unions than the craft type. A certain percentage of the dues collected by the local is paid to the national to support its activities.

Members of a local union may be working in different companies. To illustrate, Local 302 of the Cafeteria Employees Union has approximately 8,000 members who work in several hundred cafeterias in the city of New York, including many units of the Horn and Hardart chain of restaurants in the metropolitan area. Many of the larger cafeterias belong to the Affiliated Restaurateurs, Inc., which is run by a full-time manager and his staff. Their primary function is to administer the master contract which has been negotiated by a committee selected by the members and to keep the members informed of laws, rules, regulations, and so forth, which affect them. Much of their time is spent in settling employee grievances with union business agents for their members and in preparing cases that are submitted to arbitration. Local 302 and the Affiliated Restaurateurs have provided in their master agreement for a permanent arbitrator who bears the title "Impartial Chairman." He is named in the contract, serves for its duration, and is empowered to hear and decide on all disputes arising under the terms and conditions of the master collective bargaining agreement.

The members of a local union may work at only one company if its size warrants this. To illustrate, Local 600 of the United Auto Workers represents only the employees of the Ford Motor Company.

In contrast, American Airlines negotiates contracts with the Transport Workers of America, the International Association of Machinists, Airline Dispatchers Association, Allied Pilots Association (Ind.), and Flight Engineers International Association.

The various local unions whose members work in hotels in New York City have joined together into a Hotel Trades Council. The council negotiates with the New York City Hotel Association, which represents a large number of hotels. Their master contract also provides for a permanent arbitrator.

The elected officials of a local union may vary, but generally consist of a president, a secretary-treasurer, and an executive board. Union officers of very small local unions are not usually compensated or may receive a nominal sum of money for expenses and hold regular jobs. In the larger unions the officials spend all their time on union affairs, and their compensation usually varies with the size of the union. In very large unions like the Teamsters the president is paid a large salary, but in others his compensation is related to the earnings he would receive on his regular job in industry.

The shop steward, elected by the union members working in a particular department of a company, receives a token compensation or nothing at all; but he performs several critical functions. Employees discuss their complaints with him, and those that are justified are processed by the shop steward as grievances. He also makes certain that the foreman in his department abides by the terms and conditions of the contract.

Whether a good or bad relationship exists between company and union depends, in large measure, on the character of the relationship that exists between the shop steward and foreman. If either or both of these men are aggressive, unreasonable, domineering, or emotional, serious labor-management problems will ensue. Realizing this, many companies are instituting supervisory training programs and many unions are sending shop stewards to training sessions and are publishing booklets for their guidance.

To deal with a union intelligently, management must be aware of union politics and political ambitions as well as the psychological factors that motivate union officials.

In brief, the functions of a local union are negotiating a collective bargaining agreement and administering its provisions, processing grievances through the various steps in the grievance procedure, and going to arbitration when necessary. The local union also participates with management in the administration of health and welfare funds, pension plans, and other negotiated benefits.

NATIONAL AND INTERNATIONAL UNIONS

Structurally and financially independent entities consisting of the locals to which they have granted charters, national and international unions receive financial support from the local unions. Organizing the unorganized within their jurisdiction and giving financial and other support to local unions during strikes are two of their principal functions.

The nationals maintain a regional organization with each region headed by a director and staffed by international representatives who work full time for the national. Each international representative is assigned to assist certain locals in his geographical area. He advises and represents these local officials during contract negotiations, grievance proceedings, and arbitration hearings. The degree of control the national exercises over the local varies from union to union.

A national union operates under a constitution which is similar in form and content to the constitutions of clubs and other associations. The supreme legislative body is the national convention, held every two to four years, to which local unions send elected delegates. Day-to-day affairs are carried out by officials elected at the national convention. They, in turn, are aided by an administrative staff of paid employees who work at the national headquarters. Many of the nationals have their headquarters in Washington, D.C. The administrative staffs include lawyers, economists, statisticians, and public relations specialists as well as a director of research, an educational director, and an editor who supervises publications.

There are two types of national unions: craft and industrial. The craft union, such as the Carpenters, consists of skilled craftsmen and apprentices in the same trade. The industrial union, such as the United Auto Workers, consists of all workers—skilled, semiskilled, and unskilled—who work in the same industry.

AFL-CIO

The AFL-CIO is a federation of 129 autonomous and independent national and international unions. However, in practice the unions usually follow federation policies, adopted at a national convention held every two years, which generally pertain to social and economic matters. Officials of the AFL-CIO are chosen at this convention. The federation is governed between conventions by an executive council composed of a president, a secretary-treasurer, and 27 vice presidents who meet three times a year. In addition to its general administrative functions the council may investigate, try, and suspend affiliates charged with corrupt practices.

A general board composed of the executive council and the presidents of all the affiliates meets upon call of the president or the executive council. The AFL-CIO is financed by a per capita tax levied on the affiliated national and international unions. An organization chart of the AFL-CIO is shown in the accompanying exhibit on page 56.

In addition to speaking for organized labor and lobbying for federal legislation, organizing the unorganized into unions is one of the most important functions of the federation. At the head of this activity is a director of organization. Another important function of the federation is the prevention and settlement of jurisdictional disputes between nationals. A jurisdictional dispute arises when two national unions claim the right to organize and represent the same workers or when there is a dispute as to which union members shall perform a certain type of work. Procedures similar to arbitration have been established to adjudicate jurisdictional disputes.

The Union Labels Trades Department promotes the use of the union label and attempts to make workers label conscious. The federation also charters city and state organizations. The state AFL-CIO organization plays an important part in lobbying for state labor legislation and endorsing candidates for public office.

City Central Labor Councils

A city central, such as the Central Trades Council of New York City, is an affiliation of local unions in a city. They select the officials of the city

AFL-CIO STRUCTURE

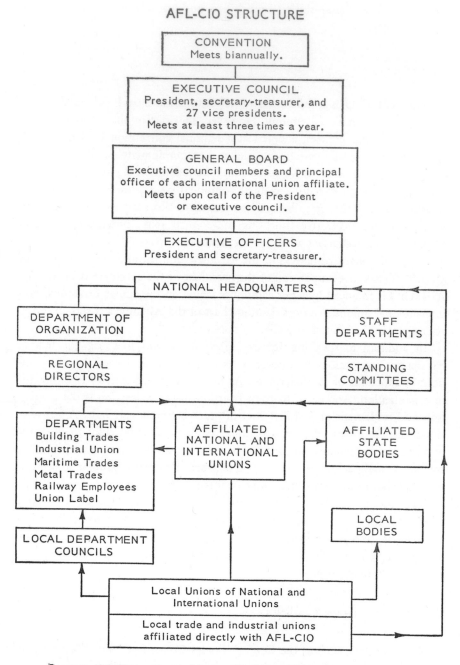

Source: U.S. Department of Labor, Bureau of Labor Statistics, 1967.

central and give it financial support. This organization correlates the activities of the local unions in the community, acts as a spokesman of labor in municipal affairs, and is active in local politics, organizational work, and social affairs.

JOINT BOARDS

Frequently, the locals of a national union that are located in the same geographical area form an organization sometimes known as a joint board. It serves to coordinate the activities of the affiliated locals and attempts to settle jurisdictional disputes among them. In the restaurant industry in New York City the various unions, all of which belong to the same national, have a joint board. Affiliated with this board are local unions representing chefs and cooks, waiters and waitresses, cafeteria workers, bartenders, and so forth.

UNAFFILIATED UNIONS

It has been estimated that in the United States and Canada about three million workers belong to unions that are not affiliated with the AFL-CIO. These workers belong to 61 national unions which have 11,877 locals and fall into three categories: large national unions such as the Teamsters (1.5 million); smaller independent unions which have organized and decided to remain independent or have broken away from the nationals; and unions representing employees of a single employer who have chosen not to affiliate with the nationals.

Some of the smaller independent unions have formed federations; one of the largest is the Confederated Unions of America, with a total of about 50,000 members.

Assembling the Facts

James F. Honzik

THE KEY TO ANY SUCCESSFUL NEGOTIATION IS KNOWLEDGE. BUSINESS ENTER- prises remain profitable over time if management decisions are consistently based upon the best available facts, information, and background material. The successful executive knows the wisdom of having a wealth of data readily available, even though it may not be used.

This need for accurate, detailed information is equally important in labor negotiations. The organized employer is bound by law to negotiate with the representative of his employees. The labor agreement differs from other business contracts in that it is the result of a statutory obligation to bargain on the mandatory subjects of wages, hours, and working conditions. An organized business cannot escape this obligation. Research and development costs are recognized as a necessary tool of business; research and planning concerning negotiations are equally necessary.

Since the duty to bargain is a continuing obligation, the assembling of information necessary for negotiations should begin the day a contract is signed and should continue until a new agreement is reached. The cycle

JAMES F. HONZIK is associated with the Milwaukee labor law firm of Lamfrom, Peck, Ferebee & Brigden.

58

should then be repeated. With facts—the management team's key tool—an intelligent approach can be taken toward every demand, and management philosophy as shown by corporate and labor objectives can be maintained.

The shop superintendent, plant manager, union relations director, attorney, or other person representing the company is usually confronted by a committee headed by a local or international union official who spends 100 percent of his time organizing, negotiating, and interpreting contracts for the employees he represents. Such officials are prepared for and experienced in their duties. Two of the biggest mistakes a company can make are to underestimate the ability of the union committee and to enter negotiations unprepared.

Unions are ready. Most internationals have large research staffs from which the union negotiating team can draw extensive, comprehensive, and exact information concerning all phases of collective bargaining. Central headquarters has computerized its research and now locals can easily obtain data and statistics from other labor agreements that they use. In addition to wage and fringe-benefit comparisons, they supply local negotiators with sample contract clauses, economic reviews, productivity studies, and even detailed reports on published profit and loss statements. Unions establish bargaining goals which they encourage each local to obtain. Using their international and local newspapers, magazines, and meetings, they endeavor to establish the bargaining climate. From this they draw their strength and get membership support for their positions and demands.

The day of the hard-nosed, let's-give-'em-nothing bargainer has passed. A look at recent settlements illustrates the full swing from company to union initiative which seems to have occurred in most industries. Bargaining based on sound facts and reasonable approaches is needed to help stem this tide. To be successful, company representatives must be better armed than those representing the union. Members of management's bargaining team must know the condition of the general economy. They must keep up with national and local trends in wages, employment, and contract settlements. They must be aware of what business in general is doing as well as what is happening within their own industry and community. They must have complete and accurate cost information about wages, fringe benefits, restrictive contract provisions, and all other conditions of employment about which they are required to bargain. Contract comparison studies are invaluable. Past bargaining history and current settlements must be a part of the bargaining arsenal.

ECONOMIC CONDITIONS

Unions are formed to represent and protect their members. One has only to read their newspapers or magazines to conclude that they are also political bodies dedicated to shaping the economic and social policies of local, state, and federal governments. This goal has become increasingly important in dictating their objectives in negotiations. What they cannot obtain through bargaining, they endeavor to get through legislation. Management must be prepared for this twin-barrel approach.

Each union local and each active member understands the labor movement drive toward a goal of higher wages, more fringe benefits, and improved working conditions. While union members are continually reminded of the need for social and economic gain, they hear little about the businessman's need for a reasonable profit to make these improvements possible.

Management representatives must be economists with statistics and facts to refute the union theory that there is always more no matter what condition exists. Each negotiation should be a class in economics. The management team must teach; to do so, facts must be available on employment and unemployment in local, national, and industry groups. Availability by skill should be known. These conditions most often dictate how serious the demands for guarantees, job security, featherbedding, and subcontracting might be. It is important to know the trends and level of earnings, hours of work, productivity, and labor turnover by locality, industry, and skill. These affect requests for pay for time not worked such as shorter workweeks and workdays, vacations, holidays, and sabbaticals. The cost of living, the purchasing power of the dollar, and the family-of-four budget are the basis for many monetary demands.

Union leaders cite excessive profits in industry to justify demands for huge increases. Union members believe them. Thus the management team must be able to discuss the profits in its industry as compared to other businesses as well as the need for profit if the company is to remain in business.

The team must decide on what is or may be important to the negotiations—then it must work to assemble the facts. Pertinent articles in newspapers and trade and industry publications should be kept on file. The Federal Government, through the Bureau of Labor Statistics, Department of Commerce, and other agencies, is the source of many statistics. State and local governments also assemble and have available much data. One source most often overlooked is the union publication. The company should subscribe to the local union newspaper, the international magazine, and other union publications.

Management has the inside and superior knowledge of its own operation. This advantage should be used to logically relate the general union goal and achievement plans to its specific demands so that the true effect on management's operation can be demonstrated. This can be done by a management team that knows the financial and operational effect of each request. If a business is publicly owned, sales and profit figures are available for use. Such reports should be utilized to measure how well the business is doing compared to its competitors and to industry in general. The return on investment and sales that the company realizes should be determined. (A note of caution: If a company claims that it is unable to pay, the union can require it to make available otherwise privileged financial reports to justify its position.)

Sales and marketing people can be of great help. They have market, sales, price, and competitive studies which can be invaluable in explaining the real management struggle to remain competitive and profitable.

The strength of the union is important. All unions must file financial reports, copies of which can be obtained from the Department of Labor. These reports should be studied to ascertain how well a union is equipped for a strike.

Whenever research and source material becomes available, it should be noted and filed. As actual negotiations near, it should be reviewed, assembled, and grouped so that the information is readily available for the management team. This team should not be left to chance. Some one person or group should be specifically assigned to and responsible for the work.

WAGE AND FRINGE STUDIES

The guts of the labor agreement are the wage and fringe-benefit provisions. To negotiate intelligently, management must know where it stands. It is essential to have the wage and fringe levels of other businesses and competitors as well as to know what the union has negotiated in its other contracts. Comparisons are invaluable.

Many employer and industry associations conduct wage and fringe-benefit surveys. The value of these surveys should be increased by supplementing them with specific private studies. Companies in the same business and locality should exchange information about and copies of their agreements. The government collects and makes available much information on wages, hours of work, and fringe benefits by community, skill, and industry. Union publications contain stories of contract settlements with other employers. Local newspapers and business publications also report on labor settlements, which can be most helpful. The spread sheet which lists on one plane the contract or location and on the other the benefit or wage classification is a good way to present information so that it is readily available and gives immediate comparisons.

Study of Contract Clauses

The wage rate and fringe-benefit aspect of labor negotiations usually gets the headlines. This is most commonly the "cost of the package" that is reported. But there is little in the labor agreement that does not have a cost. Indirect cost areas may have just as serious an effect on the profits of the company as the direct cost items which get the publicity. Seniority systems, restrictions on management rights, restricted starting times, overtime penalties, contracting out, hiring limitations, and similar restrictions can seriously affect efficiency and ability to compete.

The management negotiating team should have available contracts of competitors to insure that the union is not trying to restrict the company in a manner which will place it in unfair competition. Management's team should compare the restrictive aspects of these agreements and study and analyze its own labor agreement clause by clause. Supervisors and other key management people should do likewise. A good technique is to make available copies of the present agreement, itemized clause by clause, prepared so that there is ample space for comments next to or under each clause. Recommendations for improvement should be requested and the team should study and discuss with management what it needs to run its operation more efficiently. Contract language should be prepared covering those areas where improvement is necessary.

After the demands are received, they should be reviewed and commented on. During normal negotiations management will most likely have to give way on some of these items. Searching out those areas which will have the least effect on operations can be the way to avoid more costly changes.

ANTICIPATION OF UNION DEMANDS

Demands can be anticipated by reviewing those from past years. Many are likely to reappear. In the wage and fringe areas they will often follow established patterns; the last items dropped during previous negotiations are most likely to reappear and be very important. Studying prior grievances that have been filed will yield strong clues as to what the unions will be asking. If they have lost an arbitration, they will probably try to change the award in negotiations. From union publications can be gleaned the general goal and present objectives of the union.

It never hurts for the management negotiating team to know as much as possible about the man sitting across the table. A little knowledge about his background, conduct in prior negotiations, likes and dislikes, hobbies, and work record as an employee can help management to anticipate his conduct during negotiations and his attitude on some specific demands.

CONTRACT COSTS

A negotiator cannot do a good job unless he has cost figures. The exact cost of every wage, premium pay, and fringe-benefit provision of the present labor agreement should be available. Total cost as well as cents-per-hour cost on each item should be established. The cost of overtime and premium-pay provisions should be outlined. An increased wage rate automatically increases the cost of vacations and holidays. It is important not to overlook the compounding effect of some of these provisions. From this base the negotiator must work. After receiving the demands, similar costs for each requested change should be obtained. Just because they are unreasonable is no reason to avoid this job—the very ridiculousness can be an effective negotiation tool.

OTHER RESEARCH

The internal collection of data and information for collective bargaining is essential. But it is helpful and at times necessary to supplement this information with a purchased labor service from any one of several commercial organizations which have been especially designed to help in collective bargaining. They are extremely valuable in keeping up with the day-to-day changes by collecting, summarizing, and analyzing industry and collective bargaining information in general terms. It must be remembered, however, that such services are prepared for general use—each company must prepare for its own specific negotiations.

Assembling the facts is time consuming. Facts collected by the company, if used in negotiations, are subject to being called biased. If the story is a good one which is expected to have substantial impact, the employment of an independent researcher to prepare an economic and contract study for negotiations should be considered. Usually a college professor or economist is available to do this. He will collect much data independently, but management itself will be the prime source of much of the material he needs. Such reports, when used in connection with negotiations, are usually more readily accepted by the employees and the union than the same conclusions which result from an internal study. The success of this technique is demonstrated by the fact that some unions are hiring independent researchers to justify their demands.

Sources and Form

Every area and every industry have different specific sources of information. The following is a list of sources where information can be found:

Government Sources:
- Department of Commerce, Bureau of the Census.
- Treasury Department.
- Department of Labor, Bureau of Labor Statistics.
- Federal Reserve System.
- Department of Labor, Office of Labor Management and Welfare —pension reports.
- State and local statistical bureaus.
- Public and reference libraries.

Other Sources:
- Universities.
- Trade and industry associations.
- Chambers of commerce.

+ Research institutes.
+ Banking, financial, and investment services.
+ Newspapers and magazines.
+ Union publications.
+ Other businesses, including suppliers and customers.

Facts are useless if they are unavailable, incorrect, or not in a usable form. Extreme care must be used in the collection of data to insure the correctness of all information. Being caught in an error means losing the initiative. The following are but a few of the methods of preparation that can be helpful: a clipping file by subject; chronological or numerical listings; comparisons on spread sheets; bar and line graphs; pie and block charts; photos of areas and so forth; slides.

By using these sources, forms, and techniques, the negotiator should have available at the start of negotiations clipping files on recent settlements in the community and in the industry; recent settlements between the company and other unions; related community and industry strikes; and union trends and personalities. He should also have reports and analyses of recent grievances and arbitrations; the contract, clause by clause; and the union negotiators. In addition, a record of past union demands in the areas of wages, direct and indirect fringes, and operational changes should be readily accessible.

With proper preparation, the negotiator should also be armed with charts, graphs, and summaries of the following:

+ General economic trends.
+ Trends in the company's business.
+ Employment.
+ Business failures.
+ Strikes.
+ Number and quality of competitive businesses.
+ Capacities as related to sales.
+ Profits of industry in general.
+ Profits in the company's industry.
+ The company's profits.
+ Effects of strikes, prices, and sales on profits.
+ The company's share of the market.
+ Level of expenditures for the company's product.
+ Taxes and their effects.
+ Competitive quality and prices.

✦ Shipping costs and the company's market.
✦ Industrial production table.
✦ Hours of work and productivity.
✦ Earnings in industry.
✦ Spread sheet comparisons on wages and fringes.
✦ Cost of living and other price indexes.
✦ Wage trends.
✦ Purchasing power of the dollar.
✦ Real wage surveys.

✦   ✦   ✦

It cannot be overstressed that the key to any successful negotiation is knowledge. Since facts are necessary to counter demands, every company negotiator must be better prepared in every area than his union counterpart. This preparation, of course, takes much work and planning. But the long-term rewards of such efforts are great.

Seeking Allies

William J. Curtin

D URING THE FIRST HALF OF THE 20TH CENTURY, MANAGEMENT WAS FRE-
quently cast as the villain of the American labor scene. Recently, however, the growing economic and political strength of organized labor vis-à-
vis business has led to a much-needed re-evaluation of this assessment. Both
the Labor Board and the courts have become increasingly aware that organized labor is often more than a match for the corporations at the bargaining
table and that, consequently, the restraints against employers seeking allies
should be eased. Illustrations of this trend may be found in the judicial development of the law of employer shutdowns and in the judicial approbation
of industry's strike insurance agreements, sometimes called mutual aid pacts.

At common law the lockout was legal. Indeed, it was conceived as management's counterpart to the union's right to strike. During the early hell-for-
leather days of labor relations, therefore, companies made liberal use of the
lockout either to defeat union organizational efforts or to evade the duty to
bargain with their workers' representatives. As a weapon, the lockout proved
devastatingly effective—so much so that its use became anathema to the
unions and helped generate the antibusiness attitudes referred to earlier. In
response, the Federal Government began to regulate labor relations and, over

WILLIAM J. CURTIN is a partner in the law firm of Morgan, Lewis & Bockius in Washington, D.C.

the past several decades, established a national labor policy designed to protect and encourage representation of employees by labor unions. At the heart of this policy was, and still is, the principle that the terms and conditions of employment are best settled through collective bargaining. Consequently, the Wagner Act of 1935 (and its 1947 and 1959 amendments) proscribed business conduct which aimed at undermining the unions' right to represent their members in the bargaining process.

The fear that business would continue to thwart unionization by locking out persisted, however, and the Labor Board and the courts sanctioned a very limited use of the device prior to 1957. In effect, companies could resort to the lockout only as a last-ditch defensive reaction to a union strike threat which posed the threat of unusual hardship to either the businesses involved or their customers. In addition, it was a *sine qua non* that the employers prove that their shutdown was not intended to interfere with or undermine their employees' union links.

Thus, in the 1951 decision of *Betts Cadillac Olds, Inc.* (96 NLRB 268), the Labor Board determined that a defensive shutdown by 17 of 19 auto dealers in a collective bargaining association—after the union's threat of a selective strike had been realized against the other two members—was justified. Both sides had negotiated in good faith but reached an impasse. The crucial factor singled out by the board as the reason for its holding, however, was that the dealers could not have been expected to keep their repair shops open in the face of an imminent strike which, should it have materialized, would have tied up their customers' cars in the shops. According to the *Betts Cadillac Olds* decision, the law did not require "that the employer caught in a strike activity must be a sitting duck, stripped of his power to save himself from attendant loss or operative disruption" (id. at 285). Unfortunately, the "unusual economic circumstances" standard suggested by the *Betts Cadillac Olds* case as well as a number of other decisions of the time failed to provide employers with a truly ascertainable guideline. The test proved too nebulous for an area of conduct where the law's predictability was of the essence.

EXPANDED LOCKOUT POWER

In the *Buffalo Linen* case (358 U.S. 87) of 1957, the Supreme Court took the initiative in expanding the scope of management's lockout power beyond the narrow limits permitted by decisions like *Betts Cadillac Olds*. Factually, *Buffalo Linen* involved a whipsaw strike against one of eight linen supply companies which had formed a collective bargaining association. The association was then engaged in negotiations with the union. In response to the selective strike, the remaining seven members shut down their operations. During the ensuing litigation, the court of appeals overturned a board finding that the lockout was legal on the ground that the companies were faced with an imminent strike which threatened unusual economic harm. The Supreme Court not only reversed the court of appeals but also rejected the Labor Board's restrictive approach to determining the legality of such employer conduct. Instead, it held that a lockout was justified when undertaken to protect the integrity of a multiemployer bargaining unit threatened by a divide-and-conquer strike. The Court reasoned that the employers' legitimate interests outweighed those of the union since the companies had not shut down in order to frustrate union organizational efforts or to avoid the duty to bargain. Although the general lockout power was recognized only in defensive actions, *Buffalo Linen* was an important step forward.

The major breakthrough came in 1965 with the *American Ship Building* case (380 U.S. 300). That situation involved an employer with a long history of union recognition, collective bargaining, and strike activity. After considerable good faith negotiation with the union, a stalemate was reached and the company shut down its operations in order to precipitate a settlement rather than allow the union to strike at a moment when the corporation would—for economic reasons—be especially vulnerable. On these facts, the Supreme Court held that management had not engaged in an unfair labor practice although the obvious purpose behind the layoff was to bring economic pressure to bear on the union in order to secure prompt settlement of the dispute on favorable terms. Clearly, therefore, *American Ship Building* obliterated the old distinction between defensive and offensive shutdowns. The Court had unequivocally stated that the union's right to strike was merely the right to stop work and did not imply exclusive union control over the timing and duration of work stoppages or preclude the employer from pre-empting the strike by a shutdown.

With the *Evening News Association* case (166 NLRB No. 6), decided in 1967, the Labor Board gave new impetus to the present trend. In that decision, the board concluded that a supportive shutdown by the *Evening News* was justified in view of the strike against its only Detroit rival, the *Free Press*. The board reasoned that such an offensive use of the tactic was sanctioned by the *American Ship Building* decision and by the fact that both newspapers, although legally separate bargaining units, were engaged in essentially identical negotiations with the union involved. Thus approval was finally given to supportive lockouts where employers were not members of the same collective bargaining group.

The Labor Board also clarified its own position by enunciating a test for judging each lockout's legality. Briefly stated, the standard suggested is that the board may proscribe shutdowns "which are inherently so prejudicial to union interests and so devoid of significant economic justification that no specific evidence of intent to discourage union membership or anti-union animus is required." All other nondiscriminatory uses of the lockout for purely economic reasons would presumably be recognized as legal.

As is evidenced by the more recent cases, the trend toward allowing a wider use of the lockout is not yet entirely spent. As recently as May of 1968, for example, the board decided in the *Darling and Co.* case (171 NLRB No. 95) that an impasse in bargaining was no longer a prerequisite to a legal shutdown. Rather, the mere existence or absence of impasse was only one of numerous surrounding circumstances to be considered in deciding each case. For the immediate future, however, decisions will elaborate upon and explain the application of the principles set forth in *American Ship Building* as they are tested in the labor relations arena, rather than develop additional principles of law.

STRIKE INSURANCE PACTS

As employers have been required to seek allies in new forms because of the growing imbalance of power at the bargaining table, mutual aid agreements or strike insurance pacts—which are arrangements for financial assistance—have become increasingly significant during the past ten years. Like the multiemployer lockout, the pacts' aim is to buttress management solidarity in order to better resist the divide-and-conquer strike technique which unions frequently utilize to further their economic demands. Unlike the shutdown device, however, the strike insurance pact's mechanism is in the form of financial aid and does not have the direct impact upon the union and its members that a shutdown does.

Typically, a strike insurance plan calls for some form of contribution from all member-employers into a strike fund. If and when a union strikes one of the pact's adherents, the company may draw upon the accumulated strike fund and thus cover at least certain expenses incurred during the work stoppage. The desired result is that, by spreading the cost of the strike among all the signers of the mutual aid agreement, the group members will make it possible for the beleaguered strike victim to hold firm to his position and not capitulate to an unfavorable, pattern-setting agreement.

Although there has been scant litigation over the legality of the various strike insurance plans, it seems reasonably clear that such arrangements as currently drawn and effectuated are legal. The pact is essentially a self-help device quite similar in its aims to the multiemployer lockout which is now sanctioned. It would be inconsistent to hold, on the one hand, that offensive multiemployer shutdowns are proper and, on the other, that strike insurance plans which are primarily defensive are illegal. Nor does it appear that this will be the case.

In the 1963 decision of *Kennedy* v. *Long Island Ry. Co.* (319 F. 2d 366, cert. denied 375 U.S. 830) a union brought an action against the signers of the railroad industry's strike insurance agreement for damages allegedly sustained because of the carriers' utilization of the strike insurance plan. The union charged, among other things, that the pact was invalid under the Railway Labor Act, the Interstate Commerce Act, and the Sherman Act. The U.S. Court of Appeals for the Second Circuit dismissed the union's complaint, holding that the agreement did not breach the railroads' duty to bargain in good faith. In addition, the court described the union's contention "that the strike insurance plan adopted by the railroads undermines the Federal policies which lie at the heart of our labor and antitrust laws" as "thoroughly unconvincing" (319 F. 2d 366, 370).

Two of the principal strike insurance pacts now in effect are the airlines' mutual aid agreement and the railroads' plan. Under the airlines' agreement, whenever a pact member is struck, the other carriers turn over to the struck airline any additional revenue which they received as a result of the walkout. In addition, the operating lines are assessed a certain amount in order to reimburse the struck carrier for up to 25 percent of its overhead. Under the railroads' plan, the members set a "daily indemnity" rate for each company each year. This amount is then paid on a daily basis to each carrier that is struck. The daily indemnity rate differs for each company based on its actual daily overhead. The strike-aid payments are financed by assessing the operating railroads, with each carrier contributing an amount determined by the relationship of its daily indemnity to the total daily indemnities of all operating companies. The assessments can amount to 20 times each railroad's daily indemnity per year.

At this writing, employer mutual aid agreements are still few in number. But, in the light of the great need for employers in certain industries (for example, the transportation modes, construction, and newspaper publishing) to help one another resist exorbitant union demands, it seems logical to assume that more and more industries will investigate the advantages of such agreements and formulate plans to meet their own particular needs.

To this point, discussion has been limited to those situations where one employer seeks allies from among other employers. The experience of some companies indicates, however, that their most effective allies may be the unions themselves. Cooperation with unions has frequently proven beneficial both in strengthening a firm's internal relationship with its employees and in increasing its competitiveness in the open market. It is particularly in this latter regard that unions have served as an invaluable ally to individual companies and to the sector of the industry which has been "organized." However, management-union alliances to secure more favorable market conditions for the organized industry have often run afoul of the antitrust laws.

The Sherman Act of 1890 is the cornerstone of the nation's far-reaching antitrust legislation. It was, and still is, Congress's response to the economic doctrine of unfettered free enterprise. Antitrust law is based on the premise "that every man has the right of access to a market, and that combinations of private power do not conform to the natural competitive order; hence they are forever suspect." Section 1 of the act provides that "every contract, combination . . . or conspiracy in restraint of trade or commerce . . . is illegal" (15 USC 1). In addition, Section 2 expressly proscribes any attempts or agreements to monopolize commerce.

Antitrust Penalties

Initially, the statute's broad language caused the courts to apply the Sherman Act with equal severity against both business and labor. As a result, antitrust penalties were imposed against unions "for engaging in strikes, boycotts, and similar coercive activities having an intended or inevitable result of substantial restriction upon interstate commerce." Gradually, however, both Congress and the judiciary largely exempted unions from the antitrust laws. Congress enacted the Clayton Act of 1914, which provided that "nothing contained in the antitrust law . . . shall forbid the existence and operation of labor . . . organizations . . . or forbid or restrain . . . such organizations from lawfully carrying out the legitimate objects thereof."

In 1932 Congress again acted and, in the Norris-LaGuardia Act, prohibited the issuance of injunctions by federal courts in labor disputes. Eight years later, in 1940, the Supreme Court dealt with the question of labor's antitrust exemption in *Apex Hosiery Co.* v. *Leader* (310 U.S. 469). That case involved a strike during which the union had seized an employer's plant and refused to release finished goods produced for shipment in interstate commerce. The Court pointed out that the Sherman Act prohibited only intended restraint of competition, not restraints on interstate trade. Consequently, the union was held not liable under the act since its activity was designed solely to compel the employer to accede to its demands and had not actually affected price competition in the hosiery market. A more explicit exemption was formulated by the Court in the 1941 case of *U.S.* v. *Hutcheson* (312 U.S. 219). There, the Court concluded that Congress had intended the Norris-LaGuardia and Clayton Acts to remove the danger of antitrust prosecution for labor activities such as boycotts, picketing, and strikes.

After *Apex* and *Hutcheson* it still remained to be seen how far the exemption of labor's monopoly power would be tolerated where the union was in alliance with certain employers. This question was answered in the 1945 decision of *Allen Bradley Co.* v. *Local 3, IBEW* (325 U.S. 797). There the New York City Electrical Workers' Union had provided local manufacturers and contractors with a completely sheltered market for locally produced electrical equipment through a series of provisions in collective bargaining agreements. The predictable results were more jobs, higher wages, and shorter hours for the union, while at the same time the prices of electrical equipment and the profits of local contractors and manufacturers were artificially high.

Everyone appeared to be gaining except, of course, the New York City consumer and the out-of-city electrical producers and contractors. The Supreme Court held that the union had violated the antitrust laws, reasoning that "when the unions participated with a combination of businessmen . . . to prevent all competition from others, a situation was created not included within the exemptions of the Clayton and Norris-LaGuardia Acts" (325 U.S. 809). The conclusion to be drawn from *Allen Bradley* was that the union's antitrust exemption depended "upon whether the union acted alone or in combination with business groups" (325 U.S. 810).

Between 1945 and 1965 the Supreme Court did not further define what constituted an illicit labor-management combination. In 1965, however, the Court clarified the law in *United Mine Workers of America* v. *Pennington* (381 U.S. 657) and *Local 189, Amalgamated Meat Cutters* v. *Jewel Tea Co.* (381 U.S. 676).

In *Pennington* a small coal operator charged that the UMW and the large coal mining concerns had conspired to squeeze the smaller producers out of the market. In order to accomplish this end, it was alleged that the union and the large producers had deliberately written into the National Bituminous Coal Wage Agreement a wage scale which smaller companies simply could not afford. In addition, the union promised to impose the terms of the agreement upon all operators regardless of size. The evidence supporting the alleged labor-management combination or collusion was minimal and the Supreme Court reversed the court of appeals' finding in favor of the small operator. Yet, in the words of Professor Archibald Cox, ". . . a majority of the justices held that the agreement, if proved, violated the Sherman Act." Such an agreement "was invalid partly because it restricted the union's freedom of action outside the bargaining unit and partly because the restriction was made with the dominant purpose of affecting competition in the product market."

According to Professor Cox, *Pennington* affirms the union's right, after concluding a wage agreement with a multiemployer bargaining unit, to independently secure the same wage benefits from other employers. However, Cox also points out that *Pennington* stands for the proposition that "a union forfeits its exemption . . . when it agrees with one set of employers to impose an agreed wage scale upon other bargaining units."

The *Jewel Tea* case, which was handed down on the same day as *Pennington,* involved a provision in a multiemployer, multiunion collective bargaining agreement which restricted the retail marketing of fresh meat in the Chicago area to the hours of 9 A.M. to 6 P.M. Jewel Tea Company protested that the restriction was illegal but signed the agreement under the threat of a strike. Later, Jewel Tea brought suit against the butchers' union and the Associated Food Retailers of Chicago. It alleged that, because of its self-service facilities, the presence of butchers was not required during the evening hours. Jewel added that the marketing restriction unlawfully impeded use of its property and deprived the general public of the convenience of evening shopping.

Accepting the district court's finding that there had been no conspiracy between the Meat Cutters Union and other markets and that the union was acting in pursuit of its own policies, the Supreme Court held that the contract did not violate the Sherman Act. Speaking for the Court, Justice White declared that the key issue was whether the marketing hours restriction was "so intimately related to wages, hours and working conditions that the unions' successful attempt to obtain that provision . . . falls within the protection of the national labor policy" (381 U.S. 676, 689-690). This test was satisfied by the district court's finding that evening marketing would impair job jurisdiction or substantially alter hours or workloads.

Although the cases discussed do not settle all questions relating to labor's antitrust exemption, it seems certain that when a union joins with an employer combination in restraint of trade, the antitrust laws will be applied. As a result, the union's role as a management ally in this manner has been severely limited.

While the law has been developing to permit employer alliances for concerted economic action and financial assistance as a means of correcting the imbalance of power recognized to exist in the bargaining process, Congress has also made efforts to reduce the ability of unions to seek allies, willing or unwilling, in support of their economic demands. Both the Taft-Hartley Act of 1947 and the Landrum-Griffin Act of 1959 were intended to prohibit unions from enmeshing secondary or neutral employers in labor disputes and to regulate picketing. The Labor Board and the courts have read the statutory language restricting union activity to provide less restraint than many believe Congress intended to legislate. That question aside, however, it may be useful to illustrate the secondary boycott prohibitions of the law, their reach, and some of their notable exceptions.

SECONDARY BOYCOTTS

As a general rule, it can be stated that secondary boycotts are illegal under the Taft-Hartley Act. This point has been supported in an impressive number of decisions and can be illustrated by the 1963 case of *Local 1291, Longshoremen's Union and National Sugar Refining Co.* (152 NLRB 257). There, the longshoremen's union threatened both a sugar refining company and a stevedoring concern that they would be struck unless the refinery assigned the sampling of incoming sugar arriving at a newly constructed pier to ILA members. The refinery employed its own workers, who were members of the Sugar Workers' Union, to sample the incoming sugar, and, as a result, the ILA induced the longshoremen to walk out against both the stevedoring company and the sugar refinery. On these facts, the Labor Board held that the ILA had engaged in an illegal secondary boycott since it had struck the stevedore company—a neutral—in the expectation that the stevedoring concern would put pressure on the refinery to agree to ILA demands. This case shows a typical fact pattern where the union seeks allies, albeit unwilling ones, in its economic struggle with an employer.

There are substantial exceptions to the general prohibition described earlier. One such was handed down by the 1964 case of *NLRB* v. *Fruit Packers Local 760* (377 U.S. 58). There the Supreme Court held that "consumer picketing" at neutral retail stores for the purpose of persuading customers not to purchase the products of a particular struck manufacturer is lawful. Although the Labor Board is now in the process of "elucidating litigation" to define the practical dimensions of this exception to the secondary boycott prohibition, it seems that a union may picket any neutral employer so long as the intent of the union is to induce customers to refrain from buying the struck product at the neutral employer's premises. If, however, the intent of the union activities is to cut off all trade with the neutral employer, then it appears likely that the union will have engaged in unlawful secondary activity.

Another exception to the illegality of secondary boycotts was set forth in 1967 by the Supreme Court decision in *National Woodwork Manufacturers Ass'n.* v. *NLRB* (386 U.S. 612). There, a general contractor had an agreement with the Carpenters' Union which provided that no member of the union would be required to handle any doors that had been fitted prior to being furnished on the job. Despite this stipulation, the general contractor purchased prefabricated doors which the carpenters refused to handle. Consequently, the doors were returned and the National Woodwork Association charged that the refusal of the carpenters to install the prefabricated doors was an unlawful secondary boycott. The Supreme Court held this charge to be without merit since the objective of the boycott was the preservation of unit work for the general contractor's own employees who were represented by the union.

It is clear that, despite the statutory prohibition against secondary boycotts, unions retain significant rights to appeal to and unwillingly involve other employees and employers as allies in support of labor's demands.

Unions, of course, remain legally free to resort to other allies in order to strengthen their bargaining hand. During the 1966 airline strike, for example, the International Association of Machinists was offered considerable financial support from other unions, notably the United Auto Workers of America. Unions have also realized how much political influence they command and have often used it effectively to further their bargaining aims. Again by way of example, in July and August of 1964 the Retail Clerks

International Association asked for and secured a special Congressional investigation of a strike-lockout in the food chain industry.

In conclusion, it appears that both management and labor are making fuller use of tactics designed to secure allies in order to strengthen their relative economic positions as the bargaining table stakes grow larger. Regulatory efforts have not yet developed a full set of rules defining the areas of permissible and prohibited conduct. This aspect of labor relations law and practice, however, has received increasing attention in recent years with the radical developments in the law concerning employer shutdown (or lockouts), mutual aid or strike insurance pacts in a number of industries, judicial limitations upon employer-union combinations designed to insure labor standards uniformity in the industry, and legislation attempting to further limit unions' secondary boycott activities and equally persistent judicial interpretations limiting the reach of such statutory prohibitions.

It is predictable that the attention of the public's representatives will not waver. If free collective bargaining means that the parties to a dispute have the liberty to engage each other in economic warfare, it does not necessarily connote the license to broaden the ambit of that warfare to include as many allies as may be enlisted and thereby increase the economic injury of the public.

The Management
Bargaining Team

James F. Honzik

ONCE A UNION HAS BEEN RECOGNIZED AS THE BARGAINING REPRESENTATIVE for a company's employees, the company's obligation to bargain is established. The duty to meet and discuss wages, hours, and working conditions is becoming more regimented and regulated. Recent court and Labor Board decisions in which good faith bargaining is reviewed have greatly narrowed what once were broad rules and conditions.

The penalty for not bargaining in good faith can be extremely severe. Each day, the technicalities and implications of the duty to bargain in good faith become more complicated. Management now finds that it often does not have the unilateral prerogative to decide questions not covered by the labor agreement or to make a unilateral business decision based upon economic and competitive need alone. The "management rights" and "zipper" clauses of contracts no longer afford the protection that they did in the past.

BARGAINING CLIMATE

The duty to bargain in good faith has always meant that the company must be willing to discuss, with an open mind and at reasonable times and places, all matters concerning wages, hours, and conditions of employment. (The basic change that is occurring is the expansion of items, conditions, and circumstances which now are included.) While there is no precise definition of what authority the employer must give his representative at the bargaining table, it must be assumed that such an agent should have sufficient authority to engage in the give-and-take bargaining required under the law. There is no requirement that the company representative have full and complete authority on all subjects as long as the withheld authorities are not such that true bargaining would be frustrated. One must be extremely careful as each case is looked at in the broad light of total circumstances—quite often with the reviewers using hindsight unashamedly.

The present climate of bargaining scope and responsibility illustrates why management must always exercise extreme caution in the selection of its representative.

ATTRIBUTES OF THE NEGOTIATOR

The union cannot dictate who can or should represent a company. Management should freely select someone who understands the total business operation, who can interpret the effect of all bargaining decisions, who has knowledge of the legal duty to bargain, who is aware of current trends and legal implications, and whose ability to make decisions within the framework of company policy is unquestioned. It is difficult, if not impossible, to find a single person with all these capabilities. The larger the company or the more complicated the operation, the more difficult it becomes to select the representative. That is why a team is usually selected. In this way, management hopes to have in its representatives all the ingredients essential to successful negotiations.

The personal traits of the negotiators are most important. While not all team members have to participate in across-the-table discussions, those who do must be articulate. Most bargaining teams have a single spokesman. This person in particular must have verbal and persuasive abilities. He must be able to communicate clearly in a manner that is understood by the union representatives. The conduct, decorum, and language of the corporate board of directors do not constitute the standard which insures the best results before a union committee.

Management representatives must have patience. During negotiations, time is often the negotiator's best weapon. The making of a decision and its communication are not necessarily simultaneous. Patience is necessary so that decisions are not made in haste or prematurely. Quite often the poorest negotiators see things as black or white, as right or wrong; their approach is to seek quick final decisions; and they cannot understand another person's viewpoint.

Such people are poor negotiators not because their decisions are wrong, but because the negotiation of a contract is much like the sale of a commodity: The good salesman (bargainer) must convince the buyer (union) of the soundness of the product (offer). The good negotiator can soften the way he says "no," but still be firm; he can make the final decision, but wait until the time is right to communicate it; he can listen to and understand the other's viewpoint and give his answer within that framework; and he can understand that, no matter what the issue, there are often gray areas in every controversy.

The company negotiator must have time to participate. His time should not be curtailed by outside duties or commitments to the extent that his performance during bargaining is adversely affected. The person whose full-time duties continue during negotiations finds it difficult to make and take time when he is concerned about his effectiveness on his regular job. He will tend to want to get the negotiations over with quickly. This can result in a premature settlement—and probably a poor one. In addition, unreasonable unavailability which hinders and delays negotiations can result in an unfair labor practice charge.

An important technique of negotiation is delay. But, while delay is a good technique, unavailability is a poor one. Delay requires patience. Successful negotiations are often time consuming. Many hours are spent in caucus, waiting, and discussion. The company representative must be able to listen to the same story over and over again. He must be able to sit and wait. Long periods of no progress, irrelevant discussion, and even silence should not affect his judgment.

The size of the company, the size of the bargaining unit, and the importance of the negotiation as it affects the company are points that must be considered when determining who should represent the employer at the bargaining table. A small nonvital bargaining unit will not need the same emphasis as a unit which can effectively shut down the entire operation. The areas from which management can select the bargaining team are industrial relations/personnel, management/operations, attorneys, and outside counsel/consultants.

INDUSTRIAL RELATIONS/PERSONNEL REPRESENTATIVES

As labor relations becomes more complex, the need for people trained in all areas of management-labor relations has become universally recognized. Specialized training and specialization are now accepted as necessary functions of a business. To meet this need, schools and universities are educating and training many students in this relatively new professional field. Industrial relations departments which have evolved from the old personnel departments (which were usually limited to hiring and benefit procedures) are now being staffed by men with this training. The man from the ranks, however, is still an important candidate for this type of job. One should not overlook the capable union official or steward who, through self-training and experience, can qualify as a valuable management employee. The lawyer, because of his training, is another natural candidate for employment in an industrial relations/personnel department.

In most companies the industrial relations/personnel employee is the most important member of the bargaining team regardless of his training. He brings to negotiations his experience in day-to-day administration of the labor agreement; in hiring and firing employees; in the administration of safety, welfare benefits, and pensions; in the processing of grievances through exposure to union business representatives and stewards; in arbitrations and Labor Board proceedings; and in daily interpretation and application of seniority, layoff, and all other provisions of the labor agreement.

The industrial relations representative, because he works closely with operations in handling grievances, scheduling work under seniority provisions, and other contract interpretations, obtains a good knowledge of the total operation. While this exposure does not make him a trained machine operator, mechanic, or serviceman, it does educate him as to the function of the machine operator, mechanic, or serviceman. He knows the skill and requirements of the job and understands how each job and procedure fits into the total operation. Of course, even a representative with such knowledge may not be able to see every specific pitfall in negotiations, but his knowledge alerts him to potential trouble and enables him to check before making a decision.

The industrial relations/personnel employee does not produce direct profit for the company, but he can have a greater cost impact through his activities than many who do. He is the technician trained to protect company costs in the area of employee utilization. For this reason he is the key to most negotiations.

MANAGEMENT/OPERATIONS REPRESENTATIVES

The man from management/operations is another important member of the management team. He brings to the bargaining table his knowledge of production requirements and needs, of machines and services which produce the profit, of individual employees with whom he works, of skills required to man the shop, and of operating and scheduling problems of machines and employees.

The management/operations representative can analyze the effect of any change demanded by the union. He understands the problems that arise when working under a labor agreement. And, what is perhaps most important, his contract knowledge is from experience—not theory.

ATTORNEYS AS REPRESENTATIVES

Many companies have lawyers available from their legal or industrial relations/personnel staff. Some specialize in the field of labor law and work as house counsel. Others go into the less technical field of labor relations in the industrial relations/personnel area, where they have the advantage of a knowledge of the legal implications of bargaining and the changing court and board rules, as well as training in drafting contracts as they perform their work.

There is no question that the many legal implications involved in bargaining make it very advantageous to have a legally trained person as a member of the team. But this in and of itself does not prove that there is an actual need for an attorney at the bargaining table. On the other hand, the bargaining team cannot be without professional legal help. If this help is not available at the table, it must be available in the form of counsel; otherwise, serious mistakes can result.

While it is true that the union sits and negotiates without counsel, this does not have a serious adverse effect. The essence of bargaining is that the company gives and the union takes. At the end of bargaining the company has less than when it started. Thus it is absolutely necessary that the company fully understand all the legal and technical ramifications of the contract it negotiates. Experienced bargainers know that once a clause gets into a contract, it is extremely difficult to have it removed in future negotiations. Experience also shows that, where language is poor, arbitrators tend to interpret contracts for the benefit of the employee. On the other hand, if the union fails in a demand in one negotiation it can simply ask again the next time. Not only does the language of a labor agreement cover present conditions, but it can also become binding on future changes. Because of this, no company should begin bargaining unless it is sure that legal help will be readily available where and when necessary.

OUTSIDE COUNSEL/CONSULTANT REPRESENTATIVES

The workload of key people in many companies makes it impossible to free them to act as members of the bargaining team. Outside help is then a necessity. Industrial relations consultants who perform such work are available. But it is a more common practice to seek the help of a lawyer. Part of a lawyer's training is in negotiations and oral argument. And this is exactly what a bargainer does during labor negotiations.

The lawyer who can be of the most help is one who is experienced in the specialized field of labor law. He will know labor law; he will have had experience in negotiations and arbitration; he will understand the industrial climate; he will have worked with union officials and negotiators. He will bring his training in speech and presentation to the table. The most serious disadvantage an outside attorney has in negotiations is his lack of detailed knowledge of the plant or operations. While he may readily see the legal implication of a contract demand, he may not see the total impact of each demand as it affects operations. When using outside consultants or attorneys, the client must be able to aid them by making available people who have considerable knowledge of plant operations.

THE FULL TEAM

The industrial relations/personnel representative, the man from management/operations, and the attorney are all necessary ingredients of a full team—not in the sense that one from each area is needed, but from the broad aspect that the qualities and attributes of each are necessary. The team can be composed of one or two men in a small operation or ten or more in a large one. It is not the number of representatives that counts, but the spectrum of knowledge and experience that they encompass. Although an industrial relations man with experience may not be a lawyer, he begins to know labor law. Similarly, the lawyer, while not an operations man, begins to know production. Thus the team is built.

The key man of any bargaining team is the spokesman. He must be articulate. He must know how to present his case. He must sell. The spokesman should make all principal presentations and direct the participation of his bargaining team. He controls how, when, and to what extent each member of his team participates. He is the quarterback who must call the signals. No spokesman can be too well prepared.

Just as it is important for the bargaining team to have the bargaining authority necessary to meet legal requirements, so is it important for the team to have full internal company authority. The team members should know the extent and limits within which they can bargain and should be permitted to use their judgment within these limits and not be mere puppets. Bargaining must be recognized as a most important management function. The representative must be viewed by top management as a person in whom it can place its trust. The company that pays more attention to the purchasing of goods than to the purchasing of labor can find that it is in trouble. If the purchasing agent for goods makes a bad buy, he can look for another supplier the next time. The purchasing agent of labor starts from his last mistake—and there is seldom opportunity to look for another supplier. Mistakes of past negotiations continue to be binding for many years. A case in point is the railroads and their work-rule problems. Bargaining by capable teams can result in better contracts; it does not have to be hopeless, with the results a foregone conclusion.

In deciding who should represent management, it is well to consider that having a spokesman with the final authority at the bargaining table is usually not good. If the person representing management hits a sticky issue and is able to say, in all honesty, that he has to check it out, he is in a much better position than the person who the union knows will make the final decision himself. There *are* exceptions, however; there are times when the final word must come from the mouth of the person who makes the decision. The history and conduct of bargaining dictate such circumstances.

Management should have confidence in its bargaining team and should, prior to the first negotiation session, reach a decision as to the company's objective in the negotiations. To do the best job, the bargaining team must know the reasonable limits of its bargaining authority and how far it can go in making an economic offer. A management bargaining team which does not know until the last minute what it can do is like a one-armed boxer. Timing is one of the essential ingredients of negotiations. The circumstances of the bargaining plan may determine when an offer should be made. This timing can be lost if bargaining authority is so limited that, before any offer is made, it must be approved.

During negotiations the team should make periodic reports to top management. In this way, authorities can be kept current to keep pace with the tempo and changes can be made as they become necessary. This can avoid the 3 A.M. call to the boss.

✦   ✦   ✦

In general, the management that uses its most capable, articulate, and adroit employee and gives him full authority, within limits, to represent it at the bargaining table will most often come out with the best settlement. The management team can have one or more members; but, no matter how large or small, it should consist of the best persons available inside or outside the company. The team must be articulate, have knowledge of operations and the law, be experienced, and have full authority within reasonable limits to represent and bind the company. Only then can the company be sure it is represented as well as possible at the bargaining table.

Entering

into Negotiations

Arnold F. Campo

S INCE THE PASSAGE OF THE NATIONAL LABOR RELATIONS ACT, IT IS APPARENT
that many companies and labor unions have gained rather broad experience in negotiating contracts. They have developed their procedures,
collected much data, and built up a reservoir of valuable information so that
they are prepared when they enter collective bargaining conferences.

Employers should be aware that unions prepare well in advance of negotiations. Local unions often set up collective bargaining committees months
in advance of actual negotiation dates. Proposals are discussed with rank and
file members, contracts are exchanged with other unions, and major objectives are determined.

Union Preparations

Although unions may vary considerably in their advance preparations for
bargaining, the following procedures are quite common:

ARNOLD F. CAMPO is director of industrial relations for International Salt Company.

✦ Analyzing contracts in preparation for new demands or language changes.

✦ Reviewing grievances and arbitration decisions in order to delete, add, or modify contract provisions.

✦ Comparing the current agreement with other contracts in the area or industry and negotiated by the same or companion unions, thereby strengthening their bargaining position.

✦ Obtaining economic information on issues to be advanced in negotiations along with vital statistics affecting noneconomic proposals.

✦ Backing up demands by obtaining strike authorization from the members, thus adding power to their bargaining position.

✦ Consulting with shop committeemen and meeting with the membership before and during negotiations to provide effective support for the demands submitted.

MANAGEMENT PREPARATIONS

Management must spend a considerable amount of time gathering facts for negotiations. Representatives of management who possess negotiating know-how try to anticipate union demands, estimate costs, and weigh all proposals very carefully. Company negotiators gather much information, including wage and fringe-benefit surveys, area and industry settlements, and analysis of internal problems that have arisen during the contract period as a basis of contract changes.

The complex nature of the issues in bargaining requires thorough preparation, especially when a company is required to bargain on pension plans, group insurance, supplemental unemployment benefits, incentive pay, job evaluation, and so on. This is why it is necessary to have a negotiating policy so that a satisfactory agreement can be worked out with the union. The agreement establishes the ground rules for living together for a period of time—hopefully, in a harmonious spirit—so that the operation will remain productive and profitable or become more so.

Although companies vary in size, it is possible to summarize some techniques that are used successfully by skilled labor relations executives:

✦ Conducting meetings with supervisors and recording their experiences in working with the agreement, thus providing information for possible language changes.

+ Analyzing grievance and arbitration records—in particular those grievances that arise repeatedly under the same contract clause—and looking for poor or unworkable clauses which suggest revisions.
+ Studying other contracts in the area or industry (helpful but not always controlling in the outcome of negotiations).
+ Meeting with representatives of other companies for the purpose of exchanging viewpoints and information (may help to anticipate union demands).
+ Reviewing the labor relations policy in order to determine the course of action during bargaining sessions.
+ Studying and obtaining economic information on the company, area, and industry as a means of educating the union committee.
+ Using commercial labor relations reporting services to keep up to date on matters affecting negotiations.
+ Examining contract violations to find out if any provision of the present agreement may have caused work stoppages and slowdowns and exploring these deficiencies for possible correction.

NEGOTIATION HANDBOOK

An effective instrument for negotiating and administering a contract is a negotiation handbook. Briefly, a handbook contains specific information gathered by the company negotiator: a history of the current contract; union and company demands; statistical employee information such as seniority dates, surveys, job classifications, and rates of pay; economic data; proposals and counterproposals; tentative agreements; minutes of bargaining sessions; estimate of cost of union demands; and a copy of the final agreement.

Many companies include a great deal more information than this, such as total number of employees; hourly work schedules; yearly overtime; average straight-time hourly rate; analysis of hourly and weekly cost of fringe benefits; classification of employees by length of service—that is, those with 5, 10, 15, 20, and 25 years of service; actual and standard productivity figures; and external data, including local and national cost of living index.

The value of a bargaining book becomes obvious during negotiations as it makes for better organized bargaining. It helps to avoid emotional stress by making use of facts, and it saves time because reference material can be used at any time. Naturally, a permanent record or history of negotiations offers advantages after negotiations are completed. It may show the intent of the parties in wording a certain contract clause, which can prove valuable in settling grievances and assisting first-line supervisors in administering the agreement.

INFORMATION SOURCES

There are many sources of information available for obtaining needed bargaining statistics and material. Since a factual basis of negotiations is an essential requirement for mature collective bargaining, these sources should be utilized. Outside information can be obtained from a number of government agencies, trade associations, and international unions.

Many private research organizations that investigate labor-management problems, report on collective bargaining, and publish their findings are good sources of data, statistics, and facts. Representative of such research groups are the American Arbitration Association, American Management Association, Society for the Advancement of Management, National Industrial Conference Board, and National Association of Personnel Directors.

In addition, a number of leading colleges and universities carry on research in the field of labor-management problems. These institutions investigate numerous problems, prepare reports, and offer valuable information. Some leading educational centers engaged in labor relations research are the University of California, University of Chicago, Cornell University, Harvard University, Massachusetts Institute of Technology, University of Pennsylvania, Princeton University, University of Minnesota, Stanford University, Rutgers University, and University of Virginia.

COMMUNICATING BARGAINING DATA

There is no substitute for sound preparation and presentation in the collective bargaining process. And one of the most effective ways to make use of collective bargaining information is to practice good communication techniques during the course of collective bargaining sessions. For example, the *annual report* should be used to explain the business operation to the union committee. Union negotiators should be helped toward an understanding of bank loans, profits, reserves, depreciation, stock, and so on. Some companies prepare motion pictures to illustrate and explain annual reports. Generally, reports during negotiations take the dollar of income or sales and show how it was expended. Executives' salaries are explained, as well as the cost of fringe benefits.

Audiovisual aids—sound films, movie slides, records—have been used by many companies in negotiations. They are advantageous in describing the operation; aid in reducing the frequency, severity, and costs of unsafe practices; and are often used to illustrate how and why financial decisions are made. Some companies use these media for explaining work rules and other company regulations in order to promote better employee understanding.

PHYSICAL ENVIRONMENT

Before bargaining begins, problems must be settled regarding the physical location and setup for the sessions. In some cases, management and the union may be satisfied to conduct their bargaining on the company premises. In other situations, negotiations are held out of town. Plant negotiations require that the company furnish a suitable meeting room. Outside locations involve costs that may be met by the company alone or by both parties. In any event, whether on the company premises or away, adequate facilities are necessary. Often outside facilities can be obtained at no cost to the parties—a Chamber of Commerce meeting room, a town hall facility, or the offices of the Federal Mediation Service.

On-premises bargaining. Those who like to bargain on the premises suggest that it has two advantages: (1) convenience, because files are on hand and supervisors are on the property and can be summoned to negotiations without delay; and (2) lower costs, because no money need be spent in travel, hotel bills, or rent for meeting rooms. Some employers point out that management has an advantage because it is operating in the home park. This results in regular hours, since starting and stopping times for bargaining conform to plant schedules.

Many employers, however, contend that the disadvantages of on-premises bargaining outweigh the advantages. They report that on-premises meetings serve to stir things up, make rumors persist, and that unrest can result. Quite often, inaccurate information is reported to employees in the plant and things become hot. Management bargaining representatives may be bothered with plant problems and telephone calls and are likely to be interrupted too often to be really effective in bargaining. Some unions believe that management wants to bargain at home as a means of dominating the sessions, and, consequently, they oppose on-premises bargaining.

Off-premises bargaining. There *are* advantages for holding collective bargaining sessions off-premises. First of all, the chances of interruptions by telephone calls or business decisions are minimized. This leaves the parties free to devote full time to bargaining; consequently, strike situations can be prevented. It can also help in avoiding hasty decisions which might be made because of business pressures. There may be disadvantages according to some employers—they claim that sessions get to be too long, and often the negotiators resort to marathon bargaining in order to get the contract settled and get out of town. Sometimes issues become overstated because one or the other of the parties may have to make a big production out of bargaining merely to justify the costs of off-premises bargaining.

Facilities. Whether a company engages in on- or off-premises bargaining, adequate facilities are essential. The room must be large enough to accommodate a table with sufficient space for all members of both bargaining groups and should be properly illuminated, ready for day or night sessions. Location is important—the room should be removed from disturbances or interferences. It should be well ventilated. Ash trays should be provided for those who smoke. Clerical needs such as paper, pencils, blackboards, and chalk must be included. Water glasses must be provided. Often typewriters and projection equipment are used and should be available. The table should be adaptable to seat either a small or a large number of participants. In some cases, stenographic services are used; if so, arrangements should be made well in advance of the first bargaining session. Telephones must be available for conference calls as well as for personal messages, which can be handled during a recess or at the end of a session. A rectangular table is most commonly used, and sometimes two rectangular tables are placed together. This enables the teams to face each other, yet be sufficiently removed.

Caucus rooms. Private meetings among the respective negotiating teams require separate caucus rooms; in some instances one room is set aside for this purpose. The caucus room is also used in the event that a mediator joins the negotiations. It affords him an opportunity to discuss demands or positions with either of the parties in private. The caucus room enables the company team to develop internal bargaining strategy and evaluate the union demands in private.

Recording the Sessions

There are various methods for keeping records of collective bargaining sessions. In some cases, management keeps a record and the union maintains a record. At some point, clauses agreed upon are drawn up as tentative agreements, the tentative agreements are reviewed and approved, and both sides initial what they have agreed upon. Thus at the end of each day there is a record of negotiating progress. Sometimes negotiators prefer to agree in principle on each contractual provision that is to go into the collective bargaining agreement. Then, after final agreement is reached, each provision is rewritten and put into more formal language. Many companies will assign two members of their bargaining team to take notes during the sessions. (Since notes are generally taken in longhand, the two-member note-taking team provides a check in the event that items are overlooked.) But whether one or two records are kept, the proposals agreed upon must be typed and discussed, corrections and modifications must be made, and a final draft must be prepared.

It is customary in a great many companies to take longhand minutes. The minutes are typed after the day's bargaining, and in many cases copies are given to the union committee. It is also a practice for management and union negotiators to sign the minutes, thereby indicating acceptance. The minutes are distributed the next day. Some companies prefer to keep minutes for management's use only. Many business firms believe that verbatim reporting does not permit the parties to speak out on the issues and is not conducive to obtaining a settlement, as there is a chance that negotiators will speak for the record. Other companies use tape recorders or stenographic verbatim reporting. Everything that is said during these negotiations is either recorded or taken down by a stenographer, and the transcript actually becomes part of the agreement. Often, excerpts from the record are used in arbitration proceedings or in reviewing the contract with supervisors or shop stewards. Tape recorders are used rather infrequently because of the tendency to speak for the record and a temptation to engage in lengthy speech making. When this happens, real issues are not faced and negotiations can be unduly prolonged.

Notes should be taken down, since they enable the negotiator to examine contract language, make necessary revisions, and maintain a record of proposals, counterproposals, and agreements so that a final contract can be prepared. The notes are valuable in demonstrating that good faith bargaining in fact took place, in the event that a charge of failure to bargain is made at a later date.

PAYING FOR NEGOTIATING TIME

The question of who pays for negotiating time can be very explosive. Some employers oppose paying union committeemen because they believe it is wrong in principle and does not permit a businesslike approach to the collective bargaining process. Other companies are willing to pay on the premise that meetings can be held during normal business hours rather than after the regular workday, especially if the meetings take place on company property.

There are other companies that make the payment of committeemen a bargainable issue at each negotiation. Generally speaking, when a company pays for time spent in negotiations, the amount is limited to the straight-time rate of pay up to a maximum of eight hours, and in no case is overtime pay included. Some labor relations executives state that there is a psychological advantage in paying union committeemen for contract negotiations. Despite this opinion, strikes have been called in companies where union committeemen were paid for negotiations.

It is interesting to note that some union officials do not approve of having a company paying committeemen for contract negotiations because they are opposed in principle—they believe it is wrong. One thing is certain: If ever the practice gets started, it is difficult to stop. In an overwhelming majority of cases, the union pays for the time spent in negotiations.

There is one precaution to take in the event that a company prefers to pay union committeemen for bargaining sessions: Make certain that the number of union committeemen is determined in advance of contract talks, as well as the amount of time that will be paid for. If this safeguard device is not followed, the union may try to add committeemen during the course of contract discussions, which could be fairly costly.

THE FIRST MEETING

Since the objective in collective bargaining is to arrive at an agreement in good faith, a gracious, friendly attitude is essential. The first meeting enables the enlightened negotiator to establish a good-humored attitude. The employer is aware that the union has made broader demands than will be met. The union also knows that the employer's position does not represent the last and best offer. Negotiators know their positions well, particularly where a union submits its demands and the employer makes its counterproposals prior to negotiations. The answer for settlement lies somewhere between the union's proposal and the employer's counterproposal. The precise point of settlement depends on many factors, such as the skill of the negotiators, the economic position of the company and the union, the cost of living, the economic conditions in the nation, and so on.

At the opening of the first meeting, after the negotiators and the bargaining teams have been properly introduced, it is customary for one of management's negotiators to make a friendly opening statement. The spokesman may state how important the meetings are and how essential it is for the parties to try to arrive at an agreement in good faith. He may also stress the importance of having each side demonstrate a sense of fair play, honesty, and reasonableness. Often a union spokesman will also address the group. The informal aspect of the first meeting often has a salutary effect on all the sessions that follow. The introduction can emphasize the importance of arriving at a contract that is fair and based on sound economic arguments, not in a hostile spirit or horse-trading environment.

At the initial meeting the union generally presents its demands first. Each point is studied and explained so that the full meaning of the contractual provision is understood. The same procedure is followed when considering the company's counterproposals.

DEFINING AUTHORITY

Both company and union negotiators should have sufficient authority to make decisive commitments in the course of negotiations. Unions differ because of the requirements of the various constitutions and bylaws on this point. In some unions, the negotiator may have the authority to make a final agreement or may be permitted to make a tentative agreement subject to ratification by the members. Certain unions provide that the negotiating team be given broad guidelines within which a settlement will be acceptable to the union membership, and, as a result, final agreement can be reached at the bargaining table. Today in many labor organizations it is becoming popular to limit the authority of the bargaining team by withholding the authority to sign an agreement until the membership accepts the terms of the contract.

If the company engages in companywide or industrywide bargaining, the acceptance of an agreement by the union may be up to the international union. Labor lawyers, economists, and research personnel are common in industrywide bargaining, and their services are provided by the international union.

Some labor organizations submit final agreements to a wage policy committee which may be composed of the union's executive board and elected members from various local unions. The wage policy committee votes acceptance or rejection of the negotiated agreement.

The ratification problems develop out of the separation of authority to make an agreement from the power to make it binding. This process is clearly incompatible with the principles of sound collective bargaining. It exists, nevertheless, and employers should fully understand the process used by the union involved in order to determine an appropriate course of action. Whenever a union representative says an agreement must be submitted for ratification, it is a good policy to receive assurance that the committee will effectively recommend ratification to the union membership.

Management negotiating teams are usually composed of industrial relations personnel assigned to handle collective bargaining. In some companies the management team may include, along with the industrial relations group, operating personnel, and legal counsel. Smaller companies often follow the practice of having all negotiations conducted by operating personnel.

Management negotiating teams may operate within guidelines established by top management with authority to make a final agreement, or they may be required to submit a tentative agreement to top management for final acceptance. It is advisable for company negotiators to have the power to bind their principals, and top management should give the authority.

The parties should understand their respective positions on the subject of authority at the outset so that misunderstandings can be minimized. Management can help the situation by designating a spokesman who can inform the union that the team is empowered to enter into an agreement. This will make it difficult for a union to request that someone in authority be brought in or that the president of the company be on hand. It avoids attempts by the union to bypass the bargaining team and deal with top management. A competent management team should possess the authority to meet the union on equal terms so that the company's interest is protected.

Negotiating frustrations can be spared if authority is clearly defined.

From management's standpoint, a great deal of spadework can be done in advance of negotiations so that the matter is resolved. One approach is for top management to define limits for bargaining and then leave as much flexibility as possible to the negotiating team. For example, it is wise to determine in advance just how much of a wage increase the company is prepared to grant as well as the basic question as to the issues for which the company is willing to take a strike. Once these types of questions are decided, the management team should have flexibility without interference.

ESTABLISHING GROUND RULES

Oral agreements. The matter of oral or written agreements is covered by the Labor-Management Act of 1947—the Taft-Hartley Act—which states specifically that "the parties must sign a written contract incorporating the terms of agreement (if any), if requested by either party."

Besides the law there are other sufficient reasons that should be examined. Since collective bargaining covers the negotiation, administration, interpretation, application, and enforcement of joint understandings as to wages and conditions of employment, written agreements are essential for maintaining industrial peace. Years ago when the scope and nature of bargaining was limited, oral agreements existed in some industries. Today oral agreements are outdated because the scope of collective bargaining is broad, complicated, and often difficult—especially when language is needed to cover such items as pensions and hospital and surgical group insurance. Imagine trying to cover collective bargaining understandings without a written document! Moreover, three-year agreements are fairly common in industry. Hence all the major questions as negotiated between the parties should be recorded somewhere. The parties propose to conclude a collective agreement; if they are to avoid future disputes as well as provide information for supervisors and employees, a written contract is essential.

It is true that not all negotiations need result in a written agreement. Wages and conditions involving public employees are often decided without a written contract. Civil service employees and others engaged in public employment may receive higher compensation and have vacation plans improved and other conditions of employment adjusted without a written agreement. But this is an exception to sound industrial practice.

Some companies follow a combination technique in bargaining by entering into an oral agreement and finally reducing the oral agreement to writing. This is how it works: The parties do not attempt to arrive at a final agreement during the course of negotiations. Instead, they agree orally on contract terms in principle and then rely on company and union attorneys to draw up the agreement. The final contract is reviewed by negotiators from both sides. Experienced lawyers help to put the principles arrived at by the parties into understandable language. They try to avoid legal terminology and language that would be likely to confuse the employees as to the meaning of the contract.

Partial agreements and tentative agreements. It would be unusual to negotiate a partial agreement. There have been a few isolated cases where contracting parties have executed a partial agreement and later concluded a complete contract. In those cases, all contract provisions were agreed to except for the pension section—the principals agreed that once pertinent information was accumulated a pension plan would be developed and made part of the agreement. The same has applied to a supplementary unemployment benefit plan and group insurance. A partial agreement becomes extremely cumbersome if provision is made for allowing the union to strike in the absence of agreement. The company may be faced with crisis bargaining twice in the same year or twice during the contract term, whatever period it may cover.

It is a very good and well-accepted practice to agree with the union that all agreements reached during negotiations be tentative, subject to reaching a full agreement. Since the purpose of negotiation is to obtain an agreement that will work, actual procedures covering tentative agreements and other forms of variations will differ considerably from company to company. But, if it works well for the company, it should certainly be used.

Some negotiators simply list the agreed-to contract changes and agree that the changes will be incorporated in a contract—called "an agreement to enter into an agreement." This is a helpful technique where ratification of union membership is required. The method is effective and often saves time.

Retroactive agreements. The collective bargaining process is flexible. On many occasions, if the negotiators for the company and the union cannot conclude an agreement and the contract expires, arrangements may be made to extend the contract for a fixed period, perhaps 30 to 60 days, or on a day-to-day basis. In a majority of cases the parties agree in advance that any increase negotiated will be retroactive to the expiration date of the contract. The parties may wish to leave the issue of retroactivity unresolved until agreement is reached on all contractual clauses. Providing retroactivity on issues other than the general wage increase can be costly and should be avoided, especially if retroactivity is granted for inequity settlements, vacation benefits, holidays, pensions, insurance, and so on.

Order of contract discussion. The pattern of contract negotiations and procedures will vary considerably from one situation to another, depending on the history of prior relations between the contracting parties, and it is therefore difficult to set down a surefire method for successfully discussing the order of contract clauses. Techniques that make for successful negotiations in one case may prove highly unsuccessful in another situation. This is so because there is almost no limit to the ingenuity which skilled negotiators use in attempting to create an agreement pattern. At best, successful company and union negotiators can only suggest an approach.

At the outset, it may be practical to discuss the contract clauses in the order in which they appear. The negotiators should first resolve the least controversial issues before proceeding to negotiate the difficult issues. Then they should divide the difficult issues into economic and noneconomic demands and resolve all noneconomic issues on their merits without tying them to economic considerations. A package approach should be used on economic issues. Not all negotiators agree on this approach. Nevertheless, it is prevalent in many industries.

Publicity. There should be, if possible, an agreed-upon procedure to follow in releasing to the press terms of the negotiated settlement. It is customary in some negotiations for the company to prepare a press release, review the write-up with the union committee, and then give the story to the newspapers.

Agreement should also be obtained about progress reports to the press during negotiations, as well as advance information to the rank-and-file union members. Although arrangements differ, often no information is released until a complete agreement is concluded. Terms of a settlement and often pictures of the participants appear in company and union papers or magazines.

Other forms of publicity are noteworthy. Providing a printed copy of the agreement to all employees helps to publicize the terms of the agreement. Reviewing the contract with the supervisory force can prove beneficial in the administration of the agreement because the supervisors will then be informed on all provisions of the contract along with the correct interpretation and meaning. Some companies bring the foreman and shop stewards together to hear the principals review the terms of the labor agreement. The understanding about publicity should be agreed to prior to actual bargaining

—it saves valuable time in the end and is a businesslike facet of sound collective bargaining procedures.

CONTRACT TEXT

It is advisable for management to negotiate from its own text. Getting the union to agree to this contract text may cause a problem. On the other hand, if management prepares its draft properly, the chances that it will be used are enhanced. There are several solid reasons why a company should use its own text, and these should be pointed out to the union. (Unions, on the whole, have accepted these reasons.)

The first reason involves a rewrite of language proposed by the union—the company should simply state that it has studied the proposal, agrees in principle, and will include revised clauses in its contract. Second, the company should state that it is willing to include union proposals agreed to in the course of bargaining. Third, management should suggest that it wants to make some improvements in the proposal and that those rewritten items are included in the company draft. Fourth, management should profess a willingness to provide copies of the contract text to the union, allowing adequate time for review.

No matter who writes the contract text to be used for discussions, the draft should be prepared in the simplest possible terms. Whoever drafts the agreement should recognize the basic fact that unfamiliar words and lengthy sentences may cause confusion and can lead to unnecessary grievances and arbitration. Contracts are designed to stabilize labor relations for a definite period; they are not written for the purpose of creating confusion and disturbances in the area of employee relations.

Possible Settlements

Edward J. McMahon

As THE COLLECTIVE BARGAINING PROCESS MOVES FROM THE PREPARATION STAGE
through the actual negotiations with the union, a transformation begins to evolve. The ultimate objective of this whole process is the achievement of an agreement embodying the terms and conditions of employment. But, while the initial stages of bargaining and the negotiation activities represent a manifestation of a rational, objective analysis of the many factors previously discussed, the final stages take on a far more emotional and subjective nature.

The settlement *sought* reflects the conclusions of the bargaining team arrived at after long hours of careful study and preparation. The settlement *reached* is a function not only of this most desirable settlement but also of what the parties can in fact achieve through a skillful use of tactics and strategies within the context of each one's bargaining power. This very important distinction must be learned and remembered during negotiations. The emphasis placed on preparation and study—and justly so—must not be allowed to obscure the importance of the final stages of negotiations during which tactics must be developed and redeveloped as the situation changes.

EDWARD J. McMAHON is vice president and director of industrial relations at St. Regis Paper Company in New York City.

This chapter will deal with these final negotiation moves and the attempt to develop, arrange, and rank possible settlements.

In the subsequent development of a framework for reaching an agreement, it is important to maintain the proper perspective. In creating a conceptual model for the bargaining process the assumption is made that an agreement is possible. There are times, however, when a strike or lockout will be inevitable and will precede the bargaining climax itself. Management often knows that the union will insist on a point which it cannot grant; or the union may operate on an assumption of strike first and bargain later. In these situations, the bargaining procedures may take place after a strike or may never come into play before a plant is shut down. It is inevitable, however, that proper negotiations will require working within some framework if and when an agreement is to be reached.

Essentially, the collective bargaining contract reflects those terms and conditions under which the employers agree to employ and the employees agree to work. In its simplest form, the contract sets out the wages, hours, and working conditions of the bargaining unit involved. How these terms are worded, the amount of the wages and fringe benefits, and, in general, the degree to which they favor one party depends in great part on what takes place as the bargaining climax approaches.

AVAILABLE ALTERNATIVES

As the bargaining process approaches the point of climax, many alternatives are open to each party. To emphasize a previous point, the assumption is that the ultimate objective is to reach an agreement. Both company and union representatives adhere to this objective and each move is made with it in mind. Too often the bargainer loses sight of the fact that the other side is operating under the same assumption; that is, an agreement can and must be reached.

When negotiations reach the final stage, the employer has several alternatives. If there is no contract in existence or, indeed, if the current contract is about to expire, he may decide not to operate beyond a specified deadline. The lockout or plant shutdown is quite often an effective weapon in the hands of an experienced negotiator. He can declare that as of a specified date, if no agreement has been reached, he will cease production and order the doors to the plant locked.

The alternative to the employer is to operate without a contract. In this instance, the decision will be to offer employment either under existing conditions and at the current rate of pay or at the terms of the final employer offer once an impasse has been reached. The employer in effect is telling the employees the choice is theirs. Again it is important to point out that this choice does in fact exist. When bargaining reaches the point of impasse and one or more bargainable issues remain unresolved, the employer can bring a great deal of pressure to bear by offering its employees an alternative to the strike. In effect, the company says *work and continue to earn your current or the offered wages while negotiations continue. You can strike and we all know it. You therefore give up very little in terms of bargaining power while avoiding the sudden shock of a complete loss of earning power.*

Assuming that the employer offers to operate without a contract, the union is then forced into a strategic decision. It can accept the offer to work or can try to shut down the plant. The decision is a difficult one to make, and most international union constitutions or bylaws require a strike vote of the membership. If authority exists for the negotiating committee to call a strike, it will have to weigh the various factors involved before deciding to do so. The issue or issues separating the parties, the relative degree of economic strength, and the tenor of the labor relations picture as a whole are all important.

If a strike is called, the employer is again faced with a choice. It can take the strike by shutting down the plant or attempt to keep it open and invite the employees to continue to work. Again the choice is a difficult one. Violence and severe damage, often irreparable to both personnel and physical property, can follow a back-to-work movement. Furthermore, the damage to future labor-management relations can be incalculable in terms of the employees' relationships with each other and with management.

In the early post-World-War-II period, the back-to-work movement was a favorite tool of many companies. The strategy was to divide and conquer by enticing those employees who were never really in favor of the strike (especially when union shops were far less common than they are today) to cross the picket lines. Armed guards were hired to protect them, with results as brutal as the employer expected them to be. As violence erupted, state court injunctions were easy to obtain. Under the police power of the state, these courts were quick to enjoin the entire strike, order a return to work, and destroy the backbone of what was in many cases a rather weak strike anyway.

The consequences of such employer decisions were and often still are accompanied by strained or nonexistent union relations. The motive often was to break the union or to weaken resolve while breaking the strike. To-day, the unionization of many company operations is an accepted fact. The alternative to fighting a strike through continuing to operate must be chosen from this perspective. It can be an effective weapon, but it has attendant dangers to the future well-being of the entire operation.

EFFECTS OF BARGAINING POWER

The available alternatives pose serious and difficult questions for each party in collective bargaining—questions which do not offer simple answers. The employer must ask: What are the effects of my decision on local man-agement, on the employees, on the relationship with the international union, and on the community itself? The union must ask the same question as it relates to the members and to the organization itself. Furthermore, the question must be asked of the effect upon the problem at hand—the raison d'être for the negotiations. Unless the decision is aimed at reaching an agreement or forcing the union to recede from its extreme position, it may not be justified.

The term "bargaining power" is used to describe and define the frame-work within which these answers must be found. The ability or right to strike on the part of the union combined with the decision to lock out or to take a strike by the employer is not itself equated with bargaining power. Certainly, the possible *effectiveness* of a strike and the degree to which one party or the other can sustain its bargaining position operate as a limitation upon the decision of this party to accept or reject a given result of negotia-tions. It is really the ability to impose an economic cost on the opposing party and the consequences of this cost resulting from failure to reach an agreement that determine the bargaining power of one party vis-à-vis the other.

Many factors determine bargaining power and its effect on negotiations. It is usually defined in terms of all forces which enable an employer or union to set and maintain the terms and conditions of employment with which it can live. Tastes, goals, and motives of the parties; skills and techniques of negotiation; and external factors such as competition from other employers and unions broadly define bargaining power.

As a starting point for an analysis of the effect of bargaining power on contract negotiations, it will be helpful to discuss the concept of a "conces-sion schedule" which would relate the willingness to take or call a strike to the potential gain from such a strike. A concession schedule can be set up for both the employer and the union; with it, the demand for a particular wage gain can be weighted against the economic loss resulting from a strike. On the employer's side, a schedule would be set up showing wage changes which he would be willing to pay rather than face a strike of a given length. The wage increments would vary in direct relation with his willingness to take a strike. A similar schedule called the "resistance schedule" would be set up for the union. For a higher wage it would refuse to strike; at lower wages it would call a strike and maintain it for varying lengths of time depending on the amount of the offer.

This analysis is helpful in our discussion. It is limited to the economic aspects of collective bargaining, however, and implies that this issue would be determinative. Thus, when the point is reached in the size of the wage package where the employer's concession equals a point in the union's resistance schedule, the best possible bargain for both sides will have been arrived at. At any higher wage demand, the employer would prefer to take a strike since he believes that the employees would not hold out for as long as would be necessary to make the strike as costly to him as the wage demanded. At a lesser wage level, the union would call a strike; the employer would be willing to grant an increase since the expected strike would cost him more than the settlement at the higher rate.

Such a cost analysis can be extended to all the issues in collective bargaining. When the bargaining power of the union and the employer is weighted against the cost of settlement or nonsettlement of *all* economic and noneconomic issues, a point can be reached where the cost to each dictates that the maximum benefits for both can be obtained by settling. The effect of bargaining power, then, is to provide the motive for settlement. It is the catalyst in reaching an agreeement between two parties in an adverse relationship.

The Deadline

Given the framework of alternatives available and the relative bargaining power of each party, the negotiation process becomes a medium by which each term in a labor contract is evolved. The first contract often requires a greater length of time to negotiate. Each article is new; each must be explained as to purpose and intent. Yet the point must be reached where discussion is no longer useful, where each issue has been subjected to a complete reassessment.

At this point, one party must elect to switch from one alternative to another. Rather than continue to negotiate while working without a contract, the union, for example, may decide to call a strike. As of a specific date, it will attempt to shut down the plant. The deadline is set, management is put on notice that it must decide whether to try to keep the plant open, and bargaining power is wielded in its ultimate form.

Possible Settlements

The cost analysis described earlier must be carried out carefully and completely. It should be noted that cost as used here means more than financial or pecuniary cost. It implies disadvantage and refers to economic and noneconomic costs. Immediately the problem becomes one of defining those elements which represent some cost or gain to each side and then reducing these elements to a common denominator for purposes of comparison.

Initially, the assumption is that some agreement is possible. In general, each side feels that it is better to reach agreement through collective bargaining without resort to a strike or to the legal manipulations within the Labor Board or the courts. A second assumption is that there is some point at which the employer would offer to hire and the employees would offer to work; that is, a point at which both sides can agree to sign a contract without the necessity of a strike or of some third-party dictation of terms. Neither assumption is always true. There are times when employees desire to hit the street and no offer by the employer will prevent them from getting it out of their system. Moreover, employers who cannot or will not live with the designated union may be dedicated to breaking the union through a refusal to reach an agreement. Similarly, there are unions whose demands far exceed reality and who set a lower limit on these demands which is above the point at which a company will be forced to shut down its operations.

The concept of the acceptable settlement is essential to collective bargaining. Each party would like to get what it considers the best of a group of possible settlements. The employer, for example, in the absence of a union and in the absence of market restraints from competitors, would set its wages and working conditions at some level—call it Point E. The union, were it to have complete control over the employer's practices and the best area rates in the industry, would set these same rates and working conditions at a higher level—Point U. Somewhere between levels E and U there is a point of agreement which the employer can live with and the union can accept.

Let us analyze the acceptable settlement further. The employer's spokesman is facing a newly organized plant. Usually he can set relatively low wages in return for giving the new union some form of union security clause and making concessions on job security—generally in the form of seniority provisions. Fringe benefits, grievance arbitration clauses, and general plant rules and practices are also important. The negotiator can put together a package containing all the major points he would like to convince the union to accept. But he can also vary this package in several ways. He can reduce all the elements proportionally in terms of their being less desirable from his company's point of view, or he can reduce some more than others. In this way, he prepares a schedule of acceptable settlements, ranking them from the most desirable down to the least desirable. Above this point he cannot go. His company would prefer to take a strike rather than concede any further.

How can this ranking take place in light of the many variables involved? It is at this point in the negotiation process that collective bargaining requires skillful and exacting analysis. It is really at this point that the rational, objective cost analysis becomes less important than the intangible intuition of the negotiator. Each specific issue left unresolved by the negotiations must be balanced against the possibility and cost of a strike. But the possibility of a strike is a subjective determination made in view of the personalities of the international representatives, the local committee, and the membership as a whole. It will include consideration of the time of the year, the weather, market factors in the industry, and the mood and temperament of key employees.

Ranking the possible settlements from the employer's point of view is only the first step. The union is going through the same procedure and, consciously or unconsciously, must relate its rankings to the opinion it holds of the employer's deliberations. The final and most important task facing the company representative is to relate the various possible settlements to those determinations being made by the union. It is in this way that he himself can realistically set the line of settlement acceptable to his company which he can hope to achieve.

It is worthwhile carrying this concept further to develop a model, as it were. First, the company negotiator ranks the various settlements he feels he can achieve. Second, he sets that settlement above which he cannot go in terms of cost of the settlement balanced against the cost of a strike. This might be called the company's least acceptable settlement. His third step is to speculate upon and analyze the union's deliberations on possible settlements in order to determine the settlement he might realistically expect to achieve above this least acceptable settlement.

It is this third step which distinguishes the highly skilled negotiator from a less capable spokesman and which involves the utilization of those intangible characteristics that are so indigenous to collective bargaining.

If we could take a picture of this ranking process on both sides of the bargaining table we might see the following line diagram.

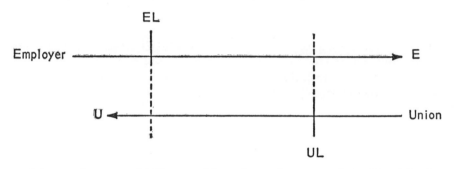

The employer would like to achieve the settlement at Point E, while the union feels that Point U is the maximum point at which it is aiming. Each party ranks the possible settlements below these points and establishes the point of least acceptable settlement, designated by EL on the employer's ranking and UL on the union's. A common result during such negotiations is that Point EL corresponds to some point at or near the most desirable settlement from the union view; that is, at or near Point U. Similarly, Point UL corresponds to a settlement on the employer's line at or near E—the employer's most desirable settlement.

It seems obvious that an employer that correctly identifies Point UL can decide to set this as its bargaining objective. Put another way, knowledge of where UL is on a ranking of possible settlements by the union can enable an employer to fix EL, its point of least acceptable settlements, at exactly that point. Conversely, the same reasoning would hold true for the union negotiator. If he fixes his objective at the point to which the employer will go before taking a strike, he can achieve the best possible settlement. The employer will concede the issues to the union at EL because he has determined that up to that point it is better to concede than to take a strike.

The adversary system embodied in collective bargaining has evolved into a contest at two basic levels. The distinction has been drawn between the cost analysis approach in terms of a rational, objective balancing of economic and noneconomic costs and the relation of this cost analysis to the more subjective determinations involved in arriving at a ranking of possible settlements and an acceptable settlement which the negotiator will seek. In a very real sense, then, this process is a useful tool in the development and maintenance of successful union-management relations. Through proper preparation, the newly organized employer can initiate a long relationship with this outside employee representative in the most beneficial way. There is no reason to give away a plant through unrealistic wages or unnecessarily prohibitive contract language because of inadvertence or inattention. Nor should a costly strike be forced upon the employees through the hit-or-miss setting of a settlement well below their expectations. Doing it properly from the beginning will establish a precedent for future negotiations and will create the type of atmosphere within which the business at hand can be carried on; that is, efficient and profitable operation of the plant.

MUTUALLY ACCEPTABLE SETTLEMENT

In the last analysis, one mutually acceptable settlement must be reached. As has been discussed, each party must rank possible settlements in order of desirability. More than one settlement may be and usually is acceptable to each party, and each tries to achieve that settlement most desirable to it. In the bargaining model, no attempt was made to quantify the factors by which the settlements are to be ranked. No mathematical formulas can or should be developed to try to simulate real-world situations in laboratory circumstances. In this sense the concepts being discussed are simply that—concepts, not models in any operations research sense of the word.

This model approach, however, is useful for discussion, bringing into focus the relationship of these concepts to the actual problems of dealing with the union. As new and more complex constraints are added to the real-world situation, it becomes even more imperative to maintain the orderly, logical thinking that this approach entails. It is easier to adapt the model and alter the solution when in fact the negotiations process requires such adaptation. In achieving the mutually acceptable settlement, this approach may still be considered a viable one.

As bargaining brings the parties down to the wire, the traditional bargaining procedure is to eliminate each issue upon which there has been an understanding, usually conditioned upon a final complete settlement. One or more issues will remain. The negotiator must re-evaluate the possible settlement in light of what he has given up and what he has received up to this point and in light of those issues remaining unresolved. Each possible course of action must be traced from this point in time in light of these fixed variables. In other words, the preceding line diagram may be redrawn; it is a picture at a given point in time only and not a continuous design over the whole negotiation period. This factor is essential in our analysis. The flexibility necessary to effective negotiations cannot be sacrificed for some aesthetic desire to quantify a model of action in some scientific way.

The employer again determines Point UL, where the union will accept a settlement without striking but below which it will not. As another issue is resolved or as one issue is conceded in return for an agreement on another, the re-evaluation continues and begins to move the parties toward a mutually acceptable settlement. If each party has done his homework well and if the negotiations have been conducted in an orderly and professional manner, an agreement can be reached which is the best possible settlement that each side can expect. At this point, when each side feels it has achieved the best possible position in its ranking of possible settlements, an agreement will be reached between the negotiating parties. While the obvious necessary last step is ratification by the union membership, this give-and-take of collective bargaining is the only way an agreement can be reached without a dictation of terms by some third party. In order to maximize the desirable conditions which are embodied in this agreement, the orderly ranking of settlements aimed at determination of a realistic acceptable settlement is proposed as the best available method.

Ranking and seeking one of many possible settlements require more than an accurate appraisal of bargaining power in a particular situation. A general framework has been provided for the selection and resolution of a collective labor agreement through the development of a conceptual model within which the negotiation process can reach its climax. Mention has been made of the issues between the parties which must be evaluated and balanced against each other in the determination of the possible settlements and final agreement. These issues themselves require a ranking process. The next chapter discusses this important aspect of dealing with the union. It seeks answers to the question, What are the vital interests of union and management?

Vital Interests
of Employer and Union

Edward J. McMahon

THE NATURE OF THE OPPOSING PARTIES IN COLLECTIVE BARGAINING IN LARGE measure influences the interests each considers vital. The circumstances surrounding the particular negotiation are also major factors in determining which interests the parties will place in a high priority status. In each bargaining situation a different set of values will emerge to dictate the relative importance of each bargaining issue.

The election campaign conducted by the union will itself act to set the framework for the first bargaining attempt. Before the passage of the Wagner Act in 1935, if unions desired to represent employees in a plant where management did not choose to recognize them, the only recourse was to strike for recognition. With the establishment of the right of workers to organize and bargain collectively and with the formation of the Labor Board to regulate the process of union organization, union efforts were aimed at winning elections rather than closing down plants.

Representation elections and organizing campaigns aimed at securing a majority vote in a unit deemed appropriate by the Labor Board did not spell the end of bitterness and violence, however. When the dust cleared and a union was designated the exclusive representative of all the employees in a bargaining unit, the result was often a highly emotional unbalancing of worker-management relations. By its very nature the union campaign was aimed at upsetting these relations and establishing a need for outside representation. The human relations and sociological implications of why workers feel the need for representation have filled volumes. It is sufficient to point out that a very real task facing the negotiating committees in their first attempt is to establish the type of relationship desired and set the tenor for many years to come. Further, those interests which each considers vital will bear a direct relationship to this long-term objective.

The Opposing Parties

The intensely political labor union reflects the traditional collectivism by which a majority vote determines the goals and decisions of the unit. In this country, the labor movement has been unique in its conceptual basis. The development of labor organizations grew out of the private enterprise system, and this growth has resulted in the acceptance of the profit orientation characteristic of American business. The idea behind employee unions became one of having a say in the terms and conditions of employment. Rather than taking over the means of production as advocated by Marxism, American labor unions preferred collective bargaining as a voice in the relationship of these means of production to the workers. In other words, while accepting the concept of profit making in private enterprise, labor unions aim at securing a say in the terms and conditions under which the employees will work within this system.

A union's representatives thus purport to reflect the view of the majority of its members. The Wagner Act provided the means of establishing this representation. At the same time this law demanded that such a representative act for *all* the members of the bargaining unit involved. Thus, when a majority of the employees vote for Union A, this union is certified as the exclusive representative of all the employees in the unit for purposes of collective bargaining.

When a union negotiating committee enters the bargaining room, it must be prepared to take a position on many issues which may be distasteful to a large minority of its members. Also, the nature of the organization lends itself to rather quick changes in mood with attendant changes in the majority view. Every issue that comes up during negotiations requires resolution to the satisfaction of this majority. When negotiations reach a climax and the ranking process discussed in the preceding chapter boils down to one or two sticky questions, the difficult task facing the union committee should be obvious. The question of economic balancing of agreement versus nonagreement requires an answer not only in terms of the bargaining developments themselves, but also in terms of the changing mood of the majority of the unit members.

One further aspect of the nature of the union must be mentioned. As a newly designated representative, the union is fighting for its own existence. In one sense the union operates as a business fighting to perform a service well enough to maintain its position in the face of tough competition. This important point has several implications. First, the question of union security is sure to arise during negotiations. This can take several forms. The concepts of union shop, agency shop, and maintenance of membership agreements will be discussed in a later section. A second implication is that a tough bargaining stance is essential to the union if it wishes to give the impression that it is trying to live up to the promises made in the organizing campaign. These are often unrealistic promises, and the initial union position in negotiations will often reflect this pie-in-the-sky approach. The dilemma facing the union in this circumstance is compounded by the fact that this is the time when it is least able to support extreme demands. As a new union, it must prove itself to a skeptical membership while simultaneously attempting to achieve some form of union security.

The employer is decidedly authoritarian. Business is structured to place authority at the level where decisions must be made and to place decision-making authority at the level best designed to achieve the objective sought. This clearly presents an entirely new set of factors in establishing and ranking vital interests. A management negotiating committee can prepare itself well enough to avoid the political complications facing its union counterpart. By establishing the objectives sought in negotiations and carefully preparing with line personnel the needs of the plant, the task of protecting vital interests rests solely with the ability of the negotiator.

The importance of having line management deal with the union must not be de-emphasized. Certainly, many companies insist that all bargaining be actually carried out by the plant manager and relegate the industrial relations representative to an advisory capacity. The point here, however, is that once the bargaining objectives are set up in light of rather clear-cut considerations of effectuating production and making a profit, this position need never change during negotiations except to move from one priority or level of desirability to another. In the usual case, the authority to make such moves is placed with the negotiating team or is easily attainable from one or two specifically identified managers. In this framework, the negotiator can react to the moods of the union and can carry out his detailed analysis of unresolved issues with a much greater degree of certainty.

Operating within this structure, management representatives will thus consider those issues to be vital which directly or indirectly affect the production objectives of the plant. Issues such as job bidding, no-strike clauses, and the right of management to operate the business are discussed in detail later. The major concerns are to establish a good working relationship with the union and to provide for the orderly continuance of production with a minimum amount of union interference.

LEGAL ISSUES

The passage and subsequent interpretation of federal labor laws has thrust the government into the collective bargaining process in an important way. Any discussion of the negotiation process, the subjects treated, and the tactics used must include some background discussion of the role of the courts and the Labor Board. This role has grown to the point that all union-management confrontations take place with one eye on the board and the courts. In a very real way, the government has become an active partner in labor relations and the regulating agencies are an integral part of the tactics, strategies, and subject matter of collective bargaining.

The basic laws on collective bargaining are the Wagner Act of 1935 and the Taft-Hartley Act of 1947. After establishing the right to bargain collectively and a procedure for carrying out representation elections, the law sets out practices and procedures of both labor and management which are illegal. The unfair labor practice jurisdiction of the Labor Board extends into collective bargaining in several areas.

Originally, the board was faced with the problem of a strong employer making a mockery of the election of employee representatives by refusing to engage in meaningful negotiations. It developed the concept of good faith bargaining and attempted to define the tactics of the parties which were not aimed at achieving an agreement. Not only *what* was said but *how* it was said is important, and the board acted vigorously to regulate the tactics and procedures of bargaining.

The regulation of tactics of collective bargaining was soon expanded by the regulation of scope and content of collective bargaining. The good faith bargaining requirement was developed to define the practices and procedures of the parties during bargaining. This requirement, however, led inevitably to the question of the subject matter of negotiations: *What* must be bargained followed directly the question of *how* it must be bargained.

The Taft-Hartley Act specifically excluded certain areas from collective bargaining. Essentially, Congress declared that despite the intent of either party, certain subjects could not be included in the labor agreement as a matter of public policy. These prohibited areas basically preclude agreements which provide that the employer refrain from handling, using, selling, or transporting the products of any other employer or cease doing business with any other person. Further, after 1947 it became illegal for the union and company to agree to a closed shop or preferential hiring provision, and a prohibition was set out in Section 14(b) against requiring membership in a labor organization as a condition of employment where state law prohibits it.

These areas of prohibited subjects of collective bargaining were merely a starting point of government regulation, however. Two other areas have developed from the rulings of the Labor Board. One area was called mandatory subjects of bargaining and was developed from the statutory phrase, "wages, hours and other terms and conditions of employment." Any subject that the board felt came within this rather broadly ambiguous phrase was a mandatory bargaining subject, and the parties were forced to discuss it. The second area was called nonmandatory but permissible bargaining and encompassed subjects about which the parties could negotiate if they wished. A caveat was added by the board to this nonmandatory but permissible area to the effect that these subjects could not be insisted upon to the point of impasse. The strike and lockout would be limited only to those subjects defined within the mandatory area of wages, hours, and other terms and conditions of employment.

The effect of this third-party interest on the labor relations function must not be underestimated. The specific aspect under discussion here has proved to be the most disturbing area of government regulation of labor relations. Noted experts and practitioners representing both labor and management have expressed concern lest the process described here as collective bargaining be turned into compulsory arbitration.

Perhaps the most important trend in recent years has been the expansion of the mandatory bargaining concept to changes in business operations such as plant removal, plant closing, or contracting-out of work. As technological advances are being made with consequent reduction in manpower needs and as new theories of organizational structure foster business relocations and reorganizations, the importance of this problem has increased.

Labor Board cases have developed several rules of which each employer entering the negotiation process must be aware. It is important to point out that a detailed examination of the legal aspects of collective bargaining is beyond the scope of this chapter. It is necessary, however, to understand that this factor is involved. This analysis of the negotiation process and the vital issues within its scope attempts to prescribe the constraints within which management must work. The nature of the opposing parties presents the basic framework. To this is added the nature of the third party—the public interest as expressed by the legislative and administrative regulations of the labor laws.

THE WAGE PACKAGE

The question of wages is at once the most complex and the most intriguing issue in collective bargaining. Not only how much money should be paid, but what form this payment should take present the parties in negotiations with important and difficult questions. The wage package is developed through a combination of basic wages with supplementary or fringe benefits. Within this package is included all the economic issues related to the amount of wage rate; length and payment of vacations, holidays, and other days off; group insurance; and pension benefits.

There are no strict guidelines for approaching these wage issues. The many factors involved in determining the final package will interrelate in as many different ways as there are negotiations. Essentially, the preparation of a wage proposal will entail an analysis of the current job and wage structure in the plant, the company, the industry, and related industries, especially within a geographic proximity to the plant in question.

Job evaluation studies within the plant are often important in developing a realistic, practical job structure. Such studies can place each job in its proper relation to each other job. These studies require the active participation of first-line foremen and their supervisors, producing the desirable by-product of an orderly system of rates developed by people who have to live and work with them in the future. Once the jobs have been placed in some relationship, the problem becomes one of applying the proper rates to each job. Practical considerations such as the particular personnel involved, the degree of intraplant movement to jobs with higher rates, and the need to attract good workmen will all be brought into the picture.

Of course, the structure, form, and amount of wages must be negotiated. The first bargaining effort will lean heavily on management's initiative in such preparations, however, and can be a good start to future relations with the employees and their union if done fairly and accurately. Before developing the vital interests of each side in the final form of the wage package, some definition of wages will be helpful.

The most common delineation of compensation to labor is first the *basic wage* and second the *fringe benefit*. Basic wages relate to payment for actual time worked and are based upon either a time factor or an output factor. It is possible to distinguish several forms of time payment and output payment. Hourly rated workers are the traditional manual laborers with whom negotiations are concerned. Time payments are often set by the hour, day, week, month, or year. Salaried personnel usually include those paid on the longer intervals—weekly, monthly, or annually. Those paid by the hour or by the day are usually called wage earners. Also, the basic wage related to time includes shift differentials for second and third shifts whereby workers on those shifts get the basic wage plus the stated differential. Also, overtime provisions required by law present another element by which employees are paid at some multiple of their basic wage. Both overtime premiums and shift differentials are common subjects of wage bargaining.

Output-related basic wages also take several forms. Briefly, these include incentive payments based on piecework per individual employee, group incentives on the basis of group output, plantwide incentives based on plant output, and standard hour or standard production incentives based on a guaranteed base pay for some standard output with a bonus for each unit above the standard. In general, such systems work best in industries where labor cost is a high proportion of total cost of production and where output per individual or group is easily observed.

The utilization of incentive plans presents many problems of which the negotiator must be aware. These require constant updating to insure accurate standards as methods change and machines are replaced. A poorly administered plan can prove extremely costly to management and can more than offset any gain in worker productivity. The basic wage plan adopted has to meet the needs of the particular plant which has specific scheduling problems, individual foremen and supervisors of varying degrees of capability, and different methods of production which may or may not lend themselves to incentive rating.

The interest of the unions in the basic wage question will vary as well. The common belief that all unions vehemently oppose incentive-rated work does not take into account the effect of these plans in different situations. As a general rule, unions do oppose these plans. Where the impact of such plans on a worker's take-home pay is effectively to increase that pay, however, most unions will favor incentive plans. This is especially true in plants where labor output can be effectively measured and where all jobs can be rated accurately to reduce friction between straight-base-rate employees and incentive rated employees. The thrust of unions that do accept incentives is at the manner in which these incentives work in practice. This aspect of negotiations has a profound effect on how these plans work.

The second aspect of wages is the fringe or supplementary wage benefit, so called because it does not directly affect time- or output-related wages. The term "fringe benefits" is an anachronism and might best be eliminated from the negotiations vocabulary. Fringe implies icing on the cake or some inconsequential aspect of the whole. In reality, the development of fringe benefits has been rapid. The War Labor Board, set up to regulate collective bargaining during the Second World War, provided the initial impetus as unions were able to expand the scope of bargaining beyond the basic wage. After the war, the bargaining process only started with wages. Fringe benefits began modestly but have since broadened into a substantial proportion of total labor costs. Today, fringes include vacation time and pay, health and accident insurance, life insurance, sick leave pay, pensions, and often some form of guaranteed wage or supplemental unemployment benefit. They are highly costly social benefits often adding 25 percent or more to direct wage costs and having a profound effect on our national economy and our state and federal social legislation.

The interests of the employer in the area of fringe benefits are a function of two major considerations. First, management must appraise the effect of each benefit on the total workforce in the plant. The need to operate with skilled personnel is obvious. When fringe benefits are tied to seniority, a result may be the extensive absence of key men since the most knowledgeable are often the most senior employees. Second, the cost of these benefits is vital to the profit picture. A balance must be drawn between the potential good that can come from these benefits in terms of attracting top employees and maintaining happy, well-rested workers and the cost burden these benefits present as a percentage of total labor costs.

On the union side, fringe benefits have become a very important part of the total wage package. For the newly recognized union, the biggest initial gains are often in this area. The employer more readily accedes to fringe benefits than to direct pay increases, especially in longer-term contracts, and these often look better to the membership than the proportional cost to the employer. In seeking a final settlement, a union will be motivated by a desire to match other gains it has achieved in area plants as well as gains achieved by rival unions. The total wage package will be an important part of these gains, and the new union will consider this vital to its survival.

WORKING CONDITIONS

To the newly organized plant and to the union which has obtained the right to represent a group of employees, an important function of collective bargaining is the formulation of the rules and conditions of employment. The wage package is only one of many vital interests of both union and management. A very important function that a union fulfills is providing for and protecting job security and acting as a medium by which employee grievances can be expressed. This function must be defined and set out in the first labor agreement.

There are many rules of employment in any business facility. Whether they are unilaterally imposed and administered by management in the absence of a union or are negotiated in collective bargaining, the rules and regulations of the employment relationship make up the basic foundation of any workforce. The employer desires a solid, smoothly functioning system of rules and procedures. He wants to know that his workers will meet time regulations, obey their foremen, and conform to safety and production practices he sets up. He cannot tolerate any deviation whether or not there is a union in the picture.

The new union is motivated by similar considerations. Initially, it desires stability in the work rules in order to establish its position in the plant. First, it will seek seniority provisions in promoting, transferring, and laying off employees. Second, it will seek grievance and arbitration machinery to reduce or terminate the ability of management to act arbitrarily and to enable the employees to initiate and process changes in the work rules which they do not like. Finally, the union wants security for its own survival in the plant. Basically, this means some form of dues checkoff and a recognition clause creating a union or agency shop.

These three areas—job security, grievance machinery, and union security —involve vital interests of both parties. The union often cannot agree to a settlement that does not contain some aspect of all three and will bargain tenaciously to achieve them. The employer is usually faced with a value judgment. He must first take a position on the very existence of the union in his plant. If he chooses not to accept this as a given fact, he will fight the union on every element. He must also take a position on the rights of his individual employees. In those states where a union shop is not outlawed, the employer may decide that under no circumstances should any worker be compelled to join a union as a condition of his right to work.

The issues of job security are confronted in two areas: seniority provisions and the distribution of work. By requiring that layoffs, job bidding, and overtime provisions be based on a worker's seniority, the union provides the stability the employee desires. By forcing the employer to divide work between crafts or job classes, the union adds to job security by restricting layoffs which result from combining job duties.

Grievance and arbitration procedures are commonly found in labor agreements. The idea is that when a contract has been written, many questions have been left unanswered. No agreement can be made to cover all possible contingencies. In order to take the administration and interpretation of labor agreements out of the play of economic power, no-strike clauses were added in consideration for some form of grievance and arbitration clauses. The union says to management, We will not strike during the term of the agreement, but in return you must provide some forum for any questions arising under the contract. Several steps are set out by which an aggrieved employee can meet with several levels of management, represented by his union steward or officer. The final step in the absence of a resolution of the problem is to submit it to the binding decision of a neutral arbitrator selected by both parties.

Both sides have a strong interest in maintaining continuity of work. The loss of wages and profits in a strike are unnecessary when some resolution of problems can be found without such work stoppage. The only reasons for refusing this form of alternative must stem from a desire not to accept unionism. When management believes that it can administer the agreement without the need for a no-strike clause and that the union is not powerful enough to force a change, this type of procedure can be left out of a contract. The ranking of this issue as one to be refused the union should come after a serious appraisal of these considerations.

The area of union security is a delicate issue and one to which a great deal of attention must be paid. This goes to the core of union survival and becomes a high-priority item for the union. The *union shop* provides that an employer agrees that all workers must belong to the union to keep their jobs. Once hired, they must join the union within a specified time (usually 30 days) or lose their jobs. The *agency shop* usually provides that a worker may join the union or not as he wishes, but that, if he elects not to join the union, he must pay a sum equal to the union dues. The *maintenance of membership provision* requires the employer to agree that all present and future members of the union must remain in the union for the duration of the contract in order to keep their jobs. Workers now on the job who are not currently in the union or who elect not to join in the future are not forced to do so to keep their jobs.

The employer must face this issue squarely. Granting a union shop requires membership in the union for all employees. When a union is elected by a bare majority, the decision to create such a condition of continued employment is serious indeed. The union would naturally prefer to have management appear to force union membership. In this way, it expands its bargaining power, increases the dues it can collect, and extends its power over the members. Yet there are serious employer arguments in favor of some type of union security clause. As previously discussed, the Wagner Act called upon the union to represent all members of the bargaining unit regardless of whether they were members of the union. Allowing such employees the benefits of collective bargaining without the burden of sustaining part of the costs can create serious morale problems. Furthermore, a more stable union with good support from the local members can often be far easier to negotiate with and to depend upon during the life of the contract. Assuming the employer is willing to accept the union, some form of agency or maintenance of membership clause may be worth granting in return for major union concessions.

RANKING OF EMPLOYER INTERESTS

The complex questions of wages and working conditions reflect the needs and desires of each side. The final settlement requires a ranking process of these interests just as the overall possible settlements discussed in the previous chapter do. The employer's major interest is the running of an efficient and profitable business. The considerations which must apply to the most important areas of collective bargaining have been pointed out here. It is obvious that each particular negotiation must be treated individually in light of these considerations.

Of primary concern to management is clear and strong language setting out its rights and prerogatives. It would be difficult—indeed, impossible—to try to enumerate each right that management wishes to retain. The most practical approach is a statement that management retains the right to determine unilaterally each and every matter not expressly covered by the agreement. Only in this way can the company preclude the gradual erosion of those rights essential to the maintenance of a going business. Each concession to the union must be made with the thought in mind that the union can use this concession as an inroad into ever-expanding areas in the future.

By establishing a priority of interests based on a fair and accurate evaluation of the needs of the employees and the needs of the employer in running the business, the company negotiator can reach an acceptable settlement with the union. By applying this priority of interests in a realistic manner, he can lay the groundwork for many years of satisfactory labor-management relations. It is necessary now to turn to the negotiation process itself to give meaning to the actual application of these ideas.

The Negotiation Process

Edward J. McMahon

HOW DOES AN AGREEMENT FINALLY RESULT FROM THE CONFRONTATION OF labor and management? An orderly process of ranking possible settlements has been established and interests important in arriving at a system of priorities have been described. Armed with a knowledge of what the employer needs or prefers and an accurate appraisal of the needs and desires of the union and the employees, the bargaining representatives are prepared to hammer out a contract.

It is important to place the negotiation process in its proper perspective. First, it is apparent that to reach an agreement in a bilateral, adversary situation such as this, some compromise is necessary. The give-and-take of collective bargaining is almost too obvious to require discussion, but it is this which most often leads to a breakdown of negotiations. An inexperienced or unskilled negotiator finds comfort in thorough preparation resulting in a predetermined set of bargaining objectives. He will often accompany these predetermined objectives with specific proposals on contract language and form and content of the wage package, and he will also decide on the exact extent to which he is prepared to deviate from these proposals. But maintaining flexibility, especially as the pressures of the final moments of bargaining increase, requires the ability to roll with the punch by bending where and when doing so would achieve the most good.

A second factor necessary to place this process in perspective is the recognition of the underlying assumptions pointed out in the preceding chapters. It was assumed that both parties desired to reach an agreement and that some agreement was possible. In the language of the bargaining model shown earlier, it was assumed that the least acceptable settlement of both sides was within range of possible settlements of both. Taking this fact as given, the negotiation process can be described as the methods and procedures by which representatives of both sides work out the final and specific terms of the settlement. Whether agreement comes before, during, or after a work stoppage and whether it is accomplished in one day or one year, this process will be used to work it out.

Finally, it should be clear that the negotiation process is the method chosen from many alternatives to reach a labor contract. This requires a definite commitment from each participant to maintain this process as the forum for raising and resolving all issues between them. This means that before it is completed the negotiation should bring out the problems and differences each side has and should attempt to find answers to these problems and differences. The agreement will not be able to provide for every contingency, and it is obvious that certain wording will be left vague in order to reach an agreement. The collective bargaining concept extends throughout the life of an agreement, however, and each grievance hearing will be a continuation of the process begun during negotiations.

Unless the parties are willing to maintain this perspective, it will be difficult or even impossible to conclude successful negotiations. Collective bargaining and the negotiation process can break down in many ways. Government intervention is the most common, either through Taft-Hartley emergency strike procedures or through Labor Board regulation of bargaining tactics and content. When one or both parties reject the process and run for government help, the process described here becomes weakened. Compulsory arbitration through third-party dictation of terms may become a necessary alternative either to protect the public interest or to enable management and labor to solve their problems.

OFFER AND ACCEPTANCE

The basic problem in negotiations is one of communication. Each party knows what is acceptable to it in terms of each issue and any modifications it might accept. It does not know what settlements are acceptable to the other party. The function of the offer and, eventually, the acceptance in negotiations is to communicate in gradual steps exactly what is acceptable to the parties. Each offer is proof that the settlement offered is acceptable to the offerer. By placing on the table the terms and conditions he wishes the other side to accept, the offerer is evidencing the fact that this settlement is acceptable to him.

The offer is also an invitation. It requests either an acceptance or a counteroffer. First, the offer proves that the terms are acceptable to the offerer; second, it seeks to obtain knowledge of what is acceptable to the offeree. If a particular settlement meets the approval of the other side, the representative will tell the offerer this by accepting the offer. If it is not acceptable, the offeree can make a counteroffer to tell the offerer what is acceptable to him.

Thus emerges the basic idea that the offer and acceptance can provide movement along the line of possible settlement. When an offer represents to the offeree what he believes to be the most acceptable settlement he can achieve considering the multitude of factors present, he will accept the offer. It is obvious that, while the offer and acceptance provide the method of movement and communication in the negotiation process, some inducement to accept the offer or propose a satisfactory counteroffer must be provided. For example, the offerer will try to convince the offeree that the proposed settlement represents the best he can do and that no other settlement more acceptable to the one side will be acceptable to the other. This inducement can come about through a variety of strategies from persuasion to the use of threats. These strategies must be planned and carried out within the overall tactical approach of each party and each negotiator.

TACTICS AND STRATEGIES

The area of tactics and strategies represents at once the most interesting and most subjective and personal aspect of negotiations. It includes all those intangible elements which characterize any adversary system where the skill and felicity of the opponents play a major role in the results of the outcome. It is difficult to describe the various methods of approaching the negotiation process. It is impossible and certainly undesirable to prescribe hard and fast rules for such an approach. This important aspect of negotiations, however, requires a sensible preplanning of tactics and a knowledgeable adaptation of strategical moves during negotiations within this general tactical approach.

It is essential that the actual spokesman for the employer be a professional industrial relations expert and that he do all or most of the talking during negotiations. There are several viewpoints on the makeup of the bargaining committee and the necessity for plant or divisional line personnel to take a large part in negotiations. Few disagree that it is essential that line management play a heavy role in the preparation for negotiations. Moreover, all agree that these people who must live with and administer the resulting agreement must take part in the determination of vital interests and the working out of contract language. They must raise questions, point out existing or foreseeable problems, and be consulted on the effect of potential concessions to the union.

The spokesman, however, must have certain characteristics which are not usually found in men who are capable managers of production and sales operations. The knowledge of a production process which such a spokesman needs is not the same as the technical proficiency needed to run a plant. As vital as this knowledge is to enable a person to speak intelligently during negotiations, it is more important to be able to speak the language of labor relations. This implies many things. It means the ability to speak about seniority, lines of progression, labor law, and other subjects too numerous to mention. It also means the ability to be severe even with one's employees or to be patient, listening, and observing where doing so would achieve a purpose. Many aspects of labor relations go beyond the level at which bargaining is taking place. Such issues as pensions, vacations, and holidays usually require corporatewide consideration. These have an effect on many other units and will be influenced by what the company has done or will do in other areas.

Line management is important in the development of an overall tactical approach. The determination of those issues which have priority in negotiations and which in turn determine the ranking of acceptable settlements must be made with line personnel. This determination then directly affects the tactics to be used and will influence the negotiator's approach to the union. The removal of an incentive system, for example, as part of a wage package proposal initiated by management might require one overall approach; a different one may be called for in the situation where the union is demanding a huge across-the-board wage increase. In the first case, a low-key, highly open approach might be best, with management laying on the line the earnings figures, how they are affecting production, and a company proposal on substituting base wages for the bonus system which is reasonably close to the level the company wants to arrive at. In the second case, however, the company might adopt the strong posture necessary to combat an unrealistic wage demand. Here management might come in with an offer as much below where it expects the wage to result as the union's demand is above.

What factors require an analysis in order to arrive at some decisions on tactics? As implied by the incentive removal example, the issues themselves will affect the tactical decisions. In each bargaining situation one or several issues will be major ones. These thorny problems will be obvious as negotiations get under way. The local personnel people, the supervisors, and the general tenor of the times can provide a fairly accurate picture of the interests that the union will consider vital. By a good communications effort and a strong sense for feedback in various forms, the employer should be able to know the major issues and where he must and can go during negotiations.

Another general factor in determining tactics has to do with the circumstances within the bargaining unit itself. This relates directly to the problems facing a newly elected union. The needs and desires of union and employer in a first-contract situation have been discussed in detail. These factors are important not only in the ranking of issues considered vital to each side but also in the development of a negotiating atmosphere and a tactical approach. Whether the employer desires long-range stability in union-management relations will affect the nature of his bargaining posture. A hostile and aggressive approach may be proper for the employer who is anxious to weaken or destroy the union representing his employees.

The political factors involved in the makeup and demeanor of the union bargaining committee and its relationship with the international or national representative have serious implications for the management negotiators. The objective of negotiations is to arrive at an agreement. The representatives of the employees will have to sell any company proposal to the union membership. In most situations the union will need strong reasons to convince the employees that it has achieved the best possible settlement, and this will require a unified bargaining committee. Management negotiators must be careful in their approach in negotiating with these people. A weak committee must be handled skillfully to lead it to a settlement which can be sold to the employees and which the company feels is just. A committee made up of several strong local officers and a weak international representative must be treated differently from a committee where the converse is true. To reach a desirable agreement the employer must react to the needs and pecularities—often conflicting—of each member of the union team.

Once a tactical approach is developed the negotiator must try to convince the union to accept an offer or propose an acceptable counteroffer. Strategies must be developed in particular situations which arise with respect to specific issues during negotiations. In other words, within a general tactical approach specific strategic decisions must be made as particular developments occur. The need for various strategies arises in two principal ways. First, the negotiating team must in some way persuade or convince the union representatives to accept an offer. Second, the negotiator utilizes various strategies in the determination of his own moves and countermoves as negotiations progress.

Convincing the Union

The use of persuasion predominates in collective bargaining approaches. The appeal to intelligent reasoning and rational analysis is rapidly supplanting the old table-pounding, epithet-spewing spokesman of the past. The educational level of employees, especially those chosen to represent the union, has risen rapidly over the years, and the most effective approach is on this higher level. The skillful negotiator uses this knowledge effectively in trying to persuade the other party that the settlement offered *should* be acceptable to it. By using economic data from the plant, the area, and the nation, he can appeal to the common sense of the union representatives. He tells the union, for example, that the offer is fair and reasonable in light of economic data and can be proudly presented to the membership with a sense of a job well done. Also, the negotiator utilizes his persuasiveness in convincing the union that this is the best offer it can expect to obtain. No settlement more acceptable to the union will be acceptable to the company. Not only do the economic facts indicate the advisability of accepting this offer, but this is the best offer that will be forthcoming.

The use of pressure in convincing a union to accept an offer can be an effective negotiating weapon. For purposes of analysis, pressure can be broken down into two types: direct pressure and strategic pressure. Direct pressure involves an act which would be in the interests of the pressuring party. An example of such pressure would be a refusal to work for a wage which is below the minimum acceptable level of the union. A strategic pressure is an act which is against the interests of the pressuring party, such as an employer's threat to shut down a profitable plant.

Threats are dangerous to use, and an effective utilization requires careful planning. Strategic pressure requires a high degree of credibility, and only an experienced negotiator should attempt to use it. He should be known as a strong, honest person who is not given to idle threats. Strategic pressure should be used only when an important issue is at stake and often is limited to the final impasse where strongly worded pressure is enough to tip the balance toward settlement. Again, it is important to mold the strategy to the particular situation. A set of facts, for example, may be changed or adapted to lend credibility to a threat. The threat to shut down a profitable plant, used at the final stage in a tense negotiation, can be an effective determinant when the employer commits himself to this by a strongly worded publication. He would then have to go through with it or lose face, and the union will be convinced that the threat will be carried out. This type of bargaining is recommended only in special circumstances, certainly not where the union is in good faith. In this case, even though its bargaining attitude is strong, a businesslike, factual approach is best.

DETERMINING THE MOVES

Specific strategies can be designed to enable a party to plot its own moves and countermoves. The basic approach is a thorough analysis of the opponent's past practices. What has happened in past confrontations between these two parties? What has been the opponent's pattern of practices with other parties? An employer can make extremely accurate estimates of what the union is really seeking and what it actually means in its statements by such an analysis.

An effective negotiator knows how to listen. He is characterized by a knowledge of his union counterpart and an ability to remain silent at the proper times. Very often, messages that come across the bargaining table are missed by the negotiator who is too intent on his own ability to express himself. Careful analysis of the committee attitude and feedback from the employees themselves form a major part of negotiation strategies. When one of several possible moves can be made, such feedback can prove an invaluable guide in determining the best choice.

Knowledge of the employees is a particularly strong form of strategy. It involves the aggressive search for information from the employees or within the union leadership hierarchy. Experienced location personnel managers provide a valuable guide to strategical decisions through long-range evaluations of plant employees' attitudes, hopes, and aspirations by day-to-day contacts beyond the traditional communications feedback systems. Proper contact with employees is actively sought by both first-line supervisors and personnel men during the life of the contract, which may develop a considerable amount of bargaining information.

The trend in recent years has been toward the increasing use of factual information as a basis for defining and resolving issues and determining the moves to be made to achieve the desired results. Consequently, the role of communications, feedback, and other forms of strategical approaches has increased in importance. The methods of presenting a proposal and arguing for its acceptance have been affected by this recent trend. Just as the tactical approaches being used today reflect high-level, intelligent presentations, so, too, do the strategical approaches taken in particular situations. The need for reliable sources of increasingly sophisticated factual information which results from these new approaches to the negotiation process has made it even more imperative to develop solid bargaining tactics and strategies around professional and skillful negotiators.

NEGOTIATION PROCEDURES

Actual procedures used in the negotiation process vary in as many ways as there are individual negotiators, companies, and unions. No one single set of procedures can be prescribed as the best approach to collective bargaining. Here, as in the preparation of issues, the ranking of important interests, and the adoption of tactics and strategies, there are many variables which must determine what procedures would best serve the needs of the parties. There are certain aspects, however, which should be considered in setting up procedures during the actual bargaining sessions and which play an integral part in achieving a settlement.

Negotiations are becoming more orderly and professional. The negotiators are usually professional bargainers whose knowledge and skill are projected to all members of the bargaining team.

The use of stenographic records or recording devices is unusual today. Most bargainers prefer to speak freely without fear that each word will be reviewed in detail at a later time for possible technical or legal violations.

Publicity is becoming more important in collective bargaining. It is usually desirable to refrain from public speech making or indiscriminate releases to the press on bargaining progress. This is particularly important in major negotiations of national impact. Often the parties agree on a brief written release to the press giving the current status of negotiations and restrict communication to this statement.

The bipartite nature of collective bargaining is typically reflected by two opposing bargaining committees. Spokesmen for the company and the union usually do all or most of the talking. When an impasse is reached, or when it is advantageous to one or both of the parties, state or federal mediation may be utilized. This involves one or more representatives of a mediation service whose function is to act as go-between for the parties. The mediator tries to crystallize the issues and often makes suggestions as to some compromise positions. Some negotiators employ this service to try to put pressure on the other side when they feel that it is being too adamant. Union officials have used this method to illustrate to their members just how far they have pushed management. When presenting a company package for ratification, the union can point to the presence of a mediator and to his suggestions on a settlement as evidence that this is the best offer the company will make.

Mediators can be particularly effective in dealing with subcommittees from both sides where the group is more wieldy and frankness is easier to come by. All information can be openly laid on the table and the framework of the ultimate settlement can be worked out between the smaller groups; then the larger group on each side can hammer out the total settlement.

Today, most union and company spokesmen realize their duties to the employees and try to carry them out sincerely and intelligently. The increasingly high level of intelligence of the local committee and other employees necessitates a new approach eliminating the old wheeler-dealer type of bargaining in favor of carefully documented, coldly logical methods using every legal and moral tool at the bargaining team's command.

✦ ✦ ✦

The negotiation process is a vital part of collective bargaining. Through a direct confrontation across a bargaining table the parties are able to arrive at a mutually acceptable settlement. The process is imperfect. There are no set rules of the game, nor are there even any firm or useful guidelines which are universally valid. The process of collective bargaining simply requires negotiations between the union and the company. These can be carried on in a variety of ways as determined by the parties.

Yet, for all its imperfections, the negotiation process as part of collective bargaining has proved to be the best method developed for establishing terms and conditions of employment when the employees choose representation. The crippling effects of a strike as part of this process have caused much disenchantment, and cries for compulsory arbitration are frequently being heard. The infrequent use of strikes or lockouts, however, is a necessary penalty to be paid for maintaining the freedom of employers and employees to determine their own work rules. Responsible representatives of management and unions can do much to preserve the process of free collective bargaining in general through judicious development of the process and procedure of the actual negotiations themselves.

Keeping Others Informed

Robert G. Hennemuth

EFFECTIVE COMMUNICATION IS A SINE QUA NON OF SUCCESSFUL LABOR RELA-
tions. Many other chapters in this book are concerned with the dialogue
between the labor relations department and the union. However, labor relations communicates not only with the union but with others in the company
as well. It is the purpose of this chapter to examine the communication
interchange between labor relations and the other parts of the enterprise.

As used here, the term "labor relations department" denotes the function
with primary responsibility for negotiating with the unions and administering the collective bargaining agreements. Titles and structure will of course
vary from company to company. For instance, a labor relations director may
report to an industrial relations director with broader responsibility than just
labor relations, and the industrial relations director may also engage actively
in labor relations, particularly in major negotiations.

INFORMING TOP MANAGEMENT

Financial and operating decisions that are influenced by labor costs as
well as by the restrictions of collective bargaining agreements are made by

ROBERT G. HENNEMUTH is vice president—industrial relations of Raytheon Company.

top management. Moreover, top management either makes or approves certain significant labor relations decisions. Therefore, the labor relations department has the responsibility of transmitting recommendations and information to top management.

During contract administration. During the administration of a collective bargaining agreement, labor relations will probably have regularly scheduled written communication with top management. An example would be a monthly report on labor relations activities. Depending on the corporate structure, the report would go directly to top management from the department head responsible for dealing with the union or would be part of the report sent by the head of a broader industrial relations function. If significant events occur or if approval is required on actions to be taken, oral or written contact would of course be made more frequently than the regularly scheduled activity report.

As analyzed more fully in the section on informing line management, it may be necessary to involve higher levels of management when agreement cannot be reached between line managers and the labor relations department on a labor relations problem. Depending on the significance of the matter at issue, top management may have to be informed and make the decision. The role of labor relations is to present top management with its recommendations and with the information necessary for making a reasoned judgment. A situation of this sort does not represent an antithesis between the labor relations and financial viewpoints. An action may represent a cost saving when calculated by an individual department or plant manager. However, it could very well mean an overall economic loss to the company either because of a precedent restricting other plants or because of potential labor strife.

As top management is particularly concerned with the cost aspects of labor relations and with planning for contingencies, it should be appraised of events occurring during the contract period that could have a marked effect on the course of negotiations. The union election provides an example. Well before an election, labor relations may know who the candidates are likely to be and may have predictions as to the outcome. In addition, labor relations may be able to indicate the kinds of problems the company would face if certain individuals were elected to office, including the potential difficulties in the ensuing negotiations.

Although significant events bearing on future negotiations, such as a change in union leadership, are reported to top management as they occur, a time comes when top management should be formally brought into the planning for an upcoming negotiation. It is important for the labor relations people to think out several months in advance what the likely issues will be, who the personalities on both sides of the table will be, and what the best estimate is as to the chances for a peaceful settlement.

Such thoughts and conclusions should be communicated to management at least three to six months before the start of negotiations. This early communication should be made for several reasons: to permit top management to put its own ability to work on the problems; to allow such time as may be necessary for getting material and equipment either into or out of the plants; and—perhaps the most important reason—to determine what the costs of a strike would be. The company may decide it cannot afford to take a strike under any circumstances. However, with most companies there will be some boundary line beyond which the company will not go just to avoid a strike. Early communication with top management is necessary to work out this boundary line.

During negotiation and strike. In order to be effective negotiators, the company team should be given broad limits within which it can act without having to consult with top management. This represents no derogation of the responsibilities of the executive office, as these limits are worked out in advance between labor relations and top management. Whether the unit involved is large or small, the procedure is similar: Labor relations gives its recommendations and top management decides upon a line of authority. If labor relations should see a need to go beyond the line of authority when negotiations are in progress, consultations would be necessary; otherwise, the company team can function as the responsible spokesman.

When negotiations are under way with a union representing a substantial number of employees (or when they will have a significant impact on other negotiations in a multiunit company), daily contact between the front office and labor relations becomes the rule. The exact number of contacts will of course vary with the stage of negotiations. For instance, if a negotiation should become difficult, with mediation involved, the negotiators would probably be in contact with top management after every session. During a strike, if the unit involved is a major portion of the company's workforce, top management will be devoting much of its effort to the strike problem. In that event, contact between labor relations and top management will be virtually constant.

When the contract covers many plants and divisions, line and division managers also become part of the communication process. Members of the negotiating team from the plants will be under instruction to communicate by telephone with top line managers in the respective plants and inform them of daily developments in negotiations. When a situation approaches a final confrontation and a strike is imminent, meetings that include plant and division managers, top management of the company, and corporate labor relations are likely to be held. These sessions serve the dual purpose of conveying information and evolving strategy. That is, not only are line managers posted in detail on events as they happen, but they are also encouraged to suggest ways to proceed—particularly in terms of the efficacy of various courses of action at their location.

The preceding discussion assumes a multiplant, multidivision unit. In the single-plant unit communication would be similar, but with the line manager playing a larger role than in the multiplant situation directed from corporate headquarters. At the other end of the spectrum are situations such as in the basic steel industry, where an executive from one company serves as the head of the industry negotiating team and communicates with top management of the other companies as well as of his own company.

INFORMING LINE MANAGEMENT AND SUPERVISION

In a multiplant company, corporate labor relations is responsible for maintaining a centralized, coordinated flow of information and guidance in the labor relations area. As discussed in the next chapter, inconsistent practices at various plants in a multiplant union environment can lead to erosion of management's contractual rights. Thus in all transmission of labor relations information at the line level, whether in formal training sessions or in daily activities such as grievance settlement, there should be an underlying theme of consistent administration of a contract and an awareness that the labor relations decisions at one plant can affect other plants.

Training. First-line supervision represents on a daily basis the interface between management and the bargaining unit employee. Therefore, it is essential for supervisors to be sufficiently cognizant of labor relations considerations and of the need for consistency. In their position as the only members of management many employees are exposed to on a regular basis, first-line supervisors can either assist labor relations in the conduct of its responsibilities or create more difficulties.

Thus a training program for all supervisory personnel is in order. Since a labor relations man from the particular plant will conduct most of the training sessions, a member of corporate labor relations might conduct the initial discussion with a view toward impressing upon supervisors the im-

portance of labor relations considerations. Then the instructor from the plant
can get into the details of contract administration. He should go over the
contract provision by provision, but certain subjects should receive the most
emphasis. For example, disciplinary action and promotion policy are particularly apposite to the line supervisor. In going over the various provisions of
the contract, the labor relations man should relate specific experiences in
order to make the application of a provision more understandable.

The training program affords an opportunity to explain the method for
handling grievances and to caution supervisors not to make any decisions or
put anything in writing on a grievance that could establish an undesirable
precedent for the rest of the company. Also, the labor relations man should
delineate which situations require communication with the industrial relations department. In the area of discipline, for example, a minor breach
requiring only a verbal warning need not be cleared through labor relations,
while a serious offense that may merit a written warning, a suspension, or a
discharge would usually necessitate contacting the labor relations man.

Depending on the size of the plant involved, the program should be
repeated at intervals frequent enough that new supervisors do not go for
long without receiving this training. In addition, because some changes are
usually made in contract language during negotiations, part of any training
program held shortly after negotiations should include those supervisors
who have already gone through these programs in the past, as well as the
new supervisors. A member of the negotiating committee should participate
in these sessions so that the new language in the contract can be presented in
the context of negotiations. The foreman will have a greater understanding
of a contract provision when the original language and the change are
discussed in terms of how they were arrived at in the negotiation process,
rather than merely having the new language presented as a rule to follow.

The training program should not be the end of the supervisor's education
process, however. Communication between the labor relations function and
supervisors takes place on a day-to-day basis and provides an appropriate and
effective means of continuing the labor relations training of supervisors.

As with supervisors, the education of line managers in the labor relations
area is a combination of formal training and learning through experience.
Management training programs given by companies often include an exposure to the various departments of the company through the medium of
speakers from each department. The labor relations director should seek to
impart the philosophies and objectives of his function. He will probably
discuss the organization and the assignments of his department. In a multi-

unit, multiplant company, he might briefly describe the history of each unit. The presentation will probably also include some mention of the union officials in the major units. In addition, a significant labor relations event such as a recent strike would be a relevant part of the presentation. A part of the discussion in a company with unorganized locations would include some explanation of the attitudes toward and methods of dealing with organization attempts. (Informing the others during an organization attempt offers a particular challenge to the communication abilities of the labor relations department. That topic, however, is not within the scope of this book.)

During contract administration. In addition to formal training programs, line management and supervision gain labor relations knowledge through the experience of the grievance procedure. The foreman is usually involved in the initial step. When the procedure goes beyond the foreman level, labor relations is likely to have the department head concerned participate in the grievance meeting and assist in determining solutions to the problems raised by the grievance.

Whenever a grievance becomes a matter of major significance in a plant, the director of labor relations or one of the members of his staff will normally be in communication with the plant manager and often with the division manager concerned with the particular plant. Where the matter involves more than one plant or division of a company, managers in the other plants and divisions will be informed. Depending on the gravity of the matter, it may also be appropriate to involve top management so that it can have an opportunity to exercise judgment.

On those occasions where there is a conflict between the philosophy of the labor relations function and the desires of the department head in regard to a grievance or an action to be taken, it may be necessary for the labor relations manager to take the problem to higher levels of management, such as the plant manager. Obviously, going over the department manager's head is not something to be done hastily if an ongoing relationship is to be preserved. Resort should be made to higher authority only when it is evident that there is no possibility of resolving the issue between the department head and the labor relations man. The plant manager may also disagree with the labor relations point of view, and, as mentioned earlier, it may be appropriate for corporate labor relations to involve top management.

An example of the sort of conflict that top management may have to resolve is this one in the area of subcontracting: The plant manager can buy components from outside vendors more cheaply than he can have them made in his own shop. The vending out of the work will directly result in some employees being laid off. Assume that the contract language gives management the right to subcontract, but also contains precatory language that subcontracting will be avoided when it would result in layoffs. The union, under the existing contract language, has not filed grievances challenging subcontracting except when layoffs resulted. An arbitration on the particular facts in question could compromise the company's right to subcontract. Moreover, a lengthy argument with the union about this particular action could induce the union to look into previously unchallenged subcontracting at other company plants and to seek revision of the subcontracting provisions at the next negotiation. Therefore, labor relations should inform top management of this situation and state its conclusion that from a companywide point of view this action would be economically damaging.

Aside from matters arising as a result of the grievance procedure or conflict between labor relations and a department head, it will occasionally be appropriate for the labor relations representative to visit with the plant or division manager to make sure that he is fully aware of serious problems that could develop. As discussed in the section on informing top management, a change in union administration might be the sort of topic that would require a report to the manager. A new union leader's personality or his activities before his election could signal a worsening labor climate. The plant manager should be apprised of this and of possible consequences such as work slowdowns or stoppages during the contract and a strike during negotiations.

In many ways, a plant in a multidivision company is a microcosm of a company. Therefore, the communication between plant labor relations and the manager will resemble communication between corporate labor relations and top management.

During negotiation and strike. During a negotiation it is a sensible rule to avoid anything in writing having to do with negotiations unless it is specifically approved by the corporate labor relations office. However, information may have to be transmitted that labor relations decides should not be put in writing. A device that can be used to advantage is to pass information downward by word of mouth through divisions by getting it first to the division and plant managers and having them disseminate it downward through their respective subordinates to the appropriate levels of the management organization. Generally, the lower levels of management are not kept informed of the progress of the negotiation, so this oral communication can be limited to a particular level at the discretion of the labor relations director.

A similar line of communication would be used during a strike, with information and direction coming from corporate labor relations to the division and plant managers. Organization for plant strike activities would then be coordinated from the plant manager's office, with assignments for lower levels of management being given by the plant manager after consultation with the labor relations manager. This centralized flow of instruction from company headquarters to plant manager to lower levels of management is particularly important during a strike involving more than one plant in order to keep companywide action consistent.

Informing Employees

During contract administration. One aspect of communication with employees during the administration of a contract is the interchange between management and union in the steps of the grievance procedure. As the grievant is often present at the various steps, management representatives have an opportunity to show that the company is firm but fair.

Another aspect of communication with employees has to do with programs designed to build up a healthy atmosphere among the bargaining unit employees in anticipation of the next negotiation. An example of this is a benefit booklet describing benefits—such as life insurance, health insurance, and pensions—that are paid for in whole or in part by the company. Another example is a personalized report for each employee which spells out in specific amounts of money what his individual benefits are under the company's programs. Although more costly to prepare than the generalized description booklet, a personalized report is more valuable in presenting to the employee the worth to him of the company's benefit programs and in making the employee feel that he is recognized by the company as an individual. A company newspaper and newspapers at plants within the company can also help make an employee feel that he is part of a community and thus improve morale in the bargaining unit.

The company newspaper can also be a medium through which to present to the employees the company's position in company-union disputes or in upcoming negotiations. However, using the newspaper for this purpose could lessen its effectiveness for the development of a commitment to the company on the part of the bargaining unit employee. Furthermore, the use of any communications to the employees of the company position in a dispute with the union will depend on the relationship with the union. Taking the company's arguments directly to the people could destroy a viable working relationship with the union leadership or exacerbate an already unharmonious one. On the other hand, particularly where the company-union relationship is already hostile, or where the union has made it clear that a forthcoming negotiation will be difficult, it may be to the company's advantage to take its case to the employees. (It should do this to demonstrate that the company's wages and benefits are comparable to those of other companies in the industry or area or that costs must be held down to stay competitive. Any attempt to make offers directly to the employees prior to a bargaining impasse could, of course, have unfair labor practice consequences.)

At any rate, the decision as to whether and how the company should present its case to the employees depends on a careful consideration of the particular circumstances involved. For example, if the company traditionally avoids communicating with the employees regarding negotiation issues and then suddenly communicates when a difficult negotiation makes it necessary, there may be a problem of credibility.

During negotiation and strike. As discussed earlier, a decision on whether to communicate prior to the bargaining period will require an assessment of a variety of factors. Whether to communicate directly with the employees when negotiations have begun, but before it is clear that bargaining will break down, will also necessitate a weighing of factors. Among those to be considered is the reaction of the bargaining unit employees to a communication program while their elected representatives are still negotiating with the company.

Once it is obvious that a strike is imminent, in most situations the need for communication becomes obvious. There are numerous methods available to management, including speeches by plant managers to assemblages of employees in the various plants, explanations—with the aid of electronic equipment—of existing benefits or company offers, letters from the president of the company distributed in plants or mailed to homes, and advertisements in local community newspapers. The quality of a company communication effort will be of particular consequence when employees are about to vote on accepting the company's final offer or authorizing a strike.

During a strike the company can use distributed memoranda to communicate with nonstriking employees and home mailings and newspaper advertisements to reach the strikers. Once a strike is over, it is important not to stop communication abruptly. Rather, the company should make an effort to communicate to both bargaining unit employees and management alike that it is imperative to return to a harmonious relationship and productive effort.

✦   ✦   ✦

The labor relations department in a company does not deal with the union in a vacuum. The activities of labor relations bear intimately on the rest of the enterprise, and the conduct of labor relations is influenced in turn by the actions and requirements of others. As a result of this interdependence, the communication of information regarding labor relations to the constituent elements of the organization is indispensable to a successful operation of the labor relations function.

The Un-Spelled-Out Terms

Robert G. Hennemuth

DEAN SHULMAN SAID, "I SUGGEST THAT THE LAW STAY OUT—BUT, MIND YOU, not the lawyers."[1] His remark is indicative of the view held by many arbitrators and academic commentators as to the nature of labor arbitration and the labor contract. Their position is that the labor agreement, by its nature, is not subject to the strict rules of the commercial contract and should not be regarded as such by the arbitrator.

Moreover, Shulman was referring primarily to the role the courts should take in regard to arbitration when he suggested the law should stay out. In this respect, it was a prescient comment, as it foreshadowed the Supreme Court pronouncements in 1960 in the three *Steelworkers* cases.

It is the purpose of this chapter to examine pre-*Steelworkers* attitudes of arbitrators and commentators toward extending a contract beyond the spelled-out terms; to set out the trilogy cases, which codified and extended the un-spelled-out terms; and then to evaluate the present state of arbitral and court precedent in regard to un-spelled-out terms in the context of a recommended course of action.

---

[1] Harry Shulman, *Reason, Contract, and Law in Labor Relations,* 68 Harv. L. Rev. 999, 1024 (1955).

The Collective Bargaining Agreement

The legal principle that a contract between parties is limited to the four corners of the contract has steadily eroded in its application to the collective bargaining agreement. Even with commercial contracts, it may be necessary to go beyond the written document in order to interpret ambiguities by determining the intent of the contracting parties. However, even where there is no ambiguity in the written contract, arbitrators often extend the coverage of a labor contract to situations not encompassed anywhere in the written words of the parties' bargain. For example, shop practices may be considered by an arbitrator in making a decision on a matter not included in the contract.

The familiar maxim *expressio unius est exclusio alterius* (the expression of one thing implies the exclusion of all others) is regularly ignored. It would seem that if the parties signed a written contract, that should be their bargain. Nevertheless, the argument that what is not included, the union does not have, often will not prevail.

The premise that a collective bargaining agreement is not merely a commercial contract, limited to its words, and that labor arbitration is therefore distinct from commercial arbitration, did not spring forth whole with the *Steelworkers* decisions. Commentators and arbitrators expounded the position and succeeded in developing a body of arbitral precedent well before the Supreme Court gave its imprimatur.

THE COMMENTATORS

Academicians expatiated the theory of the collective bargaining agreement as a document far removed from the commercial contract. Professor Cox stated the theory as follows:

> First, it is not unqualifiedly true that a collective bargaining agreement is simply a document by which the union and the employees have imposed upon management limited, express restrictions of its otherwise absolute right to manage the enterprise, so that an employee's claim must fail unless he can point to a specific contract provision upon which the claim is founded. There are too many people, too many problems, too many unforeseeable contingencies to make the words of the contract

the exclusive source of rights and duties. One cannot reduce all the rules governing a community like an industrial plant to fifteen or even fifty pages. Within the sphere of collective bargaining, the institutional characteristics and the governmental nature of the collective bargaining process demand a common law of the shop which implements and furnishes the context of the agreement. We must assume that intelligent negotiators acknowledged so plain a need unless they stated a contrary rule in plain words.[2]

In this one paragraph, Cox has set forth a plethora of differences from the ordinary contract. Among them—

+ A claim will not necessarily fail because it does not point to a specific provision.
+ The contract is not the only source of rights and duties.
+ There is a common law of the shop that augments that agreement.

In effect, Cox has reached the conclusion that "The resulting contract is essentially an instrument of government, not merely an instrument of exchange."

It is clear that a collective bargaining agreement does not cover every situation that may arise. It also seems obvious that if a party fails to negotiate a provision he desires in a contract, he should not have the benefit of that provision. However, according to Cox, the collective bargaining agreement should not be looked at in this fashion.

A collective agreement also covers a wide range of conduct and an enormous variety of problems. No state or federal statute, except possibly the tax laws, covers as wide a variety of subjects or impinges upon as many aspects of the ordinary company's business or a worker's life—wages, hours of employment, working conditions, health and accident insurance, retirement, pensions, promotions, layoffs, discipline, subcontracting, technological changes, work loads, and a host of minor items. Yet a collective-bargaining agreement must also be kept short and simple enough for the ordinary worker to read and understand. Verbal incompleteness is inevitable; the meticulous detail of a corporate mortgage is unsuited to administration by ordinary workers. The details must be filled in outside of the words.

[2] Archibald Cox, *Reflections Upon Labor Arbitration,* 72 Harv. L. Rev. 1482, 1498 (1959).

In other words, because the union did not cover everything it might have, and because simplicity is a desirable goal, the employer may find himself bound to things to which he never agreed.

THE ARBITRATORS

Professor Cox has stated, ". . . the very nature of the collective agreement calls for arbitrators to create and apply an industrial jurisprudence unrestricted by the bare meaning of its words. . . ." Many arbitrators have not been diffident about making the theorizing of academe a reality in the industrial scene.

Arbitrator Saul Wallen, in a 1948 decision involving General Electric, provides an example. The collective bargaining agreement limited arbitration to questions involving application or interpretation of the contract. The contract did not explicitly require that discipline be for just cause. The arbitrator still construed the contract to provide for arbitration of discharges because it contained discipline provisions (although these provisions seemingly provided for little more than notification). The following is an excerpt from Wallen's decision:

> The parties were, of course, free to contract that discharges would not be subject to arbitration except if both parties agreed in each case. Had they done so, and had they stated their intent plainly, the language of their agreement would have been upheld. But if consideration is given to the state of industrial relations practice at the time this agreement was drawn, there is every reason to believe that had such been their intent, the instrument they signed would have stated so clearly and without ambiguity or equivocation. For when this contract was written the principle of arbitration of disputes arising out of the discharge of employees for breaches of discipline was firmly established in industrial relations. It prevailed in nearly all collective agreements in force between the largest corporations and unions in the major branches of American industry. Its propriety and essential justice had been endorsed by both management and labor in such agencies as the National War Labor Board, and in the unanimously adopted resolution of the President's National Labor-Management Conference of 1945. The parties must be deemed to have had knowledge of the prevalence of this type of clause. No evidence was introduced in this proceeding that in the negotiations on this contract the non-arbitrability of discharge cases was even dis-

cussed, much less agreed upon. Under the circumstances the ambiguity in the contract they drew must be resolved in favor of the commonly prevailing practice (9 LA 757).

In other words, because the agreement did not specifically exclude a provision common in other agreements, the provision was read into the agreement by the arbitrator. The burden is surely on the employer—the union need not include the provision, but the employer fails to expressly exclude it at his peril.

Saul Wallen applied the general industrial practice in reaching his decision. More commonly, arbitrators apply past practice in the plant covered by the contract. Consequently, terms and conditions of employment in effect before an agreement is signed, even if not covered by the agreement, may nevertheless bind the employer. Moreover, an arbitrator, under the guise of interpretation, might hold that an established practice takes precedence over the express terms of the negotiated agreement. For example, assume an agreement giving management the right to assign work and a practice of assigning a particular task to bargaining unit employees. In spite of the contractual right, management might be prevented from assigning the task to engineering personnel.

Thus, even though limited by the contract to hearing disputes as to the interpretation or application of provisions of the agreement, arbitrators often go beyond the language of the collective bargaining agreement. As Professor Cox says, "The accepted practice of arbitrators shows the extent to which the functional characteristics of collective-bargaining agreements affect the process of interpretation." The arbitrator, in effect, can become a legislator rather than a judge.

Such a result is an obvious consequence of a view that labor arbitration is not equivalent to commercial arbitration. According to Arthur Goldberg:

> Labor arbitration, whether contract or grievance arbitration, fulfills one vital function: the substitute of the judgment of a third party for the use of economic force. It is not a substitute for litigation, which is the main characteristic of commercial arbitration. Labor arbitration is, rather, a device by which the parties agree to accept the judgment of a third party instead of fighting the issue out by industrial warfare—the strike or lockout.[3]

[3] Address by Arthur J. Goldberg, *A Supreme Court Justice Looks at Arbitration*, delivered at the American Arbitration Association Annual Meeting, March 17, 1965, in 20 Arb. J. 13 (1965).

Clearly this functional approach to labor arbitration, reflected in the view of many arbitrators and legal writers, ignores the fact that the parties negotiated a contract with express terms.

THE PARTIES

There *are* instances where management consciously creates the opportunity for un-spelled-out terms to arise by leaving ambiguities in the contract. Professor Cox describes the phenomenon succinctly:

> The pressure to reach agreement is so great that the parties are often willing to contract although each knows that the other places a different meaning upon the words and they share only the common intent to postpone the issue and take a gamble upon an arbitrator's ruling if decision is required.

Although a necessary part of the bargaining process, purposely leaving ambiguities in order to reach agreement has implicit dangers. For one thing, the arbitrator cannot successfully look to the intent of the parties to determine the meaning of language since the parties did not have a meeting of minds. Unable to look to intent, the arbitrator may feel free to legislate his own meaning.

Another danger arises from the manner in which ambiguous terms are sometimes agreed upon during hard bargaining. For instance, the union may be adamant about covering a certain topic. The company will devise language that on its face actually adds nothing to the language of the previous contract. However, the arbitrator may conclude that since the language is an addition, it must have some meaning. Therefore language that seems semantically meaningless may become operative. In the context of reaching an agreement and even avoiding strikes, however, purposely leaving ambiguities or adding meaningless language that may be interpreted to have substance may be well worth the risk.

The Trilogy

Arbitrators, with an assist from academicians, had proceeded prior to 1960 to fashion a labor contract of broader coverage than the commercial contract. Some arbitrators had legislated un-spelled-out terms in order to dispense what they considered industrial justice.

In 1960, the Supreme Court decided three cases involving the United Steelworkers, often referred to as the "trilogy." Justice Douglas delivered the opinion in each of the three cases. These cases gave judicial sanction to the most far-reaching concept of the arbitrator's role as contemplated by such writers as Shulman and Cox. In fact, it is noteworthy that both Shulman and Cox are quoted at length in these decisions.

The stage had been set for these decisions by the Supreme Court's 1957 decision in *Lincoln Mills* (353 U.S. 448), which gave the federal courts the power under Section 301 of the Labor-Management Relations Act to order arbitration. There were fears that *Lincoln Mills* would mean widespread federal court intervention in the arbitration process. The trilogy did away with these fears by making labor arbitration virtually independent of the courts.

THE FIRST STEELWORKERS CASE

In the first of the trilogy cases, *United Steelworkers* v. *American Manufacturing Company* (363 U.S. 564, 1960), an employee left work because of injury and his workmen's compensation claim was settled on the basis of permanent partial disability. Two weeks after that settlement, the union filed a grievance claiming the employee was entitled to return to work by virtue of the seniority provision of the agreement. The company refused to arbitrate.

Suit was brought by the union to compel arbitration. The employer defended on the grounds that the workmen's compensation settlement estopped the grievance and that the dispute was not arbitrable under the collective bargaining agreement.

The agreement had a no-strike clause and a standard arbitration provision (disputes as to the meaning, interpretation, and application of the provisions of this agreement may be submitted to arbitration).

The District Court held that the employee was estopped by the workmen's compensation settlement. The Court of Appeals affirmed, but for different reasons, holding that the grievance was frivolous, patently baseless, and not subject to arbitration under the collective bargaining agreement.

The Supreme Court cited 203(d) of the Labor-Management Relations Act: "Final adjustment by a method agreed upon by the parties is hereby declared to be the desirable method for settlement of grievance disputes arising over the application or interpretation of an existing collective-bargaining agreement." According to the Supreme Court, ". . . that policy can be effectuated only if the means chosen by the parties for settlement of their differences under a collective bargaining agreement is given full play."

The Supreme Court criticized a state decision in another case which held that, if the meaning of a provision of the contract is beyond dispute, the contract cannot be construed to provide for arbitration. Relating that decision to the case under consideration, Justice Douglas stated, "The lower courts in the instant case had a like preoccupation with ordinary contract law."

The Supreme Court considered the no-strike clause as a *quid pro quo* for the grievance clause and concluded that, since there is no exception to the no-strike clause, an exception should not be read into the grievance clause.

"Arbitration is a stabilizing influence only as it serves as a vehicle for handling every and all disputes that arise under the agreement. . . ." With these words Justice Douglas delineated a court's function as ". . . confined to ascertaining whether the party seeking arbitration is making a claim which on its face is governed by the contract." The courts ". . . have no business weighing the merits of the grievance. . . ." Realizing that this may lead to the arbitration of jejune claims, the Court mentioned that ". . . the processing of even frivolous claims may have therapeutic values of which those who are not a part of the plant environment may be quite unaware." Professor Cox was cited for the propriety of arbitrating frivolous claims because of their "cathartic value."

Having made these various value judgments, the Supreme Court reversed the lower court. It held that arbitration should be ordered on the superficial basis that a dispute between the parties as to the meaning, interpretation, and application of the agreement arose when the union claimed a violation by the company of a specific provision of the collective bargaining agreement and the company denied a violation.

THE SECOND STEELWORKERS CASE

The employer in the second case, *United Steelworkers* v. *Warrior & Gulf Navigation Co.* (363 U.S. 574, 1960), transported steel products by barge and maintained its barges at its terminal. The employees at the terminal were covered by a collective bargaining agreement. The employer laid off some employees and contracted out maintenance work. The company that the work was contracted out to hired some of the laid-off employees, some of whom worked on the barges. A grievance was filed protesting contracting out as a partial lockout. The agreement contained both no-strike and no-lockout clauses and provided a grievance procedure, including arbitration; however, it also removed matters "strictly a function of management" from arbitration.

The employer refused to arbitrate and the union brought suit to compel arbitration. The District Court and the Court of Appeals held that an arbitrator did not have the right to review the management decision to contract out work.

The Supreme Court declared, "A major factor in achieving industrial peace is the inclusion of a provision for arbitration of grievances in the collective bargaining agreement." With this statement as an underlying premise, the Court delivered the pronouncement that ". . . since arbitration of labor disputes has quite different functions from arbitration under an ordinary commercial agreement, the hostility evinced by courts toward arbitration of commercial agreements has no place here." The Court described the collective bargaining agreement as follows:

> It is more than a contract; it is a generalized code to govern a myriad of cases which the draftsmen cannot wholly anticipate. . . . The collective agreement covers the whole employment relationship. It calls into being a new common law—the common law of a particular industry or of a particular plant. . . . A collective bargaining agreement is an effort to erect a system of industrial self-government.

The Court, viewing the contract as something approaching a system of government rather than a contract meaning only what it said, quite naturally perceived that it is an incomplete system. The Court assumed that the gaps are part of the agreement and that arbitration is the process by which the gaps are filled:

> Gaps may be left to be filled in by reference to the practices of the particular industry and of the various shops covered by the agreement. . . . Arbitration is the means of solving the unforeseeable by molding a system of private law for all the problems which may arise and to provide for their solution in a way which will generally accord with the variant needs and desires of the parties.

Then the arbitrator was provided with a source of law: "The labor arbitrator's source of law is not confined to the express provisions of the contract, as the industrial common law—the practices of the industry and the shop—is equally a part of the collective bargaining agreement although not expressed in it."

Proceeding inevitably toward its disposition of the case, the Court concluded that the special expertise necessary to draw on the common law of the shop is peculiar to an arbitrator.

Justice Douglas did admit that ". . . arbitration is a matter of contract and a party cannot be required to submit to arbitration any dispute which he has not agreed so to submit." However, this is only lip-service to accepted principles of contract law. The Court ignored this sentence and prescribed the following extremely broad test of arbitrability: "An order to arbitrate the particular grievance should not be denied unless it may be said with positive assurance that the arbitration clause is not susceptible to an interpretation that covers the asserted dispute. Doubts should be resolved in favor of coverage."

Moreover, the Court made it easier to resolve doubts in favor of coverage under many contracts by stating that, when an absolute no-strike clause is included in an agreement, everything that management does is subject to the agreement.

The Court elaborated on its test of arbitrability:

> In the absence of any express provision excluding a particular grievance from arbitration, we think only the most forceful evidence of a purpose to exclude the claim from arbitration can prevail. Since any attempt by a court to infer such a purpose necessarily comprehends the merits, the court should view with suspicion an attempt to persuade it to become entangled in the construction of the substantive provisions of a labor agreement, even through the back door of interpreting the arbitration clause, when the alternative is to utilize the services of an arbitrator.

However, in its holding the Court went even further. It said that, because the grievance alleged that contracting out was a violation of the agreement, there was a dispute as to the meaning and application of the provisions of the agreement. Therefore, it held that whether contracting out violated the agreement was a question for the arbitrator. In effect, the Court has told a union that if it uses the proper incantation, the dispute is arbitrable.

Justice Douglas concludes his opinion with a comment typical of this result-oriented rather than legally reasoned decision: "The judiciary sits in these cases to bring into operation an arbitral process which substitutes a

regime of peaceful settlement for the older regime of industrial conflict."
Whittaker, in his dissent, decried the departure from legal principles:

> Until today, I have understood it to be the unquestioned law . . . that
> the contract under which matters are submitted to arbitrators is at
> once the source and limit of their authority and power . . . and that
> their power to decide issues with finality . . . must rest upon a clear
> definitive agreement of the parties, as such powers can never be implied.

THE THIRD STEELWORKERS CASE

The third case, *United Steelworkers* v. *Enterprise Wheel & Car Corp.*
(363 U.S. 593, 1960), differs from the other two *Steelworkers* cases in that it
involves enforcing an arbitration award rather than ordering arbitration. The
arbitrator directed the employer to reinstate discharged employees and awarded back pay for a period before and after the expiration of the collective
bargaining agreement. The employer refused to comply with the award. The
District Court directed compliance, but the Court of Appeals for the Fourth
Circuit held that an award for back pay subsequent to the contract termination date could not be enforced. Similarly the Court of Appeals held the
reinstatement award unenforceable because the agreement had expired.

The Supreme Court began its opinion with this statement: "The refusal
of courts to review the merits of an arbitration award is the proper approach
to arbitration under collective bargaining agreements." The Court conceded
that—

> Nevertheless, an arbitrator is confined to interpretation and application
> of the collective bargaining agreement; he does not sit to dispense his
> own brand of industrial justice. He may of course look for guidance
> from many sources, yet his award is legitimate only so long as it draws
> its essence from the collective bargaining agreement. When the arbitra-
> tor's words manifest an infidelity to this obligation, courts have no
> choice but to refuse enforcement of the award.

It is questionable, however, that this paragraph articulates any significant
limitation on an arbitrator. That the award drew its essence from the contract is probably nebulous enough to allow the arbitrator great freedom.

The holding in this case suggests that the Supreme Court did not intend
much of a limitation on arbitral awards. It reversed the Court of Appeals

and upheld the award, considering the arbitrator's opinion ambiguous as to the reasons for reinstatement and back pay beyond the date of the agreement's expiration. Yet the Court states that a mere ambiguity in the arbitrator's opinion which permits an inference of exceeded authority is not a reason for refusing to enforce the award. The Court held: "So far as the arbitrator's decision concerns construction of the contract, the courts have no business overruling him because their interpretation of the contract is different from his."

CRITICISM OF THE TRIOLOGY

Critical views of the decisions in the three *Steelworkers* cases were expressed immediately. Robert A. Levitt, labor counsel for Western Electric, was highly critical—particularly of the concepts that frivolous, completely unmeritorious claims must nevertheless be submitted to arbitration and that the arbitrator is not confined to the language of the contract in arriving at his decision. According to Levitt, the intentions of the parties are disregarded, and the Supreme Court substitutes its "own concepts of what is best for the parties and for the process of collective bargaining." Levitt exposed as sophistic the argument that the parties are free to spell out restrictions on the arbitrator in the contract. He pointed out that an attempt to modify long-existing contract language is likely to exacerbate the employer-union relationship.[4]

Professor Paul R. Hays (now a judge on the Second Circuit Court of Appeals) said in regard to the trilogy cases: "Arbitrators, who, some believe, are already too prone to become industrial statesmen, will be further encouraged to decide cases, as the Court suggests, on the basis, not of the evidence and the agreement, but in accordance with their views as to what will be most likely to increase production, heighten morale and decrease tensions."[5]

The Post-Trilogy Situation

Criticism was well founded when based on a prediction that as a result of the *Steelworkers* decisions the courts would order arbitration in almost any

[4] *Report of the Committee on Labor Arbitration,* section of Labor Relations Law, American Bar Association, in 46 LRRM 40–41 (1960).

[5] Address before the section of Labor Relations Law, American Bar Association, in 46 LRRM 47 (1960).

case. In 1962, the Court of Appeals for the Second Circuit (*Procter & Gamble*) summarized the rule on arbitrability, as expounded by the *Steelworkers* cases, as follows:

> The nub of the matter is that under the broad and comprehensive standard labor arbitration clause, every grievance is arbitrable, unless the provisions of the collective bargaining agreement concerning grievances and arbitration contain some clear and unambiguous clause of exclusion, or there is some other term of the agreement that indicates beyond peradventure of doubt that a grievance concerning a particular matter is not intended to be covered by the grievance and arbitration procedure set forth in the agreement (298 F. 2d 645).

The Labor Relations Yearbook for 1966 reported that the instances where the courts held that the subject matter was nonarbitrable were relatively few. This report is not surprising in light of formulations such as the preceding quotation.

Moreover, in 1964 the Supreme Court in *John Wiley & Sons* v. *Livingston* (376 U.S. 543) assigned to arbitrators the responsibility for deciding questions of procedural arbitrability. (An example of a question of procedural arbitrability would be whether the parties exhausted the preliminary steps of the grievance procedure.) Thus court consideration on substantive questions of arbitrability, albeit usually unsuccessful, is available to an employer, but the determination of procedural questions of arbitrability is left entirely to the arbitrator.

When it comes to review of awards already handed down by an arbitrator, some courts seem to apply more restrictive standards than those applied to the initial question of arbitrability in suits to compel arbitration. For instance, in 1966 the Second Circuit Court of Appeals, in *Torrington Co.* v. *Metal Products Workers* (362 F. 2d 677), imposed a limitation on an arbitrator's use of past practice. The employer had a practice of granting employees paid voting time of one hour on election day. The arbitrator decided that the practice was continued during the current contract as an implied condition because the employer failed to negotiate a contrary policy into the agreement. The Court of Appeals affirmed the District Court, holding that the arbitrator had exceeded his authority.

Dicta in the Supreme Court decision in *Enterprise Wheel* suggest that courts have the power to prevent arbitrators from straying beyond the terms of the agreement, and this may account for an occasional decision such as

Torrington. However, *Enterprise Wheel,* taken in its entirety, can be read to give the arbitrator almost completely unfettered discretion. The majority of courts seem to view the decision in this manner, for few attempts to upset the awards of arbitrators are successful.

In a recent case in the Fifth Circuit Court of Appeals, in which an arbitrator's decision was enforced, Judge Brown concluded his opinion with the statement, "The arbiter was chosen to be the Judge. That Judge has spoken. There it ends."

A Suggested Approach

The Supreme Court may have given arbitrators leave to be plenipotentiaries dispensing industrial justice. Nevertheless, criticism of the trilogy opinions is not in itself a constructive endeavor. For one thing, the Court merely affirmed what some arbitrators were doing anyway. Moreover, even if courts would less readily order arbitration or enforce arbitration awards, regular resort to the courts would not be efficacious in an ongoing relationship with a union. But most important is the fact that criticism does not provide a means of operating effectively within the present system.

The company with collective bargaining agreements should recognize that arbitrators do read un-spelled-out terms into agreements and that the Supreme Court has given arbitrators carte blanche and even encouragement to do so. With the possibility of un-spelled-out terms in mind, the company should take care to develop plant practices that will be favorable rather than harmful at an arbitration hearing. Particular attention should be given to insuring that grievance settlements are consistent and that they do not modify or extend the terms of the contract. In order to treat employees fairly or preserve a harmonious relationship with the union, it may be necessary to settle certain grievances even though an arbitrator would uphold the company position. However, these settlements should be arrived at in a fashion that avoids harmful precedent.

Discretion should be exercised in allowing cases to reach an arbitrator. When there is a substantial risk of losing a significant case, a settlement may be preferable to an unfavorable arbitral precedent. When a case does reach arbitration, of course it is essential to select an arbitrator who is aware of the necessities of efficiently conducting a business and of the limitations imposed on his function by the collective bargaining agreement. Just because courts and arbitrators will declare most issues arbitrable does not mean the company will necessarily lose on the merits.

Companies are faced with a challenge in confining their labor agreements to the written terms agreed upon in collective bargaining. The challenge can be met if management is aware and vigilant in its administration of the collective bargaining agreement.

Clauses Affecting Bargaining Power

Clifford R. Oviatt, Jr.

B ARGAINING AND DEALING WITH A UNION MUST BE CARRIED ON IN MUCH THE same way that countries deal with each other in the field of international relations. The party with the most power generally becomes the dominant force in the relationship and is better able to control the destiny of the relationship and even the destiny of the parties themselves. This power—or bargaining power—is a very real element of the bargaining process, not always recognized at the bargaining table for what it is, but nevertheless an active element of the negotiations. This chapter deals with a consideration of the main clauses that affect bargaining power.

Bargaining power is the ability to negotiate and conclude an agreement basically on one's own terms without the use of outside force. This is, in the last analysis, the aim of each of the parties—union and employer—in the labor-management relationship. The question, then, is—How does an employer obtain and maintain the bargaining power he needs to operate his business effectively?

CLIFFORD R. OVIATT, JR. is a partner in the Connecticut law firm of Cummings and Lockwood.

THE FIRST CONTRACT

Clearly, bargaining power immediately shifts to the union when it wins a secret-ballot Labor Board election. The size of the victory will often determine the extent of the union's power—and the proportionate task confronting management in getting the power restored to its side of the table.

Why, following an election which the union wins, is the bargaining power immediately placed on the union side of the table? Clearly because, in the first blush of success, the employees supporting the union have been successful *against* the company. They have in fact defeated the company and thus feel they have the power, within reasonable limits, to determine what are and what are not the proper means to handle various types of problems.

At this stage, then, the bargaining power is in the union's control. If the first contract negotiated between the parties embodies, in the words and phrases of contract language, that initial bargaining power possessed by the union, then clearly, management's task in regaining the bargaining power at some later date will be even more difficult. The first contract sets the stage for the new relationship between the employer and the union.

As has been noted elsewhere in this book, it is essential to be well prepared at the negotiations for the first contract. The operation should be well organized; facts should be assembled and evaluated; goals should be clearly established; and knowledge of the opponent should be as complete as possible. Above all, the management team should be confident that an agreement will be concluded and confident that such agreement will provide the company with the tools necessary to operate the facility effectively and equitably.

On the other hand, no company official should at any time appear arrogant or belligerent, for this will detract from the sincerity and effectiveness of the management team. At the first negotiations, appearances and attitudes are often most important.

MANAGEMENT RIGHTS

Turning now to the various contract clauses which affect the bargaining power of the parties, it is logical to start with the management rights clause. It is here that the struggle for power must automatically be focused, for this is the point upon which the battle is logically joined. Basically the question concerning a management rights clause is twofold:

1. How much power will the company have in making basic operational decisions, and how much will be relinquished to the union or to the intercontract bargaining process?
2. If the company is to have the basic decision-making ability, should the retention of that ability be spelled out in the agreement or should it be left to future determination on a decision-by-decision basis in arbitration?

There are clearly two schools of thought among management people with respect to the first of these questions. Some feel it unnecessary and unwise to spell out each management function in a management rights provision. They feel that a clause such as this is enough: "All rights previously and/or historically exercised by management shall be retained by management unless this Agreement provides to the contrary." According to these people, this clause is sufficient to support management's position that it has a given managerial right. This view is referred to as the *vested rights* theory.

Another growing segment of management opinion supports the position that a lengthy, somewhat specific (but not exclusive) management rights clause is essential to a strong and acceptable labor agreement. This position is supported by developing law resulting from the *Steelworkers* trilogy decided by the U.S. Supreme Court in 1960. In these cases the Supreme Court held that, unless a collective bargaining agreement provides that a specific subject or dispute *will not* be subject to arbitration, all disputes involving the agreement *will* be subject to arbitration.

In view of these decisions by the Supreme Court, the vested rights theory has been open to substantial attack. Clearly, by not spelling out in an agreement the basic managerial rights retained by management, the way is left open for a grievance and arbitration decision on the issue of whether management has the power to take specific action, as well as whether such action was taken or implemented properly and in accordance with the contract. If, on the other hand, the agreement provides that the company will have specific rights, then the only arbitrable issue is whether the company exercised these rights in such a way as to violate a specific provision of the agreement.

The bargaining power of the parties is greatly affected by the type of management rights clause found in an agreement. For if the union has the ability to veto or nullify a basic management decision on its own or through the decision of an arbitrator, it has retained the balance of bargaining power.

There are other compelling reasons for incorporating into a labor agreement a management rights clause specifying the various rights of management. The Labor Board, in a series of recent decisions, has taken from the parties the right to determine what are and what are not management prerogatives by expanding the *continuing duty to bargain* theory. The board has held that management has the duty to bargain with the union on the following management decisions which previously had been solely within the power of management to make:

+ Automating specific operations.
+ Closing down a plant.
+ Closing down an unprofitable branch.
+ Discontinuing particular production operations.
+ Abandoning manufacture of an unprofitable product line.
+ Moving manufacturing operations to a new location.

There have been numerous other decisions such as these. A management rights clause specifying which rights are those of management therefore fulfills a second purpose. It is proof to the Labor Board that the parties have bargained on the specified topics and agreed that management shall have the power to make specific decisions with regard to those topics—subject, of course, to the other provisions of the labor agreement, such as seniority and recognition. Two examples of such clauses are as follows:

1. *A.* Subject to the conditions of this Agreement, the Union recognizes the retention by the Company of the usual management rights, including the management of the work and the direction of the workforce, the right to hire, suspend, or discharge for just cause or to transfer, the right to relieve employees because of lack of work or for other legitimate reasons, and the right to determine the extent to which the plant shall be operated, including the determination of shift hours and the right to change methods or processes or to use new equipment.

B. It is the intention of the Company to provide regular employment for its employees so far as is reasonably possible. To that end the Company will endeavor to use its own working forces and equipment for work that can practicably be performed in the plant and will resort to subcontracting only when such is necessary for the efficient conduct of its business. In applying the terms of Section B all three parts of the Section will be given equal consideration.

2. The management of the business and the direction of the working forces, including the right to hire, lay off, promote, suspend or demote, discipline or discharge for just cause, and to issue and enforce Company rules, are vested in the Employer, subject to the provisions of this Agreement. The Employer will not, however, use the provisions of this Article for the purpose of discrimination against any employee, or to avoid or evade the provisions of this Agreement.

Management's ability to obtain such a strong management rights clause will in great measure determine where the power will lie during the term of the labor agreement and, to a great extent, for the duration of the relationship.

VETO POWER

While undoubtedly the management rights clause is the most effective method by which to obtain the power balance in the employer's favor, there are numerous other clauses which should be seriously considered and utilized.

One of the clauses most commonly sought by unions is the one which provides that no employee will be discharged or suspended unless the consent of the union is obtained or at least until a hearing is held on the matter that resulted in such disciplinary action. While such a provision goes to the heart of the right to manage, discharges are generally covered in specific contract provisions and the context of those clauses should be carefully studied. Nothing militates against the interest of management more than having an employee tell his fellow employees that he cannot be discharged for an insubordinate altercation with his foreman until he has had a hearing on the matter. Nothing is more dangerous to supervisory and management morale, and nothing gives the union more on-the-job power than the right of disciplinary control. The most that should be agreed to is the provision that discharge and discipline shall be for just cause. Then the arbitrator, if the union decides to take the case to arbitration, shall decide the propriety of the particular discipline.

Similarly, the union should not be given, by contract or practice, the right to veto management's decisions. The basic framework or power of management is unquestionably weakened when the union has the right to veto any managerial action such as the establishment of new jobs, promotions, and similar employee relations determinations.

Certainly, contract guidelines as to how management shall make specific decisions are generally established; but the inability to effectuate such a decision unless union acceptance is obtained merely adds to the union's bargaining power rather than containing it within specified limits. If such power is not curtailed, management's power—its ability to operate and function—is effectively weakened. Any clause providing for union veto (or union agreement before specific decisions become effective) serves no useful purpose other than to weaken management's right to manage. Furthermore, it increases and broadens the union's bargaining power both during contract negotiations and in that intercontract period when management's aim is to limit as much as possible the union's power to bargain.

MOVING THE OPERATION

Bargaining power is often gauged by fairly basic criteria. The strength of the union is determined by how effective and crippling a strike will be against the company; the company's bargaining power is determined by how well it can withstand a strike, slowdown, or other concerted union activity.

Yet another determinant is the ability of the company to move part or all of its operations. Such ability on the part of management tends to curb the excessive use of union power, since the union realizes that constant use of its bargaining power can effectively curtail management's ability to operate— thus resulting in the union's loss of the plant and its consequent loss of monthly dues.

Many companies therefore propose in negotiations a provision granting severance pay to employees whose jobs are permanently terminated. This severance pay is calculated on the basis of a negotiated formula granting a week's (or day's) pay for a specific amount of continuous service with the company. Often the employer will make a proposal on this item when, in fact, he has no intention or desire to move his operation. It is, to say the least, an "anchor to windward" against abuse of union power which usually is salable to the union committee. In the context of negotiations it appears as a negotiated benefit and thus can be sold by the union committee to the rank-and-file membership.

However, in negotiating such a clause, the employer should remember a number of points. First, the decision to close a specific plant, department, line, or operation must rest with management.

Second, severance pay should be paid only if there is a *termination* of the employee's job. Severance should obviously not apply when a specific job is temporarily shut down for lack of work, since that is a *layoff* and is covered by the layoff provisions of the contract.

Third, in certain situations, management may want to take some employees to the new location because of the skills they possess. The determination as to who goes and who does not should be made by management; those who are left behind should be granted their severance pay and terminated.

Fourth, the payment of severance pay to specific terminated employees should release the company from any liability to the union and the terminated employee. In view of recent court decisions, there is a body of law which holds that employees' seniority rights are property rights, and, if they are violated, the company will be held liable for damages resulting from the loss thereof.

A clause which embodies these principles would be similar to the one contained in a labor agreement in a large manufacturing plant which states—

Section 1. An employee with at least five (5) years of service shall be eligible for severance pay benefits hereinafter described if:

(a) the Company permanently closes the plant; or
(b) the Company permanently eliminates the employee's job and there is no other job in the plant to which the employee can be assigned in accordance with his seniority rights.

Severance Benefits

5 years of service	3 weeks' pay
6 years of service	4 weeks' pay
7 years of service	5 weeks' pay

8 years of service	6 weeks' pay
9 years of service	7 weeks' pay
10 years of service	8 weeks' pay

Section 2. It is expressly understood that employees with less than five (5) years' service shall not be eligible for severance pay hereunder and employees with more than ten (10) years' service shall be entitled to no more than eight (8) weeks' severance pay and that once an employee elects to receive severance pay benefits hereunder all his seniority and his other rights shall thereupon terminate.

Section 3. A week's pay for the purpose of this Article shall be construed to mean forty (40) hours' pay calculated at the employee's average straight-time hourly earnings, including incentive bonus, if any, based upon the second previous week's earnings. Employees may elect to receive severance benefits in a lump sum or in weekly installments.

Such a clause clearly keeps the anchor to windward and tends to be an equalizer in the game of bargaining power.

CONTRACT TERM AND COALITION BARGAINING

The bargaining power of a union can often be determined by the length of the contract term. Some unions will refuse to execute long-term contracts simply because they fear that the lack of bargaining activity over a period of years can result in loss of interest and then loss of majority status. On the other hand, many companies view long-term contracts as only an expedient in solving the everyday problem of union-management relations and feel it more economically sound to confront the union annually or biannually to have the necessary test of strength. Much depends, it would seem, on the individual corporate philosophy or on the contract duration pattern in the particular geographical area.

However, all employers must be wary of two significant points: uniform expiration dates and coalition bargaining.

Uniform contract expiration dates may have a devastating effect upon an employer or, on the other hand, may put him in a position where he can seek assistance from competitors with similar contract termination dates. An attempt by a union to obtain uniform expiration dates is usually prompted by some ulterior motive, such as a desire to strike the entire industry or whipsaw those on strike with a settlement received or forced from a weaker employer in the industry.

Generally, such a union demand for termination uniformity should be viewed with skepticism even though at first blush the proposal might appear more beneficial to management. If, on the other hand, such a union demand can be turned to the company's favor, management should not overlook this opportunity to gain more bargaining power.

For instance, if the union makes a demand for a June first expiration date for all companies in the area, management should try to form an association of all the employers in the industry in that area who have contracts with the same union. Then the union should be told that management will agree to the June first date if the union will agree to recognize the association as the bargaining agent for the employer members of the industry that have contracts with the union. Once this is established, each employer member of the association will fall within the protection of the no-whipsaw-or-legal-lockout provisions of the 1957 *Buffalo Linen* decision (352 U.S. 818), and the employer's bargaining power will generally be strengthened.

In any case, any union proposal for uniform termination dates should be considered carefully in the light of these questions: How long has the company operated under its present termination date? Have there been practical problems creating the need for a change? Is the business seasonal? A company should not give up a winter termination date without serious consideration of the additional strike power such an act may be giving the union.

Coordinated bargaining has been the target of criticism from the moment in 1965 when the Labor Board handed down its now-famous *American Radiator & Standard Sanitary Corp.* decision (155 NLRB 736). There, the Labor Board held that an employer could not refuse to bargain with a group of unions representing its employees on the ground that the company wanted to bargain with each union independently. This new union approach soon became known as *coordinated bargaining* and has added much to union statutory bargaining power.

An example of the type of activity employed by unions in the area of coordinated bargaining and uniform termination dates was the 1968 experience of the Campbell Soup Company, when the unions in its various plants refused to execute labor agreements with different termination dates. As a result, the last contract expired at the height of the tomato harvesting season. Then the various unions struck. Subsequently, the company was successful only because its bargaining power remained intact and it was able to develop a program by which it could convince the public and Campbell employees that the union was abusing its strike power. In that case, agreement as to uniform termination dates would have resulted in substantial weakening of Campbell bargaining power, since for years to come the company's many contracts would have expired at the same critical time of the year and would have left the company in a position of continually facing the possibility of losing its essential annual tomato crop.

Clearly, therefore, every company must guard against and be prepared for the demand for coordinated bargaining and must evaluate its position with respect to this issue both for the present and for the future. If there is one area where the company could lose its bargaining power forever—this could be it.

✦   ✦   ✦

Just as the use of bargaining power by a company can be most beneficial to it, the unwise or unjust use of this power can be most damaging to the company, its reputation, and its employee relations philosophy. Any power is an asset to the party that uses it wisely; but, by the same token, if such power is used only as a weapon it will no longer be an asset.

It is of prime importance, therefore, once a company has established its bargaining power, to guard it and use it carefully. The power must not be flaunted, but must be used selectively. Too many companies feel they have the advantage when they obtain the greatest bargaining power—only to find that, when they most need it, they have lost it from unwise and excessive use.

In short, bargaining power should be obtained, maintained, and conserved, and it should be used justly, realistically, and with discretion.

Third Parties

Donald E. Hock

THERE ARE NUMEROUS INTERESTED AND IMPORTANT PARTIES INVOLVED IN company operations on a day-to-day basis. However, in the union relations area the degree of importance of these parties—commonly referred to as third parties—depends upon the individual company, community, and union situations. Let us review the areas of interest and consideration that must be given to some of the more important third parties when dealing with unions.

One factor to keep uppermost in mind when pursuing this third-party area is that the individual company-union relationship alters the importance of each party in the picture and its specific area of interest. Some of the governing considerations in this regard are the size and scope of the company or operating unit, the effect it has on the community in relationship to the total community employment, its industry, and its type of production. In more recent years a whole new area has come into the picture: the public employment/public service type of union organizational problem. On the broader, larger scale, the impact of such problems on national health, welfare, and defense industries in critical times affects the economy of the country.

In discussing and analyzing third-party relationships, the best approach is

DONALD E. HOCK is director of industrial relations for J. I. Case Company.

to assume that normal day-to-day contacts and responsibilities are of one nature and are quite different from the responsibilities and relationships that arise during negotiation periods and strike situations. The key to success and failure in many of the third-party relationships revolves around proper planning and preparedness prior to critical, pressure-filled negotiations and strike situations. This has been highlighted on numerous occasions when time spent in planning, preparing, and communicating to third parties for potential strike situations has overcome hasty and expedient decisions in the tense negotiation or strike condition.

The more common third parties are reviewed here. They are not necessarily listed in order of importance, since this is governed by each individual situation and operating condition.

CUSTOMERS

The key and most pressing third party for consideration is the customer. Customers can be difficult to reach in specific situations because many distribution systems are complex and the end customer is quite removed in the system from the company involved. However, no less important are the independent distributors, franchised dealers, company-owned outlets, and all service areas that require production output from the company to service end users. It cannot be overemphasized that communications through these avenues should be on an ongoing basis so that planning time is available when the company is facing difficult negotiations and possible strike action. Advance notice may protect the dealer and permit him to build stock levels necessary to sustain operations. This is a vital consideration since, in many cases, dealers, retailers, and the rest have no second source of income; thus their complete operations are in jeopardy when their flow of goods is curtailed. Adequate planning and information to service the customer during critical market conditions, seasonal situations, and critical service parts supply problems can keep the company from losing a customer forever. The key factor is communication to the dealer outlet.

Direct service industries have a different problem and many times have to plan for shifting customer service to some allied agency or alternate sources of coverage when confronted with a curtailed supply, a secondary boycott, and so on. In recent years companies have joined forces in a limited manner to serve customers and prevent complete curtailment of service; a notable example is the airline industry. The potential for this type of cooperative effort has really not been fully exploited. In some situations, however, such effort offers the only possibility for customer service in view of the expansion of union coverage across a complete industry. A present-day example is the newspaper field, where, when the union strikes all the newspapers in a city, the public is left without a paper. The approach will require more joining of forces by companies to avert complete disruption of customer service.

The field of public employees and the impact they have across a community, state, or nation constitute the most difficult customer area to work with. Legislation at state and local levels needs prime consideration to protect the customer and prevent total disruption of services that are vital in a community, state, or national situation.

The customer is the key to any profit and loss statement. Thus, in approaching negotiations and work stoppage situations, management's chief concern should be communicating with, planning for, and servicing the customer.

SUPPLIERS

It is becoming common practice for companies to set up and maintain records with their suppliers as to contract termination date from the standpoint of both parties. Prior to the start of negotiations, the suppliers and the company should be informed of the outlook for such negotiations and a plan should be established for keeping them up to date as actual negotiations progress. In cases where purchasing procedures utilize open-order and inventory-level plans, the suppliers must be informed so they can plan and juggle their requirements when critical periods arise. A prepared follow-up, along with alternate plans of action, can save the suppliers undue pressure and can likewise prevent costly production interruptions when strike situations are involved. An additional advantage of such plans and communications is the ability to react quickly to a start-up situation following production disruptions.

Recognition by the company of each supplier and the economical impact it has on him is often overlooked, leaving the supplier in a difficult position. He feels he is not a part of the family if he is not given due recognition when problems arise. This impairs the relationship and affects the supplier's desire and ability to react in the proper manner when pressure is required.

The key to this problem is having an established plan which is communicated to the supplier and adhered to on a regular basis.

CARRIERS

In the complex systems that today's companies use to distribute their products, all types of carriers are covered. Besides the more common types such as truck and rail, air and ship are also used in many businesses. The coordination of both incoming supplies and outgoing product with the variety of carriers can present a maze of problems when a company is faced with a work stoppage. Movement of materials and product can be more or less of a problem, depending upon the planning and coordination that take place prior to any strike deadline. When preplanning distribution to dealers and customers in anticipation of interruptions, companies have built up inventories at distribution points and have established prearranged deliveries on an alternate schedule. Plans are established for interchange of product among dealers to help maintain supplies and service. Oftentimes the coordination requires the diversion of incoming raw materials to alternate suppliers. Reprocessing and the transfer of tooling and equipment are often involved, both of which rely heavily on the ability of coordinating carriers to react; and being informed of the dimensions of the problem makes both of these possible.

The increasing interrelationship of unions among carriers and the use of various forms of secondary boycott make these programs difficult to execute and dependent solely on the relationship of the company with its various carriers. It is not uncommon for companies to transfer complete inventories to outlying points when a strike situation is imminent. Important in this action is the timing and ability of reliable carriers to react. Frequently the best-laid plans for customer service can be snarled for a variety of causes, and the alternate distribution system must be ready. This could involve switching from truck to rail or air.

An adequate inventory level to service the customers is of no value so long as stock remains in a strike-bound plant. Carriers feel their responsibility to serve a customer in such critical situations, but only to the extent that they are informed so delivery schedules can be adjusted and thus be effective. Here, again, the key to the situation is good communication and proper timing for the effective utilization of any plan.

GOVERNMENT

All forms of government—city, county, state, and federal—are factors for consideration and concern in labor negotiations and strike situations. The concern and cooperation of these governmental agencies vary considerably, depending upon their individual complexion and the size of the company. It is reasonable to assume that most companies have developed sound operating relationships with their local, county, and state governmental agencies in particular. At any rate, such relationships cannot be established at the last minute when the company is confronted with strike pressures and attendant problems. Certain mandatory legal requirements placed upon every company make necessary day-to-day relations with some governmental agencies. These should be developed on a sound basis. Local and county ordinances are a matter of concern, as are state and federal regulations required in bargaining proceedings. Among these are state and federal mediation and conciliation services, state labor laws, and many others. At present, Labor Board decisions are being utilized by unions to the fullest extent in phases of labor relations from the organizing campaign to the negotiation table. This has a tremendous and frightening impact on third-party relations.

In recent years labor strikes have been the subject of government intervention at all levels, up to and including the White House. Notable examples are the airlines, steel, and copper strikes, to mention only a few. The pressures on the government—from outside sources—to intervene are becoming more pronounced. It is only reasonable to expect, in the area of public employees, that this will become an increasingly difficult problem with no apparent answer at hand for the immediate future. Companies must be very conscious of the impact and effect of Labor Board decisions and arbitrators' decisions on negotiations and strike situations. A notable example today is the impact of the government's cost-of-living index, which not only affects labor negotiations, but guides wage costs during the life of the contract. In numerous strike situations, local government officials are pressed to intercede on behalf of the union and employees and apply pressure on management for settlement.

The effects of these various forces are somewhat diminished when the company is aware of and knowledgeable about the makeup of the various governmental bodies, has communicated its position as completely as possible prior to and during negotiation periods, and keeps in touch with appro-

priate individuals whenever a strike situation develops. Such a relationship is
not developed overnight, and a basic awareness should be present if a company is to have this relationship from day to day. It is too late to call on such
governmental agencies when trouble has already arisen. Because of their elec-
tive or appointive positions, government officials are at best faced with a
difficult situation. When properly informed, individuals in local and state
government cannot ignore the importance of the company's operations in
their community and are more likely to be responsive to its needs.

The News Media

The news media consist of three basic areas: newspapers, radio, and
television. Also, some companies are involved to a greater or lesser degree
with trade journals and publications peculiar to their business and industry.
Logically, such media are interested in news; thus work stoppages, disruptions, strikes, and so forth are of great interest to them. Like many other
areas, a company's relationship with the news media cannot wait until the
company is confronted with a potential problem if the relationship is to be a
good one. Regular relations and communications with the media during
normal business periods greatly improve the type of coverage and influence
the result in times of crisis. As negotiation periods approach, it is important
to keep in mind the ever-present problem of the union releasing information
that conflicts with the company's position. This often leads to a situation
where negotiations actually take place through the news media. This should
be avoided. One approach to consider in such a situation is an agreement
with the union that joint news releases will be issued during the negotiations. It is important to adhere to this agreement during negotiations and
through contract ratification. Once contract terms are agreed to, nothing can
be more disturbing to both the union and the company than to have a
story break prior to ratification by the employees, covering in detail the terms
and conditions of the agreement.

During a strike situation, news media can be most effective in keeping
the employees as well as the general community informed in a factual
manner as to the basic issues and the progress being made to resolve such
issues. However, this is uncommon; a point uppermost for consideration
during strikes is the utilization of the news media by unions to cloud the issues and exploit areas of controversy to attain their desires. Skillful handling
of such situations is required to prevent an adverse reaction toward the com-

pany on the part of the general public and, more specifically, the employees. Strikes are front-page items; therefore, the media actively seek news of strikes. The reception given to newsmen and the manner in which they are provided with pertinent information must be of prime concern to the company. A no-comment response gets negative news coverage. In a sense the news media speak for a company whether the company likes it or not. For this reason management should cooperate with newsmen; if it does, newsmen are likely to return the courtesy and cooperate with management.

THE PUBLIC

In years past, a company went about its business with little regard for the things that went on outside its doors. Retailers, business people in the community, and the community in general had little contact with the company; therefore, word of mouth between friends and neighbors provided the company's image in the community.

Times have changed. Today, companies realize the concern of the public and feel the pressure the public exerts on their operations. In strike situations a company is subject to pressures from the public, not only in the community, but across the entire nation, in many cases. This is a difficult problem because, in general, the broad term "public" also encompasses the customer. Thus the company, feeling responsibilities toward the public, wants to maintain a proper operating atmosphere and proper control of costs, for ultimately the consumer price is affected. In service industries—public utilities, communications media, transportation, and so on—the reaction of the public is immediate when services are disrupted. This kind of pressure is increasing with the advent of union organization for public employees in schools, hospitals, community protection agencies, and so forth. An unusual transition takes place in these areas because the public in many cases is also actually a party to the negotiations. The public—being the taxpayers—has both aspects to consider when confronted with such conflicts. Additional difficulty arises because public representation in negotiations has a distinct disadvantage. Any offers, settlements, and the like must in some cases actually be ratified by public referendum in order to secure the funds required by the settlements for benefit areas and wage increases. Some more enlightened states have recognized this unique problem and have attempted to develop legislation to alleviate this unusual conflict of interest and provide equitable representation for the public in these areas.

Considerations of the public in the third-party picture is most difficult because it is all-encompassing. However, management must stress those aspects of the public that are closest to it in most situations—that is, it must realize that the customer is a part of the public, as is the community in which the company operates. If management guides its thinking with these two segments—customer and community—uppermost in mind whenever its relations with unions affect the public, it will have served its cause to the greatest possible extent.

✦　　✦　　✦

In general, then, today's communications systems dictate that increased attention be focused on the entire third-party area, which formerly received only passive attention in many companies. Failure to recognize the impact of the many third-party areas in the picture today can really make the difference between profit and loss in many operations. Society in general is in a sense involved in union relations, and it certainly must be reckoned with. There is no quick, convenient way to relieve management of its responsibilities to the third party. Management should not be continually on the defensive, but should instead carry out its program in the third-party area with imagination and aggressiveness. In such an environment, the successes will far outnumber the failures.

The Bargaining Impasse

Kenneth Roberts

Our national labor policy seeks, among other things, to maximize the opportunity for agreement without industrial strife. It contemplates that the Labor-Management Relations Act will direct the parties to the conference room with pure hearts, lofty motives, and a burning desire to reach agreement in good faith on all issues involving wages, hours, and conditions of employment. The parties use persuasion, compromise, exchange of information, and other techniques (including, perhaps, a threat—veiled or otherwise—of economic pressures) to lead one another closer and closer to the objective: a collective bargaining agreement. Once the objective is reached, industrial peace has been achieved.

If a no-strike clause is included—which, together with a grievance and arbitration procedure for resolving disputes, is common—a continuation of industrial peace for the duration of the agreement is assured. Unions, employees, and management prosper and the public suffers no inconvenience. Despite our frequent criticisms of the system, the result is often exactly as described.

Unfortunately, the collective bargaining process does not always result in a bargain being struck. If, despite good faith efforts by both parties, the

KENNETH ROBERTS is administrative manager of the refining department of Humble Oil & Refining Company in Houston, Texas.

objective is not reached, the parties will instead reach an impasse. The impasse ends—temporarily at least—the employer's plans for spending the next year or two, or longer, administering a contract and skillfully disposing of grievances and arbitrations; he must now turn his attention to a whole new set of concerns.

Many of the problems discussed in this chapter and the three succeeding ones involve complex legal problems. It is imperative that an employer who finds himself in the situations described in these chapters have the benefit of a highly competent labor attorney. It would be impossible to cover the problems here in sufficient detail to obviate the need for such counsel. All that is intended or attempted here is to describe in general terms the nature and scope of these problems in the hope that some employers will have a better understanding of what to expect should they find themselves involved in these situations.

When Does an Impasse Exist?

When does an employer know that the objective is, for the moment at least, beyond reach—that he has reached an impasse? In general, an impasse may be described as the situation that exists when there is no reasonable prospect that further discussions of outstanding proposals will produce an agreement.

Applying the rule is not easy—unless, of course, the parties agree that there is an impasse. If there is disagreement, determining whether an impasse has been reached can be a difficult legal question. One may know, or at least sense, that further attempts to reach agreement will be futile. To prove this to the satisfaction of the courts and the Labor Board is another matter. Careful documentation is needed and competent counseling for the employer is imperative.

If one of the parties is determined to show that bargaining has *not* reached an impasse, the matter of proof is particularly troublesome. That party can, by rearranging or altering proposals in a manner it knows to be unacceptable, give bargaining the appearance of being short of an impasse. Unions in particular may wish to demonstrate that an impasse does not exist. By admitting that there is an impasse, the union recognizes the right of the company to take certain types of unilateral action as discussed in the next section.

Effect of an Impasse on Bargaining Obligations

Because of the frequent difficulty of proving the existence of an impasse, the employer should carefully document the history of negotiations and obtain the advice of counsel before taking action.

If a true bargaining impasse does exist, the employer must decide (1) whether he wishes to suspend negotiations for the present and (2) whether he wishes to place into effect unilaterally one or more of his proposals that were rejected while bargaining was taking place (assuming that he has no contract in effect that would prohibit such action). In evaluating what to do at this stage, the employer must remember that while an impasse alters the bargaining obligation somewhat, the union is still bargaining agent for the employees. Generally speaking, except for the possibility of suspending negotiations or taking some kind of unilateral action, the bargaining obligation continues unchanged.

SUSPENDING NEGOTIATIONS

When negotiations reach the stage of an impasse, the parties will have made and discussed all the proposals which, for the moment at least, they are willing to make. Positions will have been stated. Reasons for positions will have been explained. Concessions which the parties are willing to make will have been revealed. Ways of resolving issues will have been fully explored. The Labor Board recognizes that in this situation the parties can only continue to restate their proposals to no avail, and either party is entitled to break off negotiations.

Even though the right to suspend negotiations may exist, neither party may wish to be the one to initiate a suspension of discussions. Frequently, a union and an employer, in the face of an obvious stalemate, continue futile discussions for fear that employees, the public, or the government will believe the collapse of negotiations was caused by the party that suspends the discussions.

If an employer is not concerned with the kind of image he presents to third parties, he may choose to suspend negotiations when it is clear that an impasse is at hand. If he is concerned about how a third party will view his action, he may wish to go on meeting with the union despite the hopelessness of the situation. Of course, if the union is unwilling to continue meeting, the employer no longer has this choice.

Regardless of which party chooses to suspend discussions, neither is entitled to refuse to resume meetings once the union or employer thereafter indicates a willingness to make a different proposal or take a different position. Negotiations must then be resumed until the new situation is fully explored. An impasse never creates a permanent right to refuse to meet.

EMPLOYER UNILATERAL ACTION

It should be noted that no discussion of union unilateral action is included here. About the only type of unilateral action available to unions is a strike or other forms of economic pressure and Labor Board decisions at the present time do not appear to require unions to bargain to an impasse before taking such action.

The employer, during negotiations, may have proposed changes in wages, hours, or other working conditions, including changes in provisions of any existing contract. While these types of changes normally cannot be made by an employer without first informing the union and giving it an opportunity to bargain, the employer can frequently make these changes unilaterally, once bargaining has reached the stage of an impasse. The situations involving employers' unilateral action following an impasse normally arise when the employer wishes to make a change in the status quo (1) when the parties are negotiating their first contract; (2) when a prior contract has expired; or (3) during the term of an existing contract but in connection with a matter not covered by a contract.

Whether the employer wants to act unilaterally is another question. Making changes unilaterally may damage what would, at this stage, already be a strained relationship with the union and the employees. On the other hand, there may be strong reasons for the employer to act unilaterally.

The proposed changes may be popular with employees and would thus enhance the employer's image. The union may have rejected the proposals not because they were unpopular, but because of pressures from outside sources or for reasons related to overall union bargaining strategy. Sometimes an employer proposes unpopular changes which are vital to the success of the business and which the union knows he must make. The union, however, cannot share the responsibility for such action and must refuse to agree to it. In this type of situation, the union may be very happy for the employer to make the changes unilaterally and thus remove the union's problem of accepting unpopular but necessary changes. The union must, of course, protest, even if it recognizes that the action is necessary.

Despite some exceptions, the employer should recognize that, as a general rule, unions bitterly resent unilateral action. Furthermore, employees generally feel that their union has been bypassed and also resent such action. Nevertheless, this device for effecting changes—acting unilaterally after fulfilling the bargaining obligation—has probably not been used by employers as a whole as often as it should have been. Frequently, it is the only way available to make changes vital to the business when union agreement cannot be obtained.

Each employer must evaluate his own situation at this stage to determine what action, if any, he should take. If the employer concludes that unilateral action is called for, he should make certain that the action taken is only what was proposed in discussions with the union. If an employer desires to take action on some matter not discussed with the union or take broader action than was proposed during negotiations, he must first notify the union and again give it an opportunity to bargain before the change is made.

This points up the necessity for advance planning in negotiations where an employer foresees that he must make some change involving a bargainable matter. He should be certain that the proposed change is discussed fully with the union during the negotiations. Otherwise, his obligation to offer the union the opportunity to bargain still exists, even though an impasse has been reached.

Before leaving the subject of unilateral action, it should be noted that the existence of a bargaining impasse is not necessarily a prerequisite to employer unilateral action in all cases. If an employer gives the union an opportunity to bargain in advance of action and the union does not ask to do so, the employer has fulfilled his obligation. Bargaining for a reasonable length of time without reaching agreement may be sufficient in some cases to free an employer to act. Of course, if a contract clearly gives the employer the right to take certain action—either during or upon the expiration of the contract—the employer need not wait for an impasse before taking action. However, no attempt is made here to discuss these situations. The concern has been only with the effect of an impasse on the bargaining obligation, not with the effect some other situation may have on the bargaining obligation.

Breaking the Impasse

Until the impasse is broken and agreement is reached, there is the danger of a strike, a product boycott, or other types of economic pressure. An employer will want to find a way to remove the impasse and reach an agreement. Of course, new discussions can be initiated at any time by making a new proposal, but this will not necessarily place the parties closer to agreement. The discussion in the next section focuses on ways that an employer can increase the chances of reaching agreement by learning why the union is adamant. The two sections that follow deal with some other factors that may influence the ability of the employer to prevent or break an impasse.

Determining the Reason for the Union Position

The employer knows why his position is fixed and whether he may be willing to change it. But what about the union? If the employer can learn why the union is adamant, he can better evaluate the possibility of finding a way to break the impasse. If the employer has prepared properly for bargaining, he will have fully analyzed the union's situation long before the impasse was reached and should know what is causing the union's reaction. However, the fact that an impasse was reached indicates that the employer may not have properly analyzed the pressures controlling the union's action, and a fresh attempt to learn the reasons for the union's position may be needed.

Of course, during negotiations the union will explain its position and the reasons for it. These may be the real reasons (particularly where there is a long relationship between the parties based on mutual respect) or they may be only surface reasons with the real force motivating the union hidden in the background. The employer must therefore look beyond what the union has been saying and attempt to analyze for himself the possible factors influencing the union.

Pressure from above. It is not uncommon for local unions to receive mandatory bargaining objectives from the international. If this is the situation, a possible method of breaking the deadlock exists. We know that in this situation the local must achieve the mandatory objectives even at the expense of yielding on other issues. This offers the possibility of the employer making concessions on the mandatory items in exchange for union concessions on the rest. If, however, the employer feels he cannot yield on the items which the local union has been told are mandatory, then a prolonged impasse may be in store. Eventually the international may relent if the pressures are strong enough; meanwhile, the employer must face the possibility of a strike or the use of other economic weapons by the union.

How does an employer determine whether a local union is under orders from the international to achieve certain objectives? It is not unusual for some publicity to be given to international union mandatory bargaining objectives. This is sometimes in the nature of information furnished union members, speeches by an international union officer, information in union publications, or other means. The employer should study what has been happening within the international prior to negotiations for clues as to what instructions may have been given the locals in the event that there has been no public disclosure. Frequently, it is possible to make an enlightened guess as to the instructions under which a local union is bargaining by the attitude that is taken on the various issues during the discussions. Another way is simply to ask the union negotiator. Perhaps he will answer truthfully, although it may be dangerous to rely solely on what he says.

Pressure from below. No matter how persuasive an employer's arguments may be, how logical his position, or how much the union's bargaining committee may feel that his position is reasonable, the union cannot reach agreement with the employer if there is strong employee opposition. The union must respond to employee pressures. Of course, the union will always indicate that its views represent the attitude of employees, and to a certain extent this is likely to be true. However, where the union position is being controlled by overwhelming pressures from employees, it is important that the employer know this and plan accordingly.

Lateral pressure. Sometimes the bargaining position of the union is closely related to other negotiations, such as those being conducted by the same local with other employers in the area or those being conducted by sister locals. This situation can cause one union to weaken the bargaining power of the other if it settles for less than what the other union is seeking. Furthermore, the union may also feel that its bargaining position will be strengthened and its chances of obtaining greater concessions increased if it allows pressures to build through settlements with other employers. Of course, this lateral pressure may also be in combination with pressure from above since the international may, in this situation, attempt to keep all the locals in line.

Typically, an employer may find it very difficult to remove this type of lateral pressure and clear the way for the impasse to break. Cooperation between employers is a possibility; but, with the exception of a few industries, this has not often been attempted. While there may be little that can be done by an employer to break an impasse while lateral pressure exists, he can, by determining this to be the cause of his union's fixed position, conclude that serious negotiations with his union are likely to resume only after negotiations at the other locations are concluded.

Misunderstood position. The union and the employer always have much in common. For example, both know that a sound, profitable business is a necessity for their survival. Both know that pay and working conditions necessary to produce employee job satisfaction are important in keeping the business healthy. Despite this common base from which any enlightened union and management must operate, there are frequently sharp differences in the philosophy of how to achieve the common objectives. Mutual distrust is still very common.

This is further complicated by the fact that many unions and employers still view negotiations as a contest to determine who is the sharpest trader rather than as an attempt at problem solving. It is therefore very easy for communications to break down entirely.

Facts that seem crystal clear to the one presenting them may not be believed by the other. Arguments that are compellingly persuasive may never really be understood when they are presented. Furthermore, the nature of bargaining is such that the parties are frequently constrained from making their points clearly and openly; sometimes attempts at communication are through hints, suggestions, and other indirect methods that may fail to establish a point clearly.

When negotiations reach the point of an impasse, it is very helpful for the employer to review the course of negotiations and all the statements made by both parties. In this way, he can attempt to evaluate whether his arguments were, in fact, understood by the union and whether he has really understood everything the union has been trying to tell him. Where there is any likelihood that poor communication has occurred or a misunderstanding of positions exists, the employer's position should be restated and his arguments should be remade, supported to the fullest possible extent with detailed, factual information. In addition, the employer should question the union in detail on the union's position in an attempt to make certain that it is fully understood by the employer.

Finally, and perhaps most important, it is in this atmosphere that the Federal Mediation and Conciliation Service can be the most effective. Where the parties have communicated poorly with one another, the situation is ripe for a skilled mediator to break the impasse.

Other causes. There are many other reasons why a union may adopt a fixed position. Perhaps personality conflicts and distrust so charge the emotions of the negotiators that the desire for agreement has been replaced by a desire to exact a penalty. Perhaps the union is intentionally creating an impasse, hoping that the resulting strife will help solidify its position with employees. However, the examples previously discussed are probably the most frequent causes and represent a starting point for an employer attempting to analyze why the union is adamant.

Whatever the cause may be, it is important that an employer identify it if he can. Identifying the cause may help him find a way to break the impasse. Even if it does not, knowledge of the cause is essential in evaluating the possibility of a strike and planning for the future.

Determining Employee Attitudes

An employer who is attempting to analyze what has caused an impasse and how to break it must devote considerable attention to the prevailing attitude of his employees concerning the issues involved in the negotiations. This attitude can have a major impact on the employer's efforts to end the impasse.

Employee pressure on union negotiators has already been mentioned. It represents one of the most common causes for a fixed position by a union. Where employee restraining pressures are strong enough, a union cannot make the concessions necessary to reach agreement. Not only is a settlement agreed upon in the face of employee opposition likely to be rejected in an employee ratification vote, but the union negotiators reaching such an argument may be voted out of office.

Sometimes the employee pressure is generated by union negotiators themselves in an attempt to create employee support that can be used as a lever to pry additional concessions from an employer. Union negotiators may make statements and furnish information to employees designed to inflame and agitate them sufficiently to create pressure of this type. If the union negotiators have miscalculated and the company is still unwilling to make the desired concessions, the union negotiators may be entrapped by the pressure which they themselves created.

While the employer has quite limited influence on what union negotiators may say to employees, he should, as far as possible, guide negotiations in a way that discourages the negotiators from making statements that build employee pressures on the union negotiators. The most skilled and experienced union negotiators are not likely to be caught in this trap; it is the inexperienced who may commit themselves to such an extent that they cannot later retreat in the face of an unyielding employer.

Having an understanding with the union negotiators at the outset of bargaining that neither side will communicate what is taking place during negotiations is seldom the correct approach. However, some candid discussions at the beginning of negotiations, with at least the key negotiators, may be desirable at times.

Employee pressure, whether arising spontaneously from employees or artificially generated by negotiators, may force the union into a fixed position. But there is a corollary to this that works in the employer's favor. No matter why the union has taken a fixed position, if employee support for an offer rejected by the union builds to a sufficient extent, the union must respond. Despite pressure from above, lateral pressure, or whatever may have created the impasse, the union cannot maintain its position where there is strong employee opposition. Employers must therefore recognize employee attitude to be of paramount importance, both in preventing an impasse from developing and in determining whether an impasse that has occurred can be ended without employer capitulation.

What an employer can do to influence employee attitude has been the subject of much controversy. It has become controversial because any employer attempting to influence employees is usually resented to some extent by unions. At this time, the famous *General Electric* case is still in the courts and amendments to the law dealing with employer free speech are being proposed by various groups. While this leaves some uncertainty concerning the extent to which employers can communicate with employees in the future, it is likely that two basic principles of the past will continue substantially unchanged.

First, an employer cannot design communications to his employees for the purpose of undermining or undercutting the union with the objective of destroying the union's effectiveness or causing it to lose its representative status. Second, an employer can report factually to employees his own and the union's proposals made during negotiations. In reporting on these proposals, the employer can explain the positions of both parties and the reasons for those positions. An employer does, therefore, have the opportunity to influence employees in a noncoercive manner by communicating his position and the reason for it to employees.

While there are many devices, both oral and written, for communicating with employees, the most important is given insufficient attention by most employers—through the first-line supervisor. This is not to imply that supervisors should be sent out to sell a management position or undermine a union's proposals. They must simply understand fully management's position and the reason for it and be able to answer questions intelligently and participate knowledgeably in discussions initiated by the employees.

It is not enough to wait until an impasse exists and then turn to the supervisors for help. An employer should keep supervisors fully informed before negotiations begin and at every step of the way. In addition, the employer must rely heavily on the evaluation of first-line supervisors as to the attitudes of employees and the extent to which pressure from employees on a particular issue is influencing the union position.

Nevertheless, if an impasse exists and the supervisors still have not been utilized by management, it is not too late to take advantage of their valuable position. In attempting to evaluate the cause of a fixed position by the union, conferences with first-line supervisors should almost always be the first step. If they are good supervisors with close, unstrained relations with employees, they will almost surely know the way employees feel about the issues.

If pressures on union negotiators are caused by a lack of understanding of management's position or lack of understanding of pertinent facts, supervisors can be a big help in removing pressures that have caused the union to adopt its position. In the same way, if the union's position has been fixed because of pressure from above, lateral pressure, or other reasons, a fully informed group of supervisors will help place employees in a position to determine more objectively for themselves whether they wish to allow their negotiators to continue to remain fixed.

DETERMINING PUBLIC AND GOVERNMENT ATTITUDES

More and more in recent years both the general public and the government have become influencing factors in the outcome of certain types of collective bargaining. This is particularly true where negotiations have a significant impact on the economy or upon public convenience. Thus an employer whose negotiations have reached the state of an impasse must evaluate whether the attitude of either the public or the government is likely to influence the manner in which the impasse is ultimately ended.

Today, big nationwide negotiations in key industries are frequently preceded by statements from both sides designed to generate public support for the negotiations to come. If an impasse occurs or is threatened, the possibility of a strike causing major inconveniences to the public is likely to produce greater appeals by both sides for public understanding and support of positions. While the public cannot directly control the outcome of negotiations, neither the union nor management wishes to alienate the public. A public unsympathetic to management makes product boycotts and other weapons much more effective for the union. A public unsympathetic to the union generates union fears of reprisal legislation and fears that union-oriented candidates for public office will lose votes.

As for government influence, the Federal Mediation Service has long been involved in negotiations as a neutral party. However, a new type of government participation has developed in recent years, directed partially toward the prevention of inflationary settlements and partially toward protection of national defense. This new participation has taken the form of pressures on the negotiators through direct intervention by the President, through the appointment of bodies by the President or by Congress to make recommendations, and various other techniques. Such government participation, unlike that of the mediation service, is directed not only at achieving a settlement without economic warfare between the parties, but also at achieving a settlement which the government considers to be in the public interest.

While a very small percentage of negotiations are likely to involve the general public or the Federal Government, there is probably a growing number of negotiations in which the attitudes of these parties play a part. Furthermore, it is not uncommon for the general public, in the sense of a local community, and for government, in the form of local officials, to be major factors in influencing the position of both parties in a local industry that is particularly important to its geographic area.

When an impasse develops, it is now necessary for an employer who is in a business sensitive to pressure from the public or from government to determine where he stands with the public, either generally or locally, and also to determine whether intervention from any level of public officials should be expected. If an employer is faced with this type of problem, he must attempt to prevent such pressures from forcing him to accept an unsound settlement in order to end the impasse. He must also evaluate whether support of these outside parties can help him maintain his position.

Operating Without
a Contract or Strike

Kenneth Roberts

T HE PROBLEMS AN EMPLOYER WILL FACE WHEN HIS CONTRACT EXPIRES SHOULD
be planned for much in advance, for what the employer is entitled to
do when the contract expires depends largely on what the contract says or
does not say and on what has taken place during bargaining. Some of the
questions that arise when the contract has expired, assuming that no strike is
taking place and that negotiations are continuing, are examined in this
chapter.

EFFECT OF CONTRACT EXPIRATION

In recent years the concept has grown through Labor Board and court
decisions that the labor contract, unlike other agreements, doesn't really end
when it expires. While this is not a new theory, its application has been
extended and we can expect still further decisions by the Labor Board and
the courts clarifying the rights of various parties after expiration of the
contract.

There would be little purpose here in trying to analyze in detail the complex tangle of decisions, rules, theories, and arguments related to rights of the parties upon expiration of the agreement. A basic principle and one exception to it are touched on here.

The basic principle referred to is that, once a contract expires, the provisions of the contract remain the terms and conditions of employment, with the employer required to give a Section 8(d) notice and to bargain with the union prior to making changes. [A Section 8(d) notice is a statutory notice required before making any changes in contract terms—that is, in practices covered by contract provisions. As for bargaining with the union prior to making changes, see the discussion of employer unilateral action in the preceding chapter.]

The exception to this basic principle exists whenever the contract states clearly that a particular provision is applicable only during the term of the agreement. Theoretically, under this exception the contract could be so written that the union clearly agrees, upon signing it, that should it expire before a new contract is negotiated, the employer is free at that time to make unilateral changes without notice to or prior bargaining with the union. For example, the vacation provision could state that the employer is required to give vacations only while the contract is in effect and not thereafter. A similar provision could be made applicable to any other portion of the contract or to all of it.

As a practical matter, contracts are seldom written in this manner, and there has been little litigation testing this type of provision except with respect to union security provisions. However, it is not uncommon to provide that union shop or checkoff clauses are applicable only during the term of the agreement. Litigation has established that this language is sufficient to free the employer to terminate union security arrangements without notice or bargaining.

There is also a contention that the employer should be free to cease complying with union security and checkoff provisions when the contract expires, regardless of whether these provisions are specifically related to the term of the agreement; but this is still in litigation at present. The theory here is that the law is, or should be, different with respect to certain union-oriented rights as opposed to more substantive employee rights. Regardless of the outcome of this litigation, the basic principle and the one exception to it are likely to continue to be applicable to most contract provisions, with very clear contract language an essential requirement if the exception is to apply.

SPECIAL PROBLEMS

In examining some of the decisions an employer must make at the expiration of his contract, it is assumed that he is free to make changes—either because he has given an 8(d) notice and bargained with the union before the contract expired or because the contract permits the changes. (The word "changes" is used in this chapter to mean a change in some existing practice covered by a provision of the expired contract.) What the employer *should* do if he can is considered, rather than attempting to pursue the question of what he *can* do. An employer should not, of course, proceed with any changes until he has determined that he is free to make them.

If an immediate change is necessitated by business conditions, obviously the employer should place it into effect as soon as possible. In making possible changes which are not business necessities, the employer should proceed with caution. Among other things, he should decide what effect the change is likely to have on the negotiations and on employee and union relations. These are a few of the areas in which these decisions frequently arise.

Special privileges for union officers. Such things as pay for attending conferences with management during working hours, time off to attend union meetings or taking care of other union business, bulletin-board privileges, special parking privileges, and the like are included among the special privileges for union officers.

Despite protests to the contrary, most union officials and employees can understand the reluctance of an employer to support a union financially (even in the limited manner permitted by law) when he is not required to do so by contract, particularly when negotiations have become so difficult that a contract has expired without a new agreement being reached. An employer is taking a reasonable position when he refuses to penalize himself financially by helping the union to continue advocating positions unacceptable to him. For most unions, the economic effect of the employer's refusal to pay for time spent conferring with management is probably not sufficient to have any significant impact on negotiations. Nevertheless, as a matter of principle many employers feel they should not provide this type of support to union representatives who are attempting to negotiate a new contract on terms unacceptable to management.

On the other hand, eliminating bulletin-board privileges or in-plant park-

ing privileges may serve no purpose other than to inconvenience and irritate
the union officers. This is likely to be interpreted as an attempt to penalize
and harass the union and could create ill will toward the employer without
offsetting benefits to him.

Other possible withdrawals of privileges should be measured in the same
manner: Is the action primarily a harassment of the union with no benefit to
the employer, or is it action which is reasonable for the employer to take
because it helps put pressure on the union to settle or because there is some
fundamental matter of principle involved?

Checkoffs and union security provisions. A suspension of checkoffs may
bring real financial pressure to bear upon a union. This is particularly true
since any union shop agreement would also be suspended at the same time
and the payment of union dues would not be a condition of continued
employment. Collecting union dues could become a difficult and time-
consuming task, causing some substantial reduction in union income. Most
unions can understand that it is unreasonable to expect the employer to
continue checkoffs under these circumstances, and many employers refuse to
do so. It should be noted from the earlier discussion that this is a type of
change which the employer may clearly have the right to put into effect
unilaterally, since many contracts are written in a manner that gives the
employer this right.

Grievance procedures. The effect of the contract expiration upon grievance and arbitration provisions not only has been the subject of past litigation but also is involved in pending litigation, and further litigation can be
anticipated in the future. Whenever an employer's contract expires, he
should make certain that he is fully advised of the current state of the law in
this area.

Even if an employer is free to eliminate the grievance procedure entirely,
this action is probably not in his best interests. He may want to change the
procedure if he is free to do so, and he may want to clarify what is subject to
the grievance procedure. Usually, he will not want to deprive employees of a
grievance procedure or any other management channel into which their
problems can be directed. At the time the contract expires the employer will
probably be in difficult negotiations with the union, his normal relations
with the union and his employees may be strained, the possibility of a strike
may exist, and his usual communications with employees may be less effective. Under these circumstances, it may be advantageous to the employer to
keep open all avenues of contact with employees including the grievance
procedure. Furthermore, the withdrawal of a grievance procedure is not

likely to place any considerable pressure on the union to reach an agreement.

However, this is not as simple as merely deciding to continue the grievance procedure. It is important for the employer to understand clearly what a grievance is, either by definition or by past practice in his operation. Under most grievance procedures, claimed contract violations are subject to the grievance procedure along with other complaints. Under some, *only* claimed contract violations are classed as grievances. Theoretically at least, if there is no contract in effect, there can be no contract-violation type of grievance.

The employer may wish to take the position with the union that the grievance procedure or some form of it will continue in effect, but that the matters brought into the grievance procedure while no contract is in effect will not be treated as claimed violations. He may wish to indicate to the union that a grievance that would have involved an alleged violation of the contract will now be considered as a complaint or claim of unfair, unreasonable treatment and will, during this period, be evaluated by the employer on that basis. To continue to talk about contract violations may imply an understanding with the union that the contract, or some part of it, continued in effect past the expiration date. Because of the theories now being advocated that the contract or some parts of it do remain in effect for some purposes, the employer should not leave any implication that the parties intended this to occur.

Since many grievance procedures are directly tied to arbitration provisions, the employer must evaluate his policy on handling grievances in light of his position on arbitration. To the extent that he is free of any arbitration obligation, he will probably wish to make clear that a continuation of the grievance procedure does not mean the grievances can be appealed to arbitration.

ARBITRATION

If a grievance arises while the contract is still in effect, and if that grievance is arbitrable under the contract, it is clear that the matter is subject to arbitration even if it reaches the arbitration stage after the contract expires. This rule has been in effect for a long time and most employers have no quarrel with it. However, for disputes arising after the date the contract expired, the extent to which an employer can free himself of an obligation to arbitrate is a particularly troublesome problem.

There is some indication from Labor Board and court decisions that the arbitration clause is a very special type of provision and will remain in effect, for some purposes at least, *as a contract obligation* after the term of the contract ends. Under this theory, the arbitration clause can have a longer term than the rest of the contract, even if the contract does not say so.

Despite an indication that some courts are impressed with the theory that some arbitration obligations may survive contract termination, the concept has at this time been applied only in special circumstances. Therefore, most employers still take the traditional position that the arbitration clause expires with the contract and thus there is no obligation to arbitrate on any matter except those that arose while the contract was in effect.

At any rate, an employer can, by proper drafting of his arbitration clause, eliminate or substantially reduce the possibility of inadvertently assuming an obligation to arbitrate after the contract expires. He can specifically state that there is no obligation to arbitrate upon expiration of the contract. He can also clearly limit arbitration to claimed violations of the agreement, which should preclude any arbitration when there is no agreement to violate. The clause, which some employers have unfortunately agreed to, providing for arbitration of "all disputes between the parties" is most dangerous when a post-contract dispute over arbitrability arises.

We have assumed, of course, that an employer wants to resist arbitration after the expiration of the contract and it seems highly appropriate that he should do so. There are various theories concerning the reasons why arbitration provisions are needed in a labor agreement. One of those most frequently quoted is that it is the employer's counterpart of the union's obligation not to strike. If this is the reason for the arbitration clause, then the employer should be free of arbitration when the union's no-strike obligation has expired, leaving the union free to strike regardless of the outcome of arbitration. Even under the various other arguments that make the employer willing to agree to arbitration initially, there would appear to be no justification for him to continue this obligation after the expiration of the contract if he can avoid it. Of course, he can always agree to some form of special arbitration if it is desirable, but this is quite different from an *obligation* to arbitrate.

Publishing Rules to Replace the Contract

When a contract expires, supervisors need and expect guidance in the absence of a contract to administer. As discussed previously, as a general principle, the practices provided for in the expired contract remain the terms and conditions of employment, subject to change only after the union has had an opportunity to bargain on any proposed changes. Therefore, supervisors would usually be told to continue the same practices as existed when there was a contract with whatever exceptions may be appropriate.

However, if the period without a contract is expected to go on for some time, the employer may wish to prepare and furnish the supervisors with a set of rules to apply in lieu of the provisions of the expired contract. The rules would, of course, continue in effect the substance of the expired contract since the employer must bargain before making changes in practices. However, the rules would differ in various ways from the contract. These are examples of the differences.

+ Statements imposing a duty on the union would be deleted. Company rules could not, of course, impose a duty (such as a no-strike obligation) on the union.
+ Any changes the employer has made in existing practices in accordance with the earlier discussion in this chapter would be reflected in the rules. This might be withdrawal of checkoffs or other union security rights, withdrawal of various union privileges, or other changes—assuming, of course, that the employer is entitled to take the actions.
+ The arbitration provisions would be deleted and the grievance procedure would refer to violations of the rules rather than violations of the contract.
+ Ambiguous, unclear, or awkward language would be revised to state clearly the meaning understood by management.
+ The management rights provisions would probably be adapted to the rules concept. Company rules purporting to grant rights to the company may be illogical, but areas of management discretion could still be covered in a somewhat different manner. For example, instead of saying the company can require overtime, the rules would designate the level of supervision that is authorized to require overtime. This would perpetuate the concept of the right to require overtime and would do so in a manner that would be logical for a set of company rules.
+ Practices not covered by the contract could be included—particularly practices involving some management discretion.

There would be other changes in contract language, but these items illustrate the form the rules would take. The union should have no complaint if the employer issues rules continuing in effect the practices which could not be changed without bargaining.

Publication of the rules would, however, have certain advantages:

+ Supervisors would be administering up-to-date documents rather than an out-of-date contract supplemented by instructions identifying exceptions to the contract provisions. Also, publication of the rules would make it unnecessary to attempt to explain to supervisors the legal effect of the expired contract.
+ Management's position on matters covered by the contract but subject to possible dispute because of ambiguous language or other reasons would be strengthened by giving supervisors clear and unconfusing rules to follow, representing management's provisions. This helps to eliminate the possibility that a supervisor will inadvertently misapply the old contract provision.
+ Management's position on matters not covered by the contract could be strengthened by writing these practices into the rules. Consistency in supervisory action in these areas could be assured.
+ Publishing the rules would help to negate any claim that continued administration of the expired contract implies any management agreement that the contract continues in effect.

While the union may strongly object to the publication of rules, by following the guides just outlined the employer would not be depriving the union or employees of any rights.

Planning for Operating During a Strike

Kenneth Roberts

IF AN EMPLOYER CANNOT OPERATE IN THE FACE OF A STRIKE OR PREFERS NOT TO do so, he can shut down his operation, secure his property, and continue bargaining. This situation is not pleasant, but it is relatively simple compared with that of the employer who chooses to operate. Nevertheless, many employers have found that they can operate during a strike, either at full capacity or on a partial basis.

An employer should make this decision as early as possible to provide the maximum amount of time for detailed planning and preparation. A comprehensive plan of action should be ready to put into effect the moment the strike occurs. The problems facing an employer who decides to operate will vary greatly, depending on the employer and the nature of his business. The matters discussed here will illustrate the type and scope of the planning and preparation that may be required for many employers. We will assume that the strike has begun at some type of industrial plant, although many of the problems would also exist for other types of businesses.

Maintaining Production

The first step in strike preparation is to develop plans that provide some assurance that continuity of production during the strike is practical. Unless the employer can do this, there is no need to devote time to planning and preparing for the other types of problems.

Determining Who Will Work

The employer must begin his planning by taking an inventory of the workers who will be available during the strike. They will normally come from one or more of the following sources.

Supervisors and professionals. These employees are usually the foundation on which strike preparation plans are made. They may be the only workers certain to be available. Professionals cannot be compelled to work since they, unlike supervisors, are employees and are entitled to honor picket lines if they choose to do so. However, most professional employees are management-oriented and will cooperate with the employer.

Other nonrepresented employees. In addition to supervisors and professionals, other employees who are not represented by a union will sometimes be available to work. They are entitled to honor picket lines if they choose, but many, particularly white collar employees, may be management-oriented and want to work. Nevertheless, the employer may prefer that they stay away. Unions do not particularly resent supervisors and professional employees doing represented work during a strike. This is expected. But strikers may become bitter toward other unorganized employees who work, and this bitterness can continue after the strike. Whether an employer should encourage persons in this category to work may depend upon whether they are generally identified as management employees and whether all or only a few are willing to work.

Employees represented by a nonstriking union. If an employer has employees represented by more than one union, the nonstriking union will generally be sympathetic to the strike and want to honor the picket lines. However, if the nonstriking union is working under a contract with a no-strike clause, the employer may be able to plan for those employees to be available during the strike. If the employer anticipates that employees represented by the nonstriking union will attempt to disregard their no-strike commitment and refuse to cross the picket lines, he must decide how much pressure he is willing to exert to force them to work. This pressure, if used, would usually take the form of (1) a threat to discharge employees for violating a no-strike commitment and (2) damage suits against the union for breach of contract. Unlike others who are working during a strike, employees in this category would not be asked to perform work ordinarily performed by the striking employees.

Strike replacements. In some cases, the employer can find replacements—either permanent or temporary—for strikers. But even if replacements are available, the employer may have reasons for preferring not to use them. The extent to which an employer is entitled to utilize permanent replacements if he wishes to do so is discussed in the next chapter. Before searching for replacements, the employer should become familiar with any laws to which he is subject which might restrict the source or method of recruiting strike replacements.

Employees transferred from other locations of the employer. Sometimes an employer can obtain assistance in operating during a strike from employees—particularly those in supervisory and professional categories—assigned to other operations of the employer. If they are available, they can be a valuable addition to a workforce.

Employees represented by the striking union. A few employees may be unsympathetic to the strike and want to work even though they are represented by the striking union. An employer, in inventorying available workers during a strike, should not base any of his planning on their uncertain availability. He should, however, decide in advance what his position will be if a few employees ask to work. He may prefer that they do not do so, regardless of whether their offer is made at the beginning of or during a strike, because of post-strike problems which might be created. This is discussed further in the next chapter.

When making his plans, the employer probably will not know for certain how many employees will be available to work. However, it should not be difficult to determine the minimum number, and planning can be based on that. An attempt should be made to match the name of each available worker with the most critical job for which he is qualified. Plans can then be made for assignments to be given to other employees who may become available. This planning should be in substantial detail and should include the hours the employees will work, who will relieve each one, and similar matters.

If some training of available workers is needed, it should take place prior to the strike, but should be delayed as long as possible if bargaining is taking place. Training of supervisors or others to perform represented work may give the appearance of bad faith bargaining unless a strike threat is imminent.

SAFETY

In recent years, unions have been urging the enactment of laws that would have the effect of restricting operations during a strike. This type of law is advocated as safety legislation and covers such subjects as restrictions on operating equipment without a normal complement of men. Unions have had some success in having these laws enacted as local ordinances. The employer must determine whether such a law exists in his locality.

The legitimate safety laws should also be reviewed, of course, and the employer should take steps to insure full compliance. Even safety rules and practices that are not enforced by law should be continued in effect. An employer who attempts to operate without maintaining usual safety standards may alienate the public and seriously damage his image in addition to damaging the morale of those who are working. Risking injury to persons or major damage to property is a price too big for employers to pay in order to operate.

LICENSES

Related to safety regulations are those ordinances and laws requiring licenses for operating certain types of equipment or facilities. The employer should make certain that he obtains these licenses for supervisors, professionals, or others who will need them.

FOOD AND HOUSING

It is not unusual for those working during a strike to be scheduled for extended working hours, such as twelve hours per day, seven days per week. When long working hours are necessary, it may be desirable for the employer to provide on-premise feeding or housing or both, at least part of the time. If so, arrangements must be made to provide adequate in-plant feeding and sleeping facilities and, if possible, recreation facilities. Sometimes a caterer can be found to provide these services.

In most strike situations the employer must look to law enforcement agencies to protect persons and property and to maintain peaceful picketing. Relations with such agencies are discussed in the next chapter.

If the employer maintains a guard force of his own, it can be utilized since, under Labor Board rules, it cannot be represented by the striking union. The employer may also wish to supplement his own guard force or, if he has no guards, to employ them. However, he should consider whether hiring or contracting for new guards is desirable. The presence of a group of strangers acting as guards or security men, particularly if they are in uniform, could generate visions in the eyes of the strikers of professional strike breakers and the use of force by the employer. The extent to which this could contribute to nonpeaceful picketing is a factor that must be weighed by the employer.

In many localities, off-duty policemen or other law enforcement officers can be employed to help protect property, direct traffic, and maintain law and order. Where the police find it difficult to provide the number of officers needed, the possibility of employing off-duty officers should be investigated. Some police forces permit policemen to accept off-duty employment of this type through an arrangement under which the officers receive overtime pay from the police department and the employer reimburses the police department for the extra cost. This arrangement is frequently highly desirable since pickets will not react to local officers in uniform in the same manner as they may react to new guards or security officers brought in by the employer.

Other necessary security measures should, of course, be investigated. Unused gates should be locked and barred. If the premises are fenced, the fences should be inspected and secured. A system for admitting proper persons into the premises may be needed.

Pay and Benefits

The normal system for providing wages and benefits will be disrupted during a strike for both strikers and workers. Devising a new pay system for workers and determining the status of benefits for strikers should receive early attention.

PAY SYSTEMS FOR WORKERS

When supervisors and others normally paid on a salary basis are working during a strike, their hours are likely to be much longer than normal and their working conditions quite different—at least in the initial stages of the strike. They may even be living in the plant, separated from their families.

These conditions make it necessary for a fair system of compensation to be devised. Some employers pay regular salaries plus a large daily bonus. Others devise a new salary structure for the duration of the strike. Whatever the pay system used, it must be very generous compared with normal salaries to provide fair compensation for those working under difficult circumstances.

In devising a pay system, it is important to recognize that many wage-hour exempt employees may be performing wage-hour subject work during the strike. If so, the employer can be required to pay rate and one-half for all overtime hours worked. The base on which the rate and one-half is calculated would probably include any bonuses or special compensation other than overtime pay. An employer should not be surprised to find a federal wage-hour investigator appearing to review his pay system to determine whether the law covering overtime pay has been violated.

BENEFITS FOR WORKERS AND STRIKERS

Most employers today have benefit programs of varying degrees of complexity covering such things as hospital and medical insurance, life insurance, savings plans, pension plans, and sick pay plans, in addition to vacations and holidays. While some questions may arise as to the effect of extra pay for workers on any benefits that are related to normal compensation, the most serious problems usually arise over the application of benefit plans to strikers.

If the plans were written with a possible strike in mind, the questions should be easy to answer. If not, the employer must have his plans studied carefully to determine the rights of strikers to continued participation during the strike. These questions are frequently troublesome since strikers are still employees.

Picket-Line Activity

If something more than token picketing is anticipated, the employer must be prepared for many potential picket-line problems. He should anticipate that the extent and nature of the picketing will be quite different from what it is at the premises of a nonoperating employer.

MARKING PROPERTY LINES

Pickets cannot be trespassers on the employer's property. Picketing will generally take place on sidewalks, along a street or highway, or on other public rights-of-way near the entrance to the plant. However, the exact line dividing the privately owned property from the public right-of-way may not be marked. Property records should be investigated and the location of the boundary line should be determined. Shortly before the strike begins, it may be desirable to identify the location of this line with a sign, a painted stripe, or some other marker so that the strikers and law enforcement officers will know where picketing is permitted.

DOCUMENTING PICKET-LINE ACTIVITY

Illegal or violent picketing can frequently be curtailed or eliminated. The use of the Labor Board and the courts for this purpose is discussed in the next chapter. If relief is to be sought before the board or the courts, or by other means, the employer must make advance preparations to document very carefully the improper activity. His attorney will as a rule prepare detailed instructions for obtaining this documentation. These instructions will probably include such things as the following:

Identifying information on signs. As soon as pickets arrive, someone should note exactly what is written on the signs carried by the pickets, including the size and placement of the lettering. A photograph of each sign is very helpful. In most strike situations the signs will not contain improper wording. The exact wording is usually more important in situations involving recognition or secondary picketing. However, even in an economic strike the information on the signs should be documented.

Photographing the picketing. There is no need to photograph peaceful picketing, and to do so might be considered by the Labor Board to be evidence of improper employer motives. However, the employer should be prepared to photograph any type of massed, violent, or other nonpeaceful picketing. When the strike begins, a supervisor, guard, or other employer representative at each picketed entrance should have in his possession a camera that could be used on a moment's notice. An automatic, simple-to-operate movie camera is probably best. (The quality of the photographs is unimportant.) If more than one employer representative is available at or near each entrance, it might also be desirable to have facilities available for still photography to supplement the movies. Instructing the appropriate persons on how to use the cameras should not be overlooked.

Noting incidents. The employer's representatives at the picketed entrances should prepare written notes of all incidents or unusual activity or events at the picket lines. Where possible, the representatives should attempt to determine and write down verbatim what the pickets are saying to the persons attempting to enter or leave the plant.

Investigating strike activity. If Labor Board or court proceedings need to be initiated, trained investigators may be required to interview witnesses, take statements, and investigate other strike-related activity, both on and away from the picket lines. While it may be unnecessary to have investigators available at the site of the strike at all times, the employer may wish to have them immediately on call.

Instructing Employees on How to Cross the Picket Line

An employer will want to avoid any action that could be construed as the cause of converting peaceful picketing to improper picketing. To help achieve this objective, the employer may want to instruct those who will be entering or leaving the premises on how to conduct themselves when crossing the picket lines. They should be calm, polite to the pickets, firm in their insistence on the right to cross, but careful not to create trouble unnecessarily. Persons bringing vehicles across the picket line should drive slowly and carefully and should not attempt to force their way through. If vehicles are being blocked, police assistance should be requested. Every care should be taken not to injure anyone. These are a few examples of the types of good judgment that management representatives must use in crossing a picket line to reduce the possibility of provoking nonpeaceful picketing. Instructions on proper conduct while crossing a picket line may seem elementary, but such instructions may prevent some inadvertent inflammatory conduct.

Business Relationships

Most employers deal with many other firms. An employer who operates during a strike must recognize that many business relationships may be altered, and he should prepare accordingly.

CONTRACTORS

Certain types of contractors, primarily those engaged in construction work, may be entitled to enter the plant without being subject to picketing. The employer should determine whether he wants these contractors to continue working during a strike. If so, a separate gate must be provided for them. If the pickets appear at the separate gate, the picketing would be secondary, subjecting the picketing union to an unfair labor practice charge, a Labor Board injunction, and damage suits. The separate-gate arrangement may not be available to suppliers of goods and services or maintenance contractors. The employer should determine who is entitled to a separate gate and clearly restrict the use of that gate to the appropriate contractors.

SUPPLIERS AND CUSTOMERS

Many firms may be able to continue providing normal services without change. Others may be able to expand the scope and nature of services in order to provide additional assistance to the struck employer. Some may be forced to curtail services because their own employees refuse to cross picket lines or for various other reasons.

The employer should very carefully identify every firm from which he will want a continuation of services or new or expanded services. He should then notify all these firms of the possibility of a strike and determine the extent to which they can continue to provide normal or additional services.

In analyzing these relations with other firms, careful attention should be given to those which might be performing "struck work" and thus be "allies" of the struck employer under Labor Board rules. Such firms would become subject to picketing by the striking union. Businesses not performing struck work could not be picketed by the striking union, and plans could be made for stopping any secondary pressure brought against these firms.

Customers should, of course, be notified of any likely curtailment of deliveries. For customers who ordinarily take delivery on the struck premises, a determination should be made of the likelihood that the customer's employees will refuse to cross the picket line. If so, perhaps some alternate method of delivery can be planned, such as having supervisors bring in and take out customer trucks as discussed in the next section.

COMMON AND PRIVATE CARRIERS

A great many firms depend heavily upon common carriers for inbound shipments of supplies or raw materials and for outbound shipments of products. Continued use of common carriers presents a special problem during a strike. Common carriers are required to serve all customers impartially and are not entitled to refuse service. However, both railroads and truck lines may have union contracts that excuse employees from crossing picket lines. This makes it difficult for carriers to continue furnishing services which they are obligated to perform.

Railroads frequently solve this problem by using crews of supervisors for rail movements into and out of the plant, with regular crews operating outside the picket line. This same device could be used by truck lines to move vehicles in and out of the struck premises; but it may be more difficult for the truck lines.

In any event, the anticipated strike should be explored with common carriers in advance. If a carrier cannot or will not perform services for the struck employer, advice of counsel should be obtained on the possibility of recovery of damages or other actions against the carrier.

Whether the drivers of private carriers must cross picket lines will depend upon whether they are covered by a union contract with a no-strike clause. In the absence of a no-strike commitment, whether the drivers will enter the premises depends upon their own inclination.

If motor vehicles—whether common or private carriers or employer-owned—will not be brought across picket lines by regular drivers, the struck employer should investigate the possibility of having his supervisors or other nonstriking workers pick up the vehicles at the picket line, bring them into the plant, and return them to the regular drivers outside the picket line. If this technique is used, or if there is any other arrangement made for substitute drivers to operate motor vehicles, the substitutes should be properly licensed.

Operating
After the Strike Begins

Kenneth Roberts

PLANNING IN ADVANCE OF A STRIKE SHOULD NOT BE LIMITED TO THE MATTERS covered in the previous chapter—planning and preparation should also take into account the points that are covered in this chapter. Furthermore, after the strike begins is when the planning discussed previously will have to be put into effect. This chapter will concentrate on the rights of an employer and some decisions he will have to make after the strike has been called and his strike operations have begun.

TYPES OF STRIKES

For the purpose of determining what the employer rights are during a strike, strikes can be divided into three general categories. First is an *economic strike* in which the union uses economic pressure to obtain some legitimate bargaining concession. Second is an *employer unfair labor practice strike* in which a strike is generated by an unfair labor practice committed by the employer. Third is a *union unfair labor practice strike* in which the union uses the strike as an attempt to gain an improper objective. Since the rights of employers vary with the type of strike, the employer should determine, with the aid of counsel, which type of strike exists.

Inasmuch as an employer is deprived of some rights during an employer unfair labor practice strike, it is necessary for the employer to exercise particular care, both in the period preceding an anticipated strike and during the strike, to avoid taking any action that is a potential unfair labor practice. Such practices, which may be technical in nature and which would normally be ignored by the union, may become the basis for classifying the strike as an employer unfair labor practice strike. Even during a strike an employer unfair labor practice can, under certain circumstances, convert an economic strike into an unfair labor practice strike.

The most significant employer right affected by the type of strike is the right to discharge or replace the strikers. During an economic strike, the employer can replace strikers permanently but cannot discharge them. In an employer unfair labor practice strike, the employer can neither replace employees permanently nor discharge them; he must return them to their jobs at the end of the strike. During a union unfair labor practice strike, the employer may have the right to discharge strikers, but this right should be used with care. The right to discharge employees for violence or other types of improper strike activity will, at least to some extent, exist in all types of strikes.

The difference between discharging and replacing strikers can be quite confusing. A striker is *replaced* when a permanent replacement for him is hired. A striker is *discharged* when the employment relationship is severed without a replacement being hired. In the case of an economic strike, for example, this means that the employer cannot discharge all the striking employees and then seek replacements. He can, as he finds replacements, hire them on a permanent basis, leaving the replaced strikers unemployed. If, before a replacement is found, an employee unconditionally offers to return to work, the employer must reinstate the striker and is no longer entitled to replace him. The difference between the right to discharge and to replace is, therefore, primarily one of timing—whether the employer can terminate the employee before a replacement is obtained.

Whether an employee was discharged or replaced also becomes significant with respect to voting rights in a representation election growing out of a strike. This is discussed later.

The extent to which an employer is able to exercise his right to use temporary or permanent replacements is, of course, controlled by the extent to which replacements are, in fact, available. Small employers can sometimes replace entire workforces during a strike. Larger employers, particularly those whose employees are highly skilled, may find it very difficult to find adequate replacements; the right to hire replacements may then be more theoretical than practical.

If only a part of the workforce is replaced, the employer should recognize that those strikers who do return will be very bitter toward the replacements hired. This can cause post-strike dissension which can continue for a long time.

Discharged employees can become a major stumbling block to settling a strike—particularly when a few employees are discharged for improper picket-line activities. The union and the other employees are likely to have a strong sense of loyalty toward the discharged employees and resist any strike settlement not containing the employer's agreement to reinstate them. This is not to suggest that an employer should not discharge an employee for cause or should not file a criminal complaint against an employee for illegal activities. This is frequently necessary and desirable. However, the employer should do so with the full realization that this may complicate the strike settlement.

USING THE LABOR BOARD AND THE COURTS

Two points continue to appear as keys to successful operations of an employer during a strike: advance planning and an ability to act immediately when the need arises. These same two points are also fundamental requirements for efficient use of the Labor Board and the courts during a strike.

Before the strike occurs, the employer should consult with his attorney to identify the situations likely to arise which would raise the possibility of a court action for injunctions, criminal prosecutions, damage suits, or successful unfair labor practice charges. The employer and his attorney should then decide what action will be taken should the situation arise. Procedures for collecting and evaluating evidence can then be established—such as documentation of picket-line activity and the use of investigators mentioned previously. The attorney may be able to draft in advance at least some of his court pleadings, with only blanks to be completed.

All this assures immediate action should the need arise. Even in situations where results cannot be obtained immediately, to demonstrate an ability to respond to illegal activity within hours by initiating court or Labor Board proceedings can be a substantial psychological deterrent to further improper activity.

To illustrate an example of this approach, let us assume that on the first morning of the strike there is mass picketing that physically prevents anyone from entering or leaving the premises. If advance arrangements have been made for immediate documenting of this activity, it may be possible *during the afternoon of the same day*—

+ To obtain a temporary restraining order from a court (depending upon state law).
+ To have the individuals using force arrested by notifying police and, where necessary, filing a criminal complaint.
+ To file an unfair labor practice charge with affidavits, photos, and other evidence to support it.

The employer may have reasons for not wanting to take all these steps, even if they are available, but there should be no *delay* in taking whatever action has been previously agreed upon. Employers will usually find it desirable for psychological reasons to take every possible action—including those that do not produce any immediate relief.

Another example would be the occurrence of secondary picketing even though it is peaceful. Secondary picketing might take place at a valuable customer's place of business or at a contractor's separate gate. The struck employer will generally want to provide maximum assistance in eliminating the secondary picketing. By proper planning, arrangements can be made for the customer or contractor *within hours*—

+ To file an unfair labor practice charge with the full documentation needed by the Labor Board to obtain a federal court injunction.
+ To file a substantial damage suit.

If the struck employer has planned in advance to help his customers or contractors respond in such a prompt and forceful manner, he can strongly discourage the union from any further attempts to involve his customers or contractors in his strike.

EMPLOYER APPEALS AND EMPLOYEE OFFERS TO RETURN TO WORK

An employer who issues appeals to strikers to return—or issues notices that if strikers do not return by a certain date replacements will be employed —must proceed with care in order to avoid statements that constitute unfair labor practices. However, even assuming that the time and circumstances are such that the employer can properly issue some statement along this line, he must decide whether and when it is wise to do so.

One factor that employers sometimes fail to take into account is the allegiance to the union and the loyalty to one another that develop among strikers. Even where there has been internal union dissension over whether a strike should be called, it is not uncommon for the strike to cause a closing of ranks and full support for union objectives.

Because of this, employers who expect a mass return to work may be disappointed in the employee reaction, even if the appeal to return announces a program to hire permanent replacements. While this threat may be one which employees take seriously in a small operation, employees in general—particularly those in a large operation—may disregard it. The strikers may not believe the employer is serious or they may feel certain that the employer cannot obtain replacements even if he wishes to do so. Furthermore, there are likely to be severe pressures, social and otherwise, brought to bear against those strikers willing to break ranks by returning to work.

An employer who attempts to bring strikers back to work by threats of replacement may issue statements with a great deal of fanfare and then be quite embarrassed when few, if any, employees return on the designated day. Employers should probably avoid this technique unless they are serious about hiring replacements and know that replacements can be obtained. If the employer is truly serious and can produce replacements, the notice to employees could be effective.

The employer may be faced with a difficult decision when a relatively small number of employees offers to return, whether voluntarily or in response to an employer's appeal. If the employer is attempting to operate during the strike, a few additional employees may be very valuable. However, the employer should carefully weigh the desirability of allowing a few employees to return to work in light of the post-strike abuse, harassment, and social isolation to which those returning are likely to be subjected. If the employer decides not to allow relatively small groups to return to work, he should be sure that he does so under circumstances that do not represent an illegal lockout.

The Union Dilemma

If an employer is operating satisfactorily, the union's problems increase with the passage of time. Strike benefits may no longer be possible because of a depleted treasury, and, in any event, the costs may be growing far beyond what the union anticipated. Strikers may become restless, particularly if they have had no income or substantially reduced income during the strike. What is more, the possibility of outbursts of violence by frustrated strikers increases as the strike lengthens, and the union knows that this will cause it to lose public sympathy and could result in criminal prosecution for some of its members. If the employer remains adamant in his position under these circumstances, the union may be faced with pressures that push it toward capitulation and loss of face. Nevertheless, complete capitulation is distasteful to the union and most strikers and will be resisted despite the pressures.

The employer should consider at this stage whether he can assist the union by providing some face-saving settlement that does not interfere with his own objectives. The union may well be willing to drop its own demands if this can be done in such a way as not to make the union appear to be completely ineffective. The union must be in a position to claim some benefits from the strike, even if the employer does not retreat at all from his substantive position. Through the use of ingenuity at this point, it may be possible to work with experienced, level-headed union officers to generate a settlement of this type.

Loss of the Striking Union's Bargaining Rights

In prior years employers sometimes were able to hire replacements for strikers and then file a petition for a new representation election in which the replacements voted out the incumbent union. The union then not only lost the strike, but also lost its right to bargain with the employer.

This occurs infrequently today because replaced strikers are entitled to vote in representation elections for a period of a year. Furthermore, the right of an employer to file a petition questioning the union's majority status has been severely curtailed by recent Labor Board rulings.

Nevertheless, while an employer has less control today than he did previously over whether a representation election should take place, he should not overlook the possibility of a representation election occurring under a variety of circumstances over which he has little control. If no replacements are hired, there is a possibility that another union may attempt to supplant the striking union. If replacements are hired, it is possible that the replacements themselves will generate a decertification petition with the Labor Board or that an outside union may attempt to organize the replacements. If union officers make the mistake of calling a strike without the support of a substantial majority, the striking employees could themselves generate a decertification election. The possibility of such an election could strongly influence union strategy and may, to some extent, influence the employer's position.

Relations with the Public and Public Officials

An employer, to operate successfully, does not need the support of the public or public officers; he *does* need their neutrality and objectivity. If the public and public officials actively oppose what he is doing, continuing operations can be very difficult.

Striking unions frequently unleash a continuing flood of statements to news media in an attempt to build public support and sympathy for the strike. An employer genuinely interested in solving a strike will wish to avoid a battle of press releases since this is likely to magnify the dispute, draw outsiders into it, generate higher levels of emotion, and create problems of saving face. All this will make it more difficult to settle the dispute on the basis of logic, reason, or even expediency.

However, when the union issues public charges against the employer to which the employer feels he must reply, the reply has to be immediate if it is to be effective. Business organizations, particularly large ones, frequently find it difficult to move quickly in these situations. During a strike, it is imperative that the local manager be given full authority to issue statements without delay. If public relations assistance is needed in preparing statements or otherwise assisting with news media relations, the assistance should be provided locally—not through a public relations office at a remote corporate headquarters. If there is a delay of several days in replying to charges, several other union statements may be issued before the reply and the effect of the reply will be lost.

This same principle applies to all forms of communication during a strike, whether they are statements to the press, letters to employees, or other forms of public or private communication. Timeliness is necessary for effectiveness.

If mass picketing takes place in an attempt to block entrances, the picketing is likely to be a violation of the law. Any violence, of course, is also a violation. To curtail this activity effectively if it should develop, the cooperation of local law enforcement agencies is needed. Law enforcement agencies are naturally reluctant to become involved in labor disputes. Some agencies will enforce the law objectively, impartially, and effectively; others will act only in extreme situations. In order to obtain effective law enforcement from reluctant officials, the employer must insist that law enforcement agencies perform their duty and make clear that he expects this from them.

At the same time, it is very important for the employer to make every effort to establish the proper relationship with these agencies. He should emphasize that he does not expect law enforcement officers to support his position in a dispute and that all he wants is neutral, impartial law enforcement. Tact and diplomacy are called for. The employer should cooperate with the agencies fully, informing them of his plans where possible and alerting them to possible trouble. He should, to the extent his operations will permit, be guided by the advice of the law enforcement agencies where an explosive situation exists and consult with them on the timing of movements of goods or supplies in or out of his premises.

Some thought should be given to the question of who should act as contact with these agencies. Sometimes it is desirable for the highest level of management representatives at the locality where the strike is occurring to contact the head of the local law enforcement agencies in an attempt to insure the establishment of the proper relationship. Someone else may be more appropriate at a particular location, depending upon who is best known in the community. In any event, to avoid inadvertent damage to the relationship by a management representative who does not possess the combination of firmness and diplomacy required, some continuity of the management contacts may be needed.

Emotional Nature of a Strike

Throughout the discussion in this and the preceding chapter, references have been made to the possibility that certain actions of the employer will inflame striking employees, generate bitterness, perhaps promote violence, and so on. None of these references is intended to indicate that the employer should take only such action as will be popular with employees. The fact is that nothing he does will be popular.

No implication is intended that the employer should pamper strikers, fail to discharge them for cause, fail to prosecute law violators, refuse to bring in replacements, or otherwise adopt a soft attitude. The fact that an employer is willing to take a strike—and attempt to continue operating in the face of it—precludes a soft approach. It is likely that during the course of the strike the employer must—to operate successfully, to prevent a bad situation from growing out of control, or for other reasons—take action without hesitation even though it will be bitterly resented by employees.

Furthermore, the references to the possibility of violence and other illegal activities are not intended to suggest that strikers automatically become a band of violent anarchists. While many employees on strike can, if the occasion arises, be led into some forms of improper activity (such as mass picketing), only a few, if any, will look for an opportunity to engage in pure violence. Most employees will require severe provocation before reacting with physical violence.

What is intended by all these references is to emphasize that the employer must have an understanding of and a plan to combat the emotional turmoil, internal conflicts, and bitter frustrations that are generated by strikes.

Unless the employer is able to maintain his perspective, his own decisions are likely to be influenced as much by emotion as by logic and business necessity. He is fighting to keep his business on a sound basis—perhaps to keep it from collapsing. He may have lost much of his normal understanding of and pride in his employees and may feel that they have turned against him.

However, he should try to understand how the strikers feel. They will sincerely believe the union is right on the issues that generated the strike. They will view the employer as unfair and unreasonable. They will feel that they are fighting for a better life for their families; if the employer takes action that appears to be a threat to their jobs, they will feel they are fighting to save their jobs.

The typical striker is likely to be a law-abiding citizen, loyal to his country, active in his church, proud of his family, and proud of the fact that he is a wage earner—not a charity case. Even so, under a strike situation, he may say and do things that are not natural for him. He may be so emotionally disturbed that he will react in a manner that is inconsistent with his basic character.

The employer should recognize this. He should realize that some of the things he does may be unpopular with but at least partially understandable to the striker, such as having supervisors work; while other things—such as the appearance of strike replacements or the failure of some fellow employees to participate in the strike—may set off a violent emotional storm. For the very few wholly irresponsible employees who are violent and untrustworthy by nature, no understanding or sympathy is called for. They are probably a continuous source of problems before, during, and after a strike.

Ideally, the employer should attempt to avoid driving a deep wedge between management and the large majority of the strikers. He should keep in mind the post-strike necessity of rebuilding employee morale, teamwork, and relationships with supervisors. The employer who keeps his own emotions under control and tries to develop an understanding and appreciation of his employees' feelings and problems during a strike has a tremendous advantage in planning how to operate and then carrying out operations in a way that maximizes the possibility of a satisfactory strike settlement and an accelerated post-strike adjustment period.

Binding Up the Wounds

Eric F. Jensen

THE STRIKE IS OVER. COMPANY AND UNION REPRESENTATIVES HAVE REACHED an agreement, the union membership has ratified it, and the men are returning to work. This is the way most end-of-contract strikes conclude. It is the way some wildcat strikes end too and can also apply to a strike during the term of the agreement, where the union has the right to strike rather than arbitrate over certain issues such as incentives.

Regardless of the kind of strike, now that the workers are returning to work, the question is what to do next. Depending on the length of the strike, there are a number of considerations which must be acted upon immediately. Experienced collective bargainers recognize that planning for the men's return to work must be done during the course of the strike simultaneously with, and as part of, negotiations with the union to arrive at the agreement. These considerations involve not only tactics relating to the negotiations, but also the steps that must be taken to put the plant or plants back in operation in an orderly manner without any undue or unnecessary expense or problem.

ERIC F. JENSEN is vice president—industrial relations of ACF Industries, Incorporated in New York City.

Agreement and Recall

It is likely that each industry will have its own particular problems in resuming full-scale operations after a strike. For example, in some industries where a strike has occurred, it has been preceded by the strikers' participating in the job of shutting down the facilities—banking fires in melting furnaces, shutting down transformer banks, and the like. There are some cases where maintenance men maintain certain equipment during a strike so that, when it is over, the equipment can be restored to full operation promptly. Of course, where there are a substantial number of men involved, such as in an industrywide strike, not all strikers can come back to work on the first day after the strike is ended. Thus a strike settlement agreement should include provisions for the manner and order of recalling men to work as well as for the period during which recalls may be made without grievances claiming violations of seniority or other contract provisions governing recall.

After a lengthy strike, it is of particular importance for management to have substantial flexibility in recall, at least for a period of time—perhaps a week or more—to insure that operations resume in the order which the company feels will be best in the long run. In most strike situations there are few if any production operations conducted while the strike is in progress. Thus start-up is usually a serious problem, and the importance of establishing an agreement with the union regarding recall of the strikers cannot be overemphasized.

If recall after a strike is primarily on the basis of seniority, the company will probably have to call back many employees who will not make any real contribution toward getting the plant started again quickly in order to get the relatively few persons whose role in the resumption of operations is paramount. This is an unduly costly process. Therefore, even if departmental seniority is the rule under the agreement, management should insist upon being allowed to recall first those individuals within each department whose role in the resumption of operations is essential. It is logical, then, that establishing the order of recall and the nature of the individuals to be recalled are usually covered in the final stages of negotiations.

A common approach to the problem of resumption of operations is to include a paragraph in the strike settlement agreement stating that, during the first week after the strike is over, the union will not file or process any

employee grievances alleging violations of seniority in connection with recalling men to work. By the same token, the company normally promises
that it will not use any basis for recall other than selecting people in the
order required for resuming operations. This promise, of course, is made to
assure the union that supervisory personnel will not engage in favoritism.

Initial steps in recall after a strike of any duration are of great consequence not only from the standpoint of smooth resumption of operations,
but also because they set the stage for the first contact between supervisors
and employees in a number of weeks. Steps that supervision should normally
follow in maintaining the proper attitude and developing esprit de corps,
morale, and so on will be discussed later. At this point, however, to avoid
any misunderstanding, it should be noted that recalling unnecessary
personnel—those who do not have specific assignments and real chores to
do—serves only to complicate the initial confrontation. (The returning men,
of course, know in general which employees are necessary to resume operations, and this must be kept in mind.)

OTHER SETTLEMENT ISSUES

Thus far we have discussed what to do when the strike is over by
focusing on the strike settlement agreement and recall. There are, of course,
many other issues that should go into the normal strike settlement agreement. This agreement, which is usually in addition to the labor, pension, and
insurance settlements, normally includes not only specifics as to recall but
also a company promise not to discriminate against strikers who engaged in
the strike and a corollary promise from the union that neither it nor its
members will discriminate in any way against nonstrikers. These promises
are important and probably should be given wide distribution and publicity
in the shop.

Another item a union usually wants included in most strike settlement
agreements is a company promise to drop any charges filed against the
union, such as an unfair labor practice alleging a refusal to bargain in good
faith or a suit for damages based on an event that occurred during the strike.
Whether to include such a promise is a matter for individual management
decision. Some companies are willing to wipe the slate clean. Others are not
and would rather prolong the strike if this is the only way to avoid such a
promise. Of course, the union may have filed charges of unfair labor practices against the company, and part of the settlement agreement may be that
both parties drop their respective charges.

It is not uncommon for unions to try to exact from management a promise that employees discharged for actions during the strike, such as violence on the picket line, be returned to work. Many unions have been successful in obtaining such a promise from management in the final stages of negotiations, particularly when resolution of all agreements depends on this issue. Understandably, management may agree to a union demand to waive discipline in its anxiety to get its plants back in operation. It is natural in such a situation to say, "All right, let bygones be bygones." Even so, management should consider such a promise very carefully before agreeing to it. Attitudes during a strike are at best difficult to estimate. It is one thing to have a "friendly" strike where the basic relationships between management and employees are not drastically altered by the fact that the employees ceased work and refused to return for a long period. It is quite another thing for strikers to engage in violence; threaten supervisors, non-union or salaried employees, or others; overturn automobiles; or engage in like actions and then be taken back without penalty at the strike's end. Before waiving discipline, management would do well to weigh the possibility of prolonging the strike in the light of the effects that the relaxing of discipline might have in possible future strikes and the effect on those who suffered by the violence as well as on first-line supervisors.

Should prolongation of the strike be likely but intolerable if discipline is not waived, a company may consider as a possible solution an offer of immediate arbitration in connection with any strikers who have been discharged because of violence. This would probably be a special arbitration since there was no labor agreement in effect when the violent actions occurred. If the strike was over terms and conditions of a new contract, such arbitration would mean that management may be giving up a unilateral right to discharge employees and, in fact, would be running the risk of having the arbitrator return the fired men to the company payroll. On the other hand, the facts under arbitration may be so clear that there is a strong likelihood that management's decision will be upheld. Again, management must decide for itself which course to take; and it helps to review and evaluate the discharges well in advance of decision time. Of course, where only one or a few employees have been disciplined for strike violence, there may be a good chance that the union will not be willing to prolong the strike, particularly if the economic terms of a new contract have been resolved and only the discharges are preventing a settlement.

Another issue that may well become important in strike settlement agreements is the union's right to discipline (fine) employees who cross the picket line and go in to work. A prime case of this is *NLRB* v. *Allis-*

Chalmers Mfg. Co. (388 U.S. 175), where the union imposed fines on employees who continued to work and employees who, after a few days on strike, crossed the picket line and returned to work. Under the law, it is possible that this may be considered an internal union problem and not subject to bargaining. On the other hand, if management relinquishes its right to discipline employees for strike violence, it may well be that the union in turn can be made to agree to let bygones be bygones and thus keep to a minimum the acrimony and animosity that would otherwise result. This is a difficult area, since the union may be reluctant to let down its members who have been on the picket lines just as the company may be unwilling to let down its supervisors by agreeing to take back employees who have engaged in violence during the strike.

The major items that have been or should be included in most strike settlement agreements have now been covered. Each company and union must work out its own strike settlement agreement; the nature of this agreement and the items included can do much toward properly binding up the wounds and allowing the parties to resume their relationship on a sound basis.

ATTITUDE OF SUPERVISORS

Just as important as a good strike settlement agreement is the proper shaping of the attitude of supervisors. The extreme importance of a proper reception for the returning strikers cannot be overemphasized. Thus the attitude of supervisors must be stressed and the instruction supervisors receive on how to handle the returning strikers must be exacting and detailed.

Most companies today keep supervision informed during the strike or during negotiations as to the major issues and management's position as well as that of the union. It is now common practice for letters to be written and meetings to be held to keep supervisors informed because top management as well as company negotiators are acutely conscious of the needs of supervisors. In this respect, there are a number of matters that must be dealt with so that supervisors can be properly prepared for resuming operations after the strike. This preparation, of course, should be done in advance.

Because the first meetings between supervisors and returning employees are so critical, written instructions and guidelines should be given to each supervisor. These instructions should be reviewed with supervisors in small group meetings by the industrial relations head, the manufacturing head, or both. Management should make explicitly clear that it expects the instructions to be followed.

Each company, of course, will have its own particular items to include in the instructions to supervisors, but all such instructions should include at least the following points:

- ✦ Greet each returning employee in such a way as to indicate that you are happy he is back at work.
- ✦ Avoid discussions regarding events which occurred during the strike, such as violence, court cases, unfair labor practice charges, and actions of individual employees or union officers.
- ✦ Do not in any way characterize union officers or members.
- ✦ It is likely that many of the employees were unsympathetic toward the strike. Some may have been subject to threats or coercion, which they find difficult to forget. In such cases, you as supervisor have a real opportunity to provide guidance and leadership while improving employee relationships.
- ✦ Avoid becoming too friendly with either the returning striker or the nonstriker. (Returning strikers will undoubtedly be oversensitive to any action that could be construed as showing partiality toward employees who stayed at work.) Also consider that the employee who did not strike is in a difficult situation vis-à-vis the striker.
- ✦ Do everything possible to make sure that employees are assigned to jobs and kept busy without giving the appearance of pushing them. This must be done quickly. Also, avoid having employees gather in groups.
- ✦ At this time, it is particularly important to treat all employees impartially. Go out of your way to see that this is done and to make the employees feel that you are impartial.
- ✦ Be alert for unusual happenings. Make frequent trips through the department to see that everything is running properly.
- ✦ Make an extra effort to provide advice and assistance to the employees on their jobs, as required.
- ✦ In general, show by your actions that you are really glad to have the employees back on the job.

In addition to instructions to supervisors, many companies write letters to the employees. Some companies write welcome-back letters to the returnees only, while others write to all employees expressing appreciation that the strike is over and asking them to concentrate on the job of getting the company going again as well as before the strike, if not better.

The latter approach, since it includes all employees, does not single out the strikers and thus makes their return a little easier.

In any event, a letter to employees that the strike is over is desirable. It is a sign that management is truly glad that the strike is over and that the employees are returning to work. It should expedite the process of resuming normal management-employee relationships, which is, after all, the main purpose of post-strike planning and action.

Administering the Contract

Kenneth F. Hubbard

T HE MAJOR DRAMA IN LABOR RELATIONS SEEMS TO OCCUR DURING THE CON-
tract negotiation proceedings. This is the period in which everyone involved has a vital interest—the company employees, the public at large, and
outside communications media. The duration of the negotiation proceedings
usually ranges from two months down to the deadline and actual expiration
date of the contract. It can be a very emotional time-span because of the
nature of collective bargaining; it is also one that can lead to the formation
of attitudes that are almost unreal.

The union can propagandize and usually does, using strike threats pro-
claiming that its members will shut the place down if their demands aren't
met. The company, on the other hand, can react to these threats by indicating that it is prepared to take a strike if necessary in order to uphold its
management responsibilities and remain competitive in the pricing of its
product. Finally, the public in general can react and usually does, depending
on which side it favors or how its interests seem to be affected. The public
may actually suspend its belief in the validity of the union's demands and in
management's reaction to those demands.

KENNETH F. HUBBARD is manager of the General Management Division of the American
Management Association.

But in spite of what appears to be an impossible situation and in many cases a misunderstood one, a written agreement finally emerges between the parties—the union and management—which is formally known as a collective bargaining agreement or contract. This sets the stage for the beginning of a continuing relationship between the parties. The contract that has been negotiated becomes the basis for a working relationship between the employees represented by the union and the management representatives who are responsible for the direction of those employees in achieving overall work objectives. These two groups therefore play a vital role in contract administration. What they do and how they do it will be crucial to its success.

CELEBRATING THE SIGNING

Regardless of the type of negotiation, be it a difficult one or a relatively simple procedure (although few ever admit to this) there is, in many instances, a certain fanfare attached to the formal contract signing process and the immediate period thereafter. It is a form of celebration that signals the end of hostilities and perhaps, what's more important, alludes to future relationships in an optimistic fashion. This is looked upon by some as a public relations gesture of questionable value. However, there must be some method by which the union and company negotiators can minimize the antagonism that may have developed during the negotiations and indicate to those not actually involved in the negotiations that bygones are bygones. Thus, at least for the moment, major differences that may have existed are reconciled. To put it simply, a conclusion has been arrived at and, hopefully, a working relationship can now be developed between the parties.

It is presumed, of course, that such a relationship is desirable to the company in achieving its overall business objectives. So perhaps the signing ceremony can be defined as a public relations gesture with labor relations ramifications. The ceremonial form does not seem to be that decisive. It can be a major proceeding attended by company and union brass and a press corps or a simple approach during normal business hours attended only by the company and union representatives who will be involved in the everyday labor relations decision-making process. In any case, it is imperative that the ceremony take place regardless of the negotiation process that preceded it. It should be performed no matter how many contracts have been negotiated between the parties and regardless of the relative ease or difficulty in arriving at the settlement.

DISTRIBUTING COPIES

Duplicating and distributing the new contract in printed booklet form is a relatively uncomplicated task. Although management is under no legal obligation to do so, it may choose to print and distribute the new contract at its own expense to all its employees. Or distribution may be made to management-level employees only, down to whatever level of management may seem expedient. Often this will depend upon the size of the company or the level of management involved in implementing the contract.

Should management decide to limit distribution of copies of the new contract to the managerial group, it leaves to the union, of course, the task of making copies available to the bargaining-unit employees. This seems to be the key point and one worthy of consideration from an overall employee relations standpoint. The artistic considerations of contract format—size, color, and shape—seem to make little difference; the only suggestion is that, as a form of identification, new language should be shown in bold type to give a ready reference to those who will work with the contract.

INSTRUCTING SUPERVISORS

During the life of the contract the supporting levels of management, which in the overwhelming majority of cases were not actively involved in the negotiations, must assume active roles in the contract administration. This is a continuous process and one that has come in for a great deal of research and discussion. The supervisor has been portrayed, among other things, in such colorful terminology as management's first line of defense or the go/no-go element in carrying out a company's labor relations program. It is difficult to quarrel with this point of view, and no attempt will be made here to take issue with this premise. It is true that the supervisor is in most cases the initial contact between company and union, and, in the day-to-day administration of a contract, he is accountable for the initial company response and union demands. However, a realistic labor relations approach by sophisticated management will exercise a reasonable degree of control over the supervisor's actions, thus precluding leaving all the company's eggs in one basket, so to speak.

The control process, from the veteran labor relations practitioner's standpoint, is not an easy task. The reasons for this are many and varied; but basically a lower-level supervisory force is under pressures, self-imposed or not, that have an impact on its everyday union relationships. First, the supervisor is principally responsible for a work objective which entails a knowledge of product and processes, budget controls, quality of product, and methods improvement, among other things. Second, he may have a span of control that encompasses several employees or different types of operations. Third, his decision-making process may not allow for a great deal of reflective or in-depth thinking (the heavily production-oriented industries, for example, are extremely vigorous). Fourth, he may be confronted with a union representative who is quite inventive and who, being an elected representative, may feel a strong obligation to produce a certain amount of harassment or grievance activity. (The union representative, because of the contract agreement, may be able to devote most of his time if not full time to this activity.) Fifth, the supervisor may have a mistaken notion of his role in the administration process. Finally, no matter how adept a supervisor may be at implementing contract language, there can be a strong judgment factor involved in labor relations.

These are only some of the considerations that upper management is confronted with in trying to establish an administrative control mechanism over its labor relations. A launching point of this control is a sound development/communication program wherein contract language changes are presented to the supervisor by a management representative who can transpose the legalities into a working environment. This can be accomplished in formal training sessions with all the trappings—visual aids and the rest—or in individual counseling sessions on a personalized basis.

Obviously, the intent of the language, whether a clause is company-sponsored or based on a union demand, should be translated to the supervisor. This is based on the premise that contract language, no matter how honorable the intent, can be somewhat ambiguous and not crystal clear to those who are not experts in negotiations. No one should expect that all possible eventualities can be foreseen; but cautiously and conservatively the supervisor should be informed of possible future action that a union might take and offered a management interpretation of ways to offset the union demand. Hopefully, this will give the supervisor an intuitive feel or sixth sense and allow him a sense of projection.

Because of the scope and complexity of many contracts, it is unreasonable to expect a supervisor to be able to quote chapter and verse of all articles and sections in a contract. In the educational process, he should not be expected to become a benefits expert or to have a close familiarity with a complicated pension plan. The type of questions that he will be confronted with will probably involve the assignment of work (including overtime distribution), discipline and discharge, production standards, incentive violations, promotion, and the like. Hours of work, wages, and working conditions tend to relate to an everyday working world from the supervisor's standpoint; but, even in these areas with which he is familiar, there can tend to be shades of gray where he will require counseling.

RECORDING EXPERIENCE

The number of grievances, oral or written, that will arise during the term of the contract will undoubtedly depend on the union, management's policies and procedures, and the contract itself. It is through the grievance procedure that the company can find out what is actually going on in the plant.

A records control system can be set up which will show types and categories of grievances, date filed, who is involved, and disposition. How formal or sophisticated this should be depends of course on the size and geographic spread of an organization. It can be disturbing to find that one company location is taking a position at variance with another location on a particular issue when this could be avoided through proper communication. To this end, the lines of communication must be kept open both upward and downward. It is certain that a hard-working union will be doing the same thing to achieve uniformity of action among its members.

The supervisor should be impressed with his obligation. It is his responsibility to understand the details of the matter and to get all the facts before rendering a disposition. If he is in doubt about contract interpretation or its applications, he should be in a position to obtain competent assistance from a knowledgeable labor relations source. Without this, of course, he may resort to settling the grievance merely to avoid trouble and thereby establish precedents that may have catastrophic consequences.

Even with the various managerial information systems and controls that have been discussed, the supervisor will find himself confronted with many judgment decisions that have to be made in carrying out his part of the collective bargaining process. To a great degree, how well he does will depend on his makeup and his success in interpersonal relationships. Administratively, as many companies know, the supervisor cannot operate in a vacuum, and it is only through constant labor relations guidance that he will become consistent and effective in contract administration.

WILDCAT STRIKES

The ultimate occurrence during the term of a contract is a work stoppage, sometimes referred to as a wildcat strike. This is a flagrant violation, in most instances, presuming of course that a so-called no-strike clause is incorporated into the agreement. A wildcat strike is an action wherein employees resort to self-help rather than attempting redress through the normal channels of the grievance procedure. The reasons for such stoppages are numerous and varied, but certain characteristics can be associated with them, such as a heavy buildup of grievances, disciplinary action taken against one or more employees possibly including a union steward or committeeman, and a change in working conditions instituted by management that has not received the blessing of the union.

In the wildcat situation the supervisor is the man in the middle and is responsible, in most cases, for taking quick action to offset the union maneuver. For this reason it is wise to offer him instruction in what he should and should not do. The following are some of the measures the supervisor should take if and when he is confronted with a work stoppage:

+ Instruct the employees involved to return to work immediately. There should be no mistake about this, and, if practicable, it should be done in the presence of the employees' union representative.
+ Avoid becoming involved in judging the merits of the case at this point and refrain from any discussion until the employees have returned to work.
+ As soon as time permits, write a detailed description of the proceedings including time, date, and names of those involved—with particular emphasis on the leadership—and a verbatim account of his conversation with the employer and the union representative.
+ Communicate immediately with the management representative responsible for labor relations.

✦ Prepare for any disciplinary action to be taken against the employees involved—which will, in many cases, be performed with the assistance of the company's labor relations representative.

The ability of a supervisor to discourage a work stoppage—or other flagrant violations, for that matter—may well depend upon the extent to which the employees identify with him. If the supervisor has the necessary leadership qualities to control and direct the work of others and does not relinquish his position to an ambitious union representative who is not supposed to lead but to represent, he may be the decisive influence in solving or at least minimizing the many problems arising during the contract term.

SIDE AGREEMENTS

Although all management people should take a uniform position as to what the contract means, it is inevitable that some will like what it means less than others. The contract will be difficult to administer in some departments, easy to administer in others. Some department managers will wish that the contract said something different—at least in their departments; thus the temptation to make a side agreement with the union, applicable in the particular department and supplementing or overriding the master contract.

Such an agreement usually produces conditions of employment better suited to the local scene. But it exacts a price. It introduces competition between department heads and forces the reader to read more than one document to learn what the conditions of employment are. Accordingly, the employer should give careful consideration to the subjects, if any, on which side agreements may be made.

When any department manager or local plant manager makes a side agreement, he should make sure that two points are clear: (1) Do the general provisions of the master contract apply to the side agreement? For example, do the definitions apply? And does the arbitration clause apply? (2) When will the side agreement expire? When the term ends? After a reasonable time? Or when either party unilaterally wants to end the side agreement?

The Rival Union

Seymour Goldstein

THIS CHAPTER DEALS WITH THE PRINCIPAL PROBLEMS FACING AN EMPLOYER when he is—usually suddenly—confronted with the entrance into the picture of a new, rival union. It is presupposed that the employer has for some fair period of time had an ongoing relationship with an incumbent union. Long having accepted, with or without good grace, the presence of the incumbent union, the employer probably has adjusted to the development of an appropriate role for that union.

The employer may now be enjoying a stable relationship with the union which is, at the minimum, tolerable and, at the maximum, desirable. On the other hand, owing to his inability to adjust or perhaps even despite his best efforts to do so, the employer may have been having a difficult time of it with the incumbent union. The majority of the employees may be basically satisfied with the character of the incumbent union, its past accomplishments, and the personality of its leadership. Or they may be somewhat—or even completely—restless, dissatisfied, and clearly ready for change.

The employer and the incumbent union will undoubtedly have been parties to a series of contracts over the years. The current contract between them may yet have a considerable time to run. On the other hand, the current contract may be about to expire.

SEYMOUR GOLDSTEIN is a partner in the law firm of Kaye, Scholer, Fierman, Hays & Handler in New York City.

The rival union, newly entering the arena, may merely be engaging in the very early throes of union organizational activity with or without much inside employee support. Or it may formally request recognition of the employer almost immediately, asserting its majority status. In many instances it may even file a petition for an election with the Labor Board simultaneously with the first notification of its interest to the employer. The employer may be pleased at the reputation or record of the rival union or he may be fearful of the harm it may cause his interests.

Under all these various alternative circumstances, the sudden and often unexpected intervention by the rival union raises a number of serious problems—both tactical and legal—for the employer. It will be necessary for him to cope with these problems and to try to tailor his actions to provide satisfactory answers.

Is neutrality between the incumbent union and the rival union mandated by law? If not, to what extent can the employer legally express or act upon his preferences, and what are the outer limits of such employer intervention in a campaign between two unions?

Apart from any possible legal right of the employer to take a stand in the battle between the two unions, is neutrality toward the two unions, as a matter of policy, advisable for the employer? What discrimination or special treatment in favor of the incumbent union does its apparent majority status render justifiable? What discrimination or special treatment in favor of the incumbent union does an existing labor contract with the employer justify? Finally, when does a question concerning representation arise which compels the employer to participate in a binding determination as to which union enjoys majority support (usually through the vehicle of an election conducted by the Labor Board)?

This chapter deals with these questions. It must be stressed, however, that the solutions to these problems depend in substantial measure upon individual circumstances. Thus a creative approach which assesses "universalisms" in the light of the particular needs is essential. To the extent that legal judgments are required, there is no satisfactory substitute for consultation with qualified counsel.

LEGALITY OF EMPLOYER NEUTRALITY

From a purely legal point of view, the employer, if he desires to intervene in the organizational campaign, is *not* required to maintain strict neutrality between the incumbent union and the rival union. Of course, he may not assist, by word or conduct, one of the unions in a manner which would be deemed unlawful even in the one-union situation. Nor may he provide specific unfair advantage to one side. Thus he cannot financially support one union's campaign or pay for counsel or facilities for one union; nor may he dominate or control one union. However, he is not legally required to maintain silence in the face of a campaign between the two unions.

The employer may speak or act, within appropriate restrictions to be discussed later, for the purpose of protecting his own interests or that of his employees. Far from prescribing silence or mandating neutrality, in the National Labor Relations Act as amended Congress explicitly permits any party, including an employer, to express and disseminate any views, arguments, or opinions concerning matters covered by the statute—such as rival organizational campaigns—as long as the conduct contains no threat of reprisal or force and no promise of benefit.

It is certainly true that some of the decisions of the Labor Board are rather restrictive, limiting the statutory area of employer free speech and sometimes finding a threat or a promise lurking in what appears to be an innocent statement. Nevertheless, even the Labor Board has never required an employer to maintain strict neutrality with the entry of a rival union, but has allowed active employer intervention as long as the employer sticks to the sometimes changing and puzzling rules of the game.

The Do's and Don'ts of Employer Conduct

Since the employer is not required by law to maintain absolute neutrality in the battle between the incumbent union and the rival union, it may be fruitful to explore briefly the principal restrictions on employer participation which are applicable. In summary, it can be said that an employer in a two-union situation is subject to substantially the same kinds of restrictions as is an employer confronted with an organizational campaign by a single union. Thus, for example, the employer may not question any employee as to his leanings toward, attitudes concerning, or affiliation with one or the other union; nor may an employee be questioned concerning the leanings, attitudes, and affiliations of other employees. Even a secret private poll on these matters, however fairly conducted, must be avoided. Of course, receiving information or views volunteered by an employee on the subject of the unions' campaigns is not improper; but an employee's views should not be solicited by the employer.

Obviously, no promises of benefits to be granted by the employer can be made to any employee on the condition, express or implied, that he oppose one union or support the other. On the other hand, prescheduled benefits provided under the union contract may continue to be granted on their respective effective dates. No threats of reprisal such as discharge, lower wages, or a plant shutdown can be made to an employee because of his support of one union rather than the other. No discriminatory treatment can in fact be imposed because an employee favors the undesired union. Employees cannot be advised that selection of one particular union would be absolutely useless and futile because that union would secure nothing in collective bargaining or would secure less than the other union.

In the area of rival campaigns conducted by the respective unions, the decisions of the Labor Board provide further employer restrictions which require, not neutrality, but fair and nondiscriminatory treatment with respect to the organizational efforts of each union. Thus an employee normally cannot be prevented from wearing a union button or other modest-size union insignia in the plant. No employee can be prohibited from talking up or soliciting for one union rather than the other during his own free time, whether his efforts take place at his work station, in the lunchroom or washroom, or anywhere else inside or outside the plant—as long as he does not disturb any other employee who is actually engaged in work. However, an employee *can* be barred from such discussion or solicitation during his own actual working time, but not during his lunch periods, coffee breaks, and the like—even if he is paid for such time. An employee cannot be barred from handing out literature in the plant in favor of either union as long as he does so in nonworking areas and on his nonworking time; he may be barred from handing out literature on his own free time in any working area, however.

The employer need not open up his bulletin boards and other plant facilities to either of the competing unions (except under certain contractual arrangements to be discussed later). Generally, all nonemployee union organizers can be barred from solicitation or speech making on company premises unless there is no other point of employee access. They can, however, solicit on the sidewalks in front of the plant and at the entrances to parking lots. If employees normally drive out of the parking lot too speedily for feasible solicitation, the outside union organizer must also be permitted to solicit inside the lot.

Although the employer legally may express his partisan views if they are free of threat or promise, there are certain procedural restrictions further qualifying this right. For example, employees cannot be called one by one or in small groups into any private office or similar plant location overtly symbolizing management authority in order to discuss either union, even if the discussion is otherwise free of any taint. Such informal discussions with one or more employees may, however, be carried out in the plant at the employee's work station or other public, nonauthoritative location, such as aisles, corridors, lunchrooms, washrooms, or parking lot.

Systematic visits by members of management to employees' homes to discuss the pros and cons of either union are also considered improper. Petitions in support of one union or against another may not be circulated or instigated by the employer, although he may permit *both* unions to do so. An employee favoring one union should not be given greater privileges or a greater license to campaign in the plant than an employee favoring the other union (subject only to certain contract rights of the incumbent to be discussed later). The employer may make speeches to captive audiences of employees in the plant without granting equal time to the unions (if equal time *is* granted, *both* unions must get it), subject only to the qualification that such speeches are prohibited within 24 hours before an election conducted by the Labor Board.

In exercising his legal right to speak freely in favor of one union or against the other, the employer may make statements to the employees on the following points:

+ Employees may be reminded of existing benefits and past improvements of such benefits, and it may be pointed out to them that these and other favorable working conditions were attained through the efforts of the incumbent union.
+ Employees may be told that the rival union is unfamiliar with or not geared to handle their problems. It can be pointed out that the rival union employs as paid representatives persons who are strangers to the community, to the company, and to the particular kinds of problems present in the plant.
+ The employer may properly argue that the financial costs of employee affiliation with a particular union, in the light of its dues structure, fees, and assessments, may outweigh any advantages offered by the union.
+ The employer may cite the record of a particular union with respect to strikes and boycotts, cautioning employees as to the risks and costs of engaging in labor disputes involving cessation of work.

+ The employer may point out that a particular union pursues an unduly restrictive seniority policy, thwarting individual initiative and advancement.
+ The employer may characterize the propaganda or campaign of a particular union as false, misleading, inaccurate, exaggerated, or incomplete.
+ The employer may recite to the employees with factual accuracy the history of either union and may condemn the record, policies, or reputation of either union.

WHEN IS EMPLOYER NEUTRALITY ADVISABLE?

We have seen that the employer is legally free to reject neutrality and to take a strong partisan position in favor of or against either union in a two-union situation. The only restrictions on his conduct are of the kind previously discussed—those imposed by the Congress in the statutes and by the Labor Board in its interpretations of the statutes. Accepting this legal license, is it tactically sound for the employer to take an active and partisan role or is it better policy for him to maintain surface neutrality?

The answer to this policy question in any particular situation is obviously not an easy one. It requires a balancing of two countervailing policy considerations. On the one hand, the employer owes it to his employees, to his own interests, and to his sense of pride and integrity to proclaim his views on the often difficult matter of selecting between two unions competing for the allegiance of the employees.

Employees naturally tend to look, consciously or not, to their employer as at least one source of counsel or information in evaluating the merits of two competing choices. Despite the current cynicism as to employer-employee relations, it is still a defensible position to contend that many employees, even those who do not identify with management, still maintain considerable respect for management's judgment and sources of information.

If the employer fails to take a public position in the contest between the two unions, these employees may well presume that the employer simply does not care enough about the choice that they, the uninformed employees, are forced to make. The employees are thus left to flounder and to depend upon the propaganda efforts of each union. Silence or neutrality on the part of the employer may cause him to lose irrevocably his golden opportunity to sway even the few undecided and perhaps decisive votes in the preferred direction. In short, the employer who maintains strict neutrality despite his secret preference is undoubtedly letting down his employees and abandoning a part of his self-respect, a course of conduct which may redound to his serious detriment by permitting a bad choice to become the bargaining agent.

On the other hand, it is certainly realistic to observe that employer statements or conduct constituting a departure from neutrality by taking a partisan and even activist role in the two-union campaign do raise the serious risk of at least two possible adverse effects: First, the union that is the beneficiary of the employer's expressed preference is likely to forget that favor before long and dissipate the employer's "credit." And the union that has been the victim of the employer's partisanship—if successful in the campaign despite the employer's opposition—may be forced by pique or the need to show its muscles to retaliate against the employer. Thus failure to pick a winner can be fatal. Second, since some employees are rather independent souls who resent instruction from authority or interference with the exercise of their own free choice, a strong preference expressed by an employer may, in some instances, produce a strong backlash effect which can result in a defeat of the employer's choice.

In most instances these contradictory options can be balanced through intelligent assessment of the particular situation and all its factors and through careful determination of the safest course of action. Faced with this apparent dilemma, many employers successfully find an appropriate accommodation of the two counterbalancing choices, geared to the particular circumstances. Where the union preferred by the employer appears to face either almost certain victory or defeat, the employer generally tends to remain relatively silent or neutral. Where the outcome of the campaign is in more serious doubt, however—which is quite frequently the case—many employers exercise their legal right to take sides but manage to carry out their program in a manner which does the least harm while achieving the greatest gain.

Thus, where the favored union itself carries out a vigorous, hard-hitting, and perhaps noisy campaign, the employer finds it wise to express his views in relatively milder and less belligerent tones. Such an employer generally sets out for his employees the germane facts, obviously stressing those elements in favor of the preferred union but trying not to appear too argumentative. Then he declares in a relatively dignified manner his conclusion as to the choice he feels will best serve the interests of the employees. Such a high-road approach (leaving the low road to the favored union if that fits the union's character) generally conveys the point to the employees without ambiguity, satisfies the employer's feeling of obligation to his employees and to himself, and meets the expectations of the favored union—all done, hopefully, without creating a strong desire for retaliation on the part of the unfavored union and without creating the monster of a backlash vote.

It must be stressed as axiomatic that the specific approach utilized by an employer must be tailored for his particular situation. However, much can be said in favor of a program of controlled nonneutrality.

Special Status of the Incumbent Union

Next to be considered is the extent to which the majority status of the incumbent union or the contractual provisions between an employer and the incumbent union may justify discriminatory treatment in favor of that union. Normally, majority status on the part of one union, even without a union contract, brings with it a special standing under the law which entitles that union to special treatment of a much higher order than any of its rivals, actual or potential. Thus the incumbent union that enjoys majority status has the right to insist upon exclusive recognition by the employer, bringing with it the exclusive right to speak for all employees in their dealings with the employer, to negotiate a contract on a wide variety of subjects, to meet and confer with the employer upon all such negotiable matters, to receive detailed information permitting it to intelligently represent employees and negotiate for them, to process grievances on behalf of employees, and, generally, to represent the employees' total interests vis-à-vis the employer regarding wages, hours, and all other terms and conditions of employment.

The legal authority of the incumbent union is extensive and tends to be self-perpetuating, particularly when publicized favorably. On the other hand, the actual or potential rival union, which does not enjoy legally provable majority status, is not entitled to such recognition or to any rights which flow therefrom. The rival union's rights are pretty much restricted to an organizational campaign—a kind of selling program. Thus, under normal circumstances, an employer may treat with and, indeed, *must* treat with the incumbent majority union on a basis which is clearly far more substantial than the extremely limited role of the rival union.

However, this special position of the incumbent union presumptively enjoying continuing majority status changes radically in one circumstance: If an employer is suddenly confronted, after the first year following certification by the Labor Board of the incumbent union, with a conflicting claim of representation in an appropriate unit of employees on behalf of a rival union and that claim raises a real question concerning representation, the employer must cease granting exclusive recognition to the incumbent union and must deal with each union on the basis of equal treatment, with each representing only its own members. What constitutes a real question concerning representation will be discussed later.

The rationale behind the decisions of the Labor Board establishing the foregoing principle is this: Given the existence of a real question concerning representation which can be resolved conclusively only by a Labor Board election (if such an election is timely requested), the employer cannot unilaterally determine that question himself without such an election merely on the basis of his own presumptions or investigation of majority status. Rather, pending binding determination of the question concerning representation through a Labor Board election, the employer must withdraw discriminatory privileges (except for certain contractual matters to be discussed later) and must treat both unions as if they enjoyed equal status as contenders for the crown of ultimate exclusive recognition.

The existence of a union contract providing both substantive benefits for employees (wages, hours, and working conditions) and organizational benefits for the incumbent union (such as union security clauses, dues checkoff, grievance representation, paid time off for representation purposes, super-seniority for union officials, the right to certain notices and information, and the use of company bulletin boards and other facilities) raises serious legal problems when the rival union appears on the scene. Certainly, it is indisputable that the employer may and, indeed, *must* honor the substantive contract benefit provisions setting out wages, hours, and working conditions for employees, despite the entrance of a rival union and even if the rival union raises a real question of representation which temporarily deprives the incumbent union of exclusive recognition status. Moreover, even with regard to the contract organizational benefits which inure directly to the incumbent union, the mere existence of a rival union, however active, does not deprive the incumbent of such contractual advantages at least until a real question concerning representation is properly raised by the rival union.

The more difficult legal problem arises with regard to honoring contractual organizational advantages on the part of an incumbent union *after* the rival union has raised a real question concerning representation—for example, by filing a petition for a Labor Board election. The Labor Board and the courts have not always been clear and consistent in applying the law to this problem. However, it can probably be said with some degree of certainty that those contractual provisions which, while benefiting the incumbent union, are clearly necessary to carry out its normal functions on behalf of employees under the contract may and should be honored.

In essence, the rival union's presence does not invalidate contract provisions previously negotiated. Thus the incumbent union can certainly continue to administer the contract and carry out its functions under the grievance procedure, including, for example, enjoying paid time off to process grievances, even though the rival union does not enjoy this right.

Access to company facilities and use of bulletin boards and other physical facilities by the incumbent union may also continue, at least for union announcements and similar purposes which are authorized and necessary under the union contract. It should be pointed out, however, that while the Labor Board has permitted continued exclusive use of bulletin boards by the incumbent union without affording the rival union the same opportunity, the board has barred contract clauses which would freeze out any solicitation or literature distribution by a rival union even during nonworking time. The courts have not always agreed with the Labor Board on this point, and the matter is still subject to further litigation and consideration.

While the line to be drawn is thus a somewhat fuzzy one, it may be best depicted by saying that, even when a real question concerning representation is raised by a rival union, the incumbent union may still receive those contractual advantages which are obviously necessary to carry out specific functions under the contract on behalf of employees and which do not imply continued exclusivity of representational status—even though this may enhance the prestige of the incumbent union. On the other hand, enforcement of any contractual provisions that are privileges going with exclusive recognition but are not a necessary function benefiting employees, and that unduly emphasize exclusivity, are probably not permissible once the rival union has raised a real question concerning representation. In any event, it should be reemphasized that the law in this area is less than certain and an employer should act with great caution, perhaps erring on the side of circumspection.

QUESTION CONCERNING REPRESENTATION

The last problem to be considered is this: When does a question concerning representation arise? As we have seen, the existence of a real question concerning representation raised by a rival union requires an employer to halt exclusive recognition of the incumbent union and to deal with each union on an equality-of-treatment, members-only basis. Moreover, the existence of such a question concerning representation normally requires the employer to undergo a formal organizational campaign culminating in a Labor-Board-conducted election where one or the other union is usually the victor.

The existence or nonexistence of a question concerning representation is subject to many decisionary rules of the Labor Board. This is particularly true in rival union situations where the detailed principles of so-called contract bar prevail. Generally it can be said that a question concerning representation arises when a rival union—usually but not necessarily after oral or written communication to the employer requesting recognition and asserting an alleged majority status—files a petition with the Labor Board asking for an election. As an initial condition, such a petition must be supported by the signatures, in appropriate form, of at least 30 percent of the employees in the bargaining unit. Moreover, to raise a proper and real question concerning representation, a rival union election petition must be filed in a timely fashion; that is, it must be filed during certain specific time periods. Thus it cannot be filed during the first year after Labor Board certification of the incumbent union. Moreover, the timeliness of such a petition raises questions as to the application of the intricate contract bar rules of the Labor Board.

The principal contract bar rules of the Labor Board are as follows:

+ If there is no union contract in existence with the incumbent union at the time of filing, the rival union election petition is clearly timely filed.
+ If an existing contract with an incumbent union contains an illegal union security clause (such as the closed shop or requiring that new employees join the union in less than 30 days), the petition is timely filed despite the existence of the contract.
+ Assuming the existence of a lawful contract of any specified duration with the incumbent union, during the time of up to the first three years of any such contract a rival union election petition may be filed only between the 90th and the 60th day prior to the expiration or termination date of the contract (or prior to the end of the third year if the contract runs longer than three years).
+ A rival union election petition filed earlier than the 90–60-day

filing period will be dismissed by the Labor Board as premature and untimely.

+ An election petition filed during the last 60 days of the contract (or during the last 60 days of the third year of a longer contract) will be dismissed as untimely since this 60 days is deemed an "insulated period" during which the employer and the incumbent union may freely negotiate for a new contract (and contract bar) without being concerned with rival union intervention.

+ Once the 60-day period has expired and as long as no new contract has been executed, a rival union petition is again timely despite any continuing negotiations between the employer and the incumbent union.

+ Early extension of a contract far in advance of its prescribed expiration date will not create a new contract bar period; filing of a rival union petition during the 90–60-day period prior to its original expiration date will still be considered timely.

In the face of the filing of a timely rival union petition for election, resolution of the difficult legal and tactical problems discussed in this chapter becomes of paramount importance to the employer. For he is, in a real sense, in the middle of a situation over which he has only limited control.

Index

About the Authors

VINCENT R. D'ALESSANDRO is director of industrial relations for Sinclair Oil Corporation in New York City since 1961, having been a staff member in that department since 1946. He graduated with a B.A. from Manhattan College and received an LL.B. Fordham Law School. He is a director of the Tanker Service Committee and a member of the National Petroleum Refiners Association and the American Petroleum Institute. He is also a member of the National Association of Manufacturers Subcommittee on Labor Relations and the Industrial Relations Research Association. He has lectured at labor relations conferences for the past ten years. In addition, he has participated in numerous panel discussions and as guest speaker before various association groups throughout the country, including Industrial Relations Counselors' Williamsburg seminar and Notre Dame University's 15th Labor Conference (1967), the proceedings of which have been published.

ARNOLD F. CAMPO is director of industrial relations for International Salt Company in Clarks Summit, Pennsylvania. He is a graduate of the University of Santa Clara. Prior to joining International Salt Company, he was associated with the American Can Company in New York City. During World War II Mr. Campo served as a member of the National War Labor Board in San Francisco. In 1952 he was appointed by the President to the National Wage Stabilization Board Steel Panel. He is chairman of the National Association of Manufacturers Committee on Collective Bargaining. Mr. Campo teaches a course in industrial relations at the University of Scranton Graduate School and has written several articles on collective bargaining. He has also been a frequent speaker at leading universities and at management seminars.

WILLIAM J. CURTIN is a partner in the law firm of Morgan, Lewis & Bockius and heads the labor section of that firm's Washington, D.C. office. He specializes in the representation of management in labor relations law matters. Mr. Curtin was admitted to practice in 1956 and is a member of the Bar of the U.S. Supreme Court. He was awarded LL.B. and LL.M. degrees (concentrating in labor law) from Georgetown University Law Center. Mr. Curtin is a public member of the Administrative Conference of the United States, a member of the American Bar Association's Special Committee on Strikes in the Transportation Industries, and chairman of the Labor Relations Law Committee of the Public Utility Section of the American Bar Association. He is a recipient of the American Arbitration Association's Award for Labor Management Peace for 1966. He also serves as editor of the "Negotiated Employee Benefit Plans Service" of the National Foundation of Health, Welfare and Pension Plans, Inc.

FRANK P. DOYLE is vice president—public and employee relations of the Western Union Telegraph Company. Before joining Western Union in 1967 he served as corporate director—industrial relations at American Standard, Inc. There he planned and directed the company's successful response to union efforts to coordinate bargaining for American Standard's more than 100 separate labor contracts. At both Western Union and American Standard, Mr. Doyle was responsible for restructuring personnel organizations within rapidly changing corporate environments. He is a frequent lecturer on labor matters.

SEYMOUR GOLDSTEIN is a partner in the New York law firm of Kaye, Scholer, Fierman, Hays & Handler, specializing in the practice of labor law. He graduated with honors from the College of the City of New York and New York University Law School, where he was an editor of the *Law Review*. Mr. Goldstein was a trial attorney and hearing officer with the National Labor Relations Board prior to joining his law firm, where he represents management clients in the private sector in connection with labor relations problems. He is a frequent lecturer on labor relations.

ROBERT G. HENNEMUTH is vice president—industrial relations of Raytheon Company in Lexington, Massachusetts. He was graduated from Syracuse University and Harvard Law School. His association with Raytheon Company extends over 18 years, first in the company's law department, then in recent years as head of the company's activities in labor relations, personnel administration, legislative matters, management development, equal employment opportunities, medical services, and security. He is a member of the Massachusetts and Federal Bars.

DONALD E. HOCK is director of industrial relations for J. I. Case Company, a leading manufacturer of agricultural and construction equipment located in Racine, Wisconsin. Mr. Hock is a graduate of Grinnell College. He is a member of the American Society of Personnel Administration and the Bureau of National Affairs Personnel Forum, and he has been a frequent speaker at seminars on industrial relations.

JAMES F. HONZIK is a member of the Milwaukee law firm of Lamfrom, Peck, Ferebee & Brigden, which specializes in representing management in labor-management relations. He previously spent 15 years with the Jos. Schlitz Brewing

Co. as director of legal, economic, and labor relations. He has frequently spoken before civic and business groups. Early in his career he served on the international staff of a labor union. He obtained his LL.B. and J.D. degrees from Marquette University.

KENNETH F. HUBBARD is manager of the General Management Division of the American Management Association. Prior to joining AMA in 1964, he served in labor relations capacities with the Ford Motor Company and Merck & Company, Inc. on both line and staff assignments. He is a graduate of Cornell University.

ERIC F. JENSEN is vice president—industrial relations of ACF Industries, Incorporated in New York City. He received his B.S. degree in industrial relations from Cornell University and his LL.B. from Brooklyn Law School, and he also has completed the Advanced Management Program at Harvard. He was admitted to the New York Bar in 1956. Prior to joining ACF in 1961, Mr. Jensen was associated with Bethlehem Steel for nine years, the last five as an arbitration attorney. He is a member of the American Bar Association, the Brooklyn Law School Law Review Association, Cornell Alumni Association, and the Advisory Council of the New York State School of Industrial and Labor Relations at Cornell University, and he is a director and past president of the Industrial Relations Society of New York.

LEROY MARCEAU has counseled unions, employers, and both federal and state governments on labor law. He is author of the familiar textbook, *Drafting a Union Contract,* and is currently labor counsel for the Standard Oil Company (New Jersey).

EDWARD J. McMAHON is vice president and director of industrial relations at St. Regis Paper Company in New York City. He has been with St. Regis since 1947, starting as a personnel trainee. He has a strong interest in national, state, and local programs for the disadvantaged. He is a member of the American Paper Institute and Fibre Box Association's Personnel and Industrial Relations Committee; the Labor Relations Committee of the U.S. Chamber of Commerce; and the Commerce and Industry Committee of the National Urban League. He is also a member of the Industrial Relations Society.

CLIFFORD R. OVIATT, JR. is a partner in the Connecticut law firm of Cummings and Lockwood. He was graduated from Wesleyan University and Cornell Law School. Mr. Oviatt is a member of the Ad Hoc Committee on Practice and Procedure in Labor Arbitration of the American Bar Association; the Committee on the Improvement of the Administration of Justice of the American Bar Association; and the Connecticut Bar Association. He was admitted to practice in New York and Connecticut, the Court of Appeals for Second Circuit, and the Supreme Court of the United States. He is a frequent speaker at management seminars.

WALTER H. POWELL is vice president of industrial relations at IRC, a division of TRW Inc. He received his B.S. and J.D. degrees from New York University and his M.A. in industrial relations from the University of Pennsylvania. Mr. Powell is a past member of the AMA Personnel Planning Council and is currently on the A11 AMA Planning Council. He has been president of the Industrial Relations Research Association of Philadelphia. Currently he is a member of the American Arbitration Association and is co-director of the National Alliance of Businessmen in Philadelphia.

KENNETH ROBERTS is administrative manager of the refining department of Humble Oil & Refining Company in Houston, Texas. He is a graduate of The University of Texas, where he received B.B.A., LL.B., and LL.M. degrees. While specializing at various times in a variety of legal fields, a large part of his practice has been in labor law, representing his company on labor law problems throughout the United States. In 1965 he became head of a section in the Humble headquarters law department responsible for legal matters for the refining department and labor law for the entire company. Changing to management assignments in 1967, he served for one year as administrative manager of Humble's Baytown refinery prior to assuming his present position in July of 1968.

MAURICE S. TROTTA is a professor of industrial relations and management in the School of Commerce and of arbitration law in the Graduate Division of the School of Law of New York University. He holds an M.A. degree in economics from Columbia University and a J.D. degree in law from Fordham University, and he is a member of the New York Bar. He has arbitrated labor disputes for more than 25 years, written several books and articles, and serves as a consultant and lecturer. Dr. Trotta is a member of the panels of Mediators and Fact Finders of the New York State Public Relations Board and Office of Collective Bargaining. He was recently sent by A.I.D. to organize a school of industrial relations for a university in Lima, Peru.